Pro PHP Refactoring

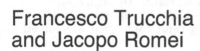

Francesco Trucchia
and Jacopo Romei

Apress®

Pro PHP Refactoring

ISBN-13 (pbk): 978-1-4302-2727-4

ISBN-13 (electronic): 978-1-4302-2728-1

Printed and bound in the United States of America 9 8 7 6 5 4 3 2 1

President and Publisher: Paul Manning
Lead Editor: Michelle Lowman
Technical Reviewer: Aaron Saray
Editorial Board: Clay Andres, Steve Anglin, Mark Beckner, Ewan Buckingham, Gary Cornell, Jonathan Gennick, Jonathan Hassell, Michelle Lowman, Matthew Moodie, Duncan Parkes, Jeffrey Pepper, Frank Pohlmann, Douglas Pundick, Ben Renow-Clarke, Dominic Shakeshaft, Matt Wade, Tom Welsh
Coordinating Editor: Anita Castro
Copy Editor: Mary Ann Fugate
Compositor: Mary Sudul
Indexer: Julie Grady
Artist: April Milne
Cover Designer: Anna Ishchenko

Distributed to the book trade worldwide by Springer Science+Business Media, LLC., 233 Spring Street, 6th Floor, New York, NY 10013. Phone 1-800-SPRINGER, fax (201) 348-4505, e-mail orders-ny@springer-sbm.com, or visit www.springeronline.com.

For information on translations, please e-mail rights@apress.com, or visit www.apress.com.

Apress and friends of ED books may be purchased in bulk for academic, corporate, or promotional use. eBook versions and licenses are also available for most titles. For more information, reference our Special Bulk Sales–eBook Licensing web page at www.apress.com/info/bulksales.

The source code for this book is available to readers at www.apress.com. You will need to answer questions pertaining to this book in order to successfully download the code.

Contents at a Glance

Contents

About the Authors

 ■ **FRANCESCO TRUCCHIA**, after taking a degree in computer science, worked for some years as a web engineer on small, medium, and large projects for some Italian companies.

He is now the co-founder and the CTO of Ideato, a PHP Italian company that is expert in web software development, systems integration, and Agile methods.

Francesco likes to develop with Agile methods. He has introduced these practices in Ideato for their software's lifecycle process, and has received a lot of positive feedback for it.

 ■ **JACOPO ROMEI** is an avowed Extreme Programming adopter and evangelist residing in Rome, Italy. He spent ten years leading his PHP based companies and most of that time testing his own agile coaching skills on the field.

Currently he supports companies in kickstarting development projects and keeping them productive and rewarding for a long time, closely cooperating with developers, interaction designers and managers. Jacopo's contributions to the Symfony framework are just a part of his steady support to open source software.

In his spare time Jacopo likes to cultivate a broad range of interests travelling, sailing, practicing downhill MTB, uploading photos on flickr and singing a cappella with his band.

About the Technical Reviewer

 Since 2001, **AARON SARAY** has been madly in love with PHP. As a Zend
Certified Engineer, Milwaukee PHP Users Group organizer, Author and
Technical Editor, Aaron continues to remain active in the PHP community.
He continues to push out new open source software as well as keep a web
development blog on aaronsaray.com.

Acknowledgments

Thanks to Gabriele Lana and Francesco for being so closely related to the writing of this book. Without the help of Giada and some true friend, though, many things would be harder now: thank you all.

J. R.

Thanks to Ideato, my company, and Jacopo, they let this project be true. Thanks to the PHP community for the great work they do every day to improve this great language. Thank to Chiara, without her patience and support nothing of this could be possible.

F. T.

Introduction

Welcome to our book on PHP Refactoring. Before starting to talk about refactoring techniques applied to the PHP world, we want to introduce you the reasons behind this book.

We think that PHP language has become an enterprise-class language over years, nowadays ready for the great world web market. Experiences like Facebook, Delicious, Daily Motion, Digg and many others show this evolution has come. We think that PHP is becoming the language of the Web, but what about the quality of web software development processes?

Today more than ever being enterprise-class requires more than a language ready for any challenge. Solid values, principles and practices, most of them shared with other contexts far from the web, are needed to be in place and empowered to support the software life cycle. Agile methodologies usually taught along with other compiled object oriented languages can also be applied to scripting languages like PHP with many benefits when adopted in the volatile context of the web development.

Refactoring is a collection of techniques that can help you to improve the quality of your PHP code during all its lifecycle, reducing costs thus improving your business performance. Learning how to identify typical anti-patterns known as bad smells, and addressing them by means of solid and safe step-by-step code changing techniques, you will deliver more value to your customers.

Starting from the refactorings collected by M. Fowler and acknowledged by the whole international agile community, this book is meant as a bridge connecting the PHP language with more traditionally object oriented environments, like Java and Smalltalk, since also PHP developers can strongly benefit from their use.

Too many companies and freelancers depend on old high-value PHP software that gets more obsolete everyday because of its hard maintainability. The reasons for this may be a badly designed software; or legacy code developed by a single cowboy programmer; or even the code belonging to the old procedural times of PHP, when it was not object oriented yet. Reading this book will provide an intermediate or advanced PHP developer with some effective tool to distill the best quality out of her lines of code.

During the last 6 years or so we learned day by day that code can always be improved and that there's always room for a better design. By writing this book we'd like to help you in discovering this or, if you are a more experienced developer, to assist you in your day to day work with a complete and reliable reference.

CHAPTER 1

■ ■ ■

Introduction

Once upon a time, a young CEO, who had just begun his own start-up company, met a young developer in order to start developing a brand new PHP-based general purpose booking system, a core product of the company itself. The CEO was coming from an exciting development experience with his own open-source PHP booking system. This, based on a procedural (though well-organized) framework and with a very low to no use of a good object-oriented architecture, had served its purpose for years with very few issues and excellent stability, even attracting unexpected money donations from the users community. The young CEO and the young developer were about to meet harsh obstacles, considering the application was based on the old but resilient PHP4[1] language, which explains why the object-oriented style was not already maturely used across the application's code. On their way to adding a whole bunch of new features to the release, upon which to base the new start-up, the inexperienced CEO and his partners decided to develop the new system completely from scratch, thinking that the old code base was too rigid and ossified to cope with the pace of the new aggressive features development. The young developer was keen (even eager) to start working on a new object-oriented PHP project, and nothing was on the horizon for a few months. Good process, bad results.

The development team started developing the application building features one by one, with lots of discipline and commitment. The main architecture was meant to be the best collection of design patterns ever seen and the development process was inspired by the best-known methodologies. The old application, in the meantime, was proudly on duty, paying back lots more than it was initially thought worth: no signs of instability, no bugs, and no performance issues. It continued converting users' usage into money.

After the first year of development, the company, still stuck in a *feature creep* that was preventing the application from being released publicly, decided to collect some real-world feedback. So they deployed the application featuring a subset of the final features on a very small subset of customers' web sites, replacing the old web service application. This one, though, was keeping to serve its users and the website owner though. The reason to replace it came as much from its defects as from the need for the new application to meet real-world requirements and get useful feedback from real users. The old application was showing no signs of breakdown, though: the company's *ROI* had always been in its hands until that day.

Another year came and went, and the same development team was on the same project with continuing problems with features deployment, development, and requirements, and there was no mass deployment yet. Fear of regressions, even just user-*perceived* ones, was too strong, and the unnecessary and uncontrolled addition of features had completely distracted them from the real target: stability and return of investment. The dismissed application was still in use on most of the customers' web sites, but time had passed, making it very hard for the company to keep itself alive.

---

[1]   Support for PHP4 has been discontinued since December 31, 2007.

Lesson Learned

At the end of the story, the CEO left the company, having never gotten a stable massive deployment, young developer having been let free to found his own consulting company months before. The start-up project failed, and the new booking system was even removed from the few web sites it had started to be used on and, as of today, the old application is still working undefeated: a few highly-valued features, stability, and a popular users community. It is probably not the best booking system in the world, but it is definitely good enough to provide value to the users' businesses.

Here is the lesson learned: never *easily* throw away working code. Would you ever throw away money? Well, if you would, call us *asap*, but it is more likely you wouldn't. Working code deployed in a production environment means money. If it means money it *is* money. So you're not willing to lose it.

Besides the value directly injected into the code by developers with their own work, the value of a working software hides around a few other corners.

Hidden Gems

The first reason more value lies in an existing working code base than the raw code itself, is about *opportunity cost*. Opportunity cost, as defined on Wikipedia, is the value of the next best alternative forgone as the result of making a decision.

Opportunity cost is a key concept in economics, first developed by John Stuart Mill in the 18th century, concerning the well-known situation of the choice between many desirable yet mutually exclusive results or goods. "Thus opportunity cost plays a crucial part in ensuring that scarce resources are used efficiently."

Time is always a scarce resource and so are good developers, good interaction designers, good graphic designers, and technological resources. It's fair to say that everything needed to build a good application is scarce. We can then recognize an opportunity cost saver in everything. A working application saves *all* of them if we don't need any additional featuress, while it can still save lots of them if we add some new, fancy feature on top of it. Opportunity cost then is the first thing to keep our focus on while valuing a working application.

The second reason a working application could be worth more than we think comes again from the world of economics[2]. Return of Investment (aka ROI) is defined on Wikipedia as "the ratio of money gained or lost on an investment relative to the amount of money invested." In other words, it is a measure of investment profitability. A less specific definition is this good old adage: a dollar earned yesterday is worth more than a dollar earned today and a dollar earned today is worth more than a dollar earned tomorrow. This means that a working application, providing dollars today, is worth more than an application under initial development expected to provide the same (or slightly higher) amount of money some day in the future.

You Don't Know What You've Got 'til It's Gone

To say it the other way around: we all know the motto "Release early, release often." Well, having a working application in a production environment to start from is like having a *free release* at the very beginning of the new project life. This is a strong argument against working code dismissal, which no IT CEO or CTO can ignore.

The CEO and the partners in the brief story at the beginning of this chapter lacked this awareness or, at least, they didn't give it the right weight in making decisions about their new booking web platform. First, after many months, the development team was still struggling to have a clear set of features on the

---

[2]   It should be no surprise since, in the end, we can and should consider enterprise software a revenue generator.

new system, paying the opportunity cost of not improving the old one with the new fancy features the start-up business was meant to be based on. On the other hand, no meaningful ROI was generated for a very long time by the new code base, consuming company back-up resources to the bone until the *de facto* final death.

We are not saying you should never consider building new software from scratch. Many valid reasons concerning technology, enterprise strategy, or even copyright, can lead to the decision of writing a whole system beginning from the very start. Some situations could then even require flushing the old code base away, and we should be ready to do that.

Our point, though, is to make you consider the option of giving the old working software another chance, given the value you already have within your existing custom applications. We think you should at least consider the waste it would be if you threw it away, since it is free. Besides all this, we want you not to miss the whole point of this book: you can reduce the negative impact of an old architecture while adding new features now and in the future, if you know how to do it. Using the right methodology, the right tools, and the right steps, you can safely bring your old *legacy* code from a condition of hard maintainability to the right supple architecture, combining the best of two worlds: new cutting edge features on top of a reliable and already operating software.

Call of Duty

For too long the PHP community avoided good software development methodologies, partly due to the easy learning curve, letting many raw coders survive spreading raw code around, partly due to the weak support in older PHP versions for the well-known and mature, though not unique, object-oriented paradigm. It's been years since the release of PHP5, so the time has come to leap ahead and *embrace change*, adopting techniques and methodologies to ease our everyday work and empower our teams to cope with big and complex enterprise class software.

Does this mean we have to leave our old-fashioned PHP applications behind? Does it mean we have to waste all of our previous effort? Does it mean we have to significantly hurt our income while upgrading our systems? No, not at all. It just means we have to learn how to *refactor* our code towards a simpler design and a better architecture. The consultant and the CEO in the brief story at the beginning of this chapter were Francesco Trucchia and Jacopo Romei, ourselves. In that experience, we learned that existing software has a great value no one should neglect. After years of managing and developing PHP projects, we want to share a few key concepts about your goal and ours: saving the value of your software. Refactoring is at the center of this methodology. But before we learn how to refactor, let's see how the code can *smell bad*.

CHAPTER 2

■ ■ ■

Finding "Bad Smells" in Code

Kent Back's grandmother once said, "When it stinks, change it." Obviously she was talking not about code, but about Back's child. Well, we do not believe it, but the same sentence should be totally applied to the development of software.

Martin Fowler talks about this strange history in his book *Refactoring: Improving the Design of Existing Code*, and Kent Back, the father of Agile Method, helped him write this book. We will take a lot of Martin Fowler and Kent Back's refactoring concepts and try to move them into a PHP context.

Why Code Can Smell

Often, we must work with code that stinks, or rather, to be polite, that emanates bad smells. These odors may result from a bad use of software design practices, from a many-hands writing of the same code, from a code that was written in different periods by different people not using best practices, and much more. Some alarm bells for recognizing that a code smells are

- Difficulty understanding or following the logic of the code
- Many inline comments within the code
- Inability to add new features for fear of introducing bugs
- A lot of files with thousands of lines of code
- Procedural code

If our software is strategic for our company and has at least one of these previous characteristics, then it smells bad. We absolutely have to use some kind of deodorant to make our code smell good again. When faced with a bad code, many software houses decide to rewrite the entire product from scratch. As we have seen, this decision can be lethal for a company. Rewriting a software that is currently a money machine for a company could be really dangerous, because we may not ever release it, fearful of not matching the old product features, or meeting customer needs and users' expectations.

When our code smells good, everything smells around him, we can make happy our leaders doing to grow rapidly the software, according to the needs of business logic, we can have more time to spend with what we value, like family, returning home quietly in the evening, without overtime, we can have better health, preventing sickness liver and hair loss. This is possible because with a clean code, we can embrace change with courage and serenity. Martin Fowler has taught us that, using a variety of code refactoring practices, odors can be easily recognized and eliminated.

Now we will consider the bad smells frequently encountered in a PHP development career. We'll not report all the bad smells listed by Martin Fowler, but only the most representative for the PHP world according to our point of view. For every bad smell, we will learn how to recognize it and what practices we can use to eliminate it. All recommended practices are the official practices taught by Martin Fowler in his book *Refactoring: Improving the Design of Existing Code* [FOW01]. In this chapter we will not go into details of the practice, as each case will be detailed in following chapters.

Duplicated Code

The most hostile enemy of our code is code duplication. It can cause many problems with software maintenance and performance. For example, if we have duplicate code in the same method of two sibling classes, or if we have the same pieces of code in different methods of the same class, or if we use different algorithms to do the same thing in different methods, and we make a change only at one point and not at all points where the code is duplicated, we can change all the behaviors in a consistent manner, reducing the risk of bugs. We should never forget that software is written in the right way when it is enough to change something in one place in order for the entire system to accept and follow the change uniformly.

To refactor our code we can use various strategies. For example, when we have two equal code blocks within the same class, we can simply **extract the method** and invoke the call in both places. If instead we have two identical methods in different classes that extend the same class, we can **move the method** in the parent class and delete it from the other two subclasses. If the code is similar but not exactly the same, we must first **extract the method** with the equal parts and then move it to the parent class. If we have two methods that do the same thing but with two different algorithms, we can choose which algorithm is the best and use only it and **substitute the algorithm**. If you have duplicate code in classes that are not related, we can think of creating a parent class and **move the method**, or if the objects cannot be children of the same class, we may decide to keep the method in a single class and invoke it from a related class, or to create a third class and invoke the method of this third class in the other two. The strategies can be varied—it's up to us to understand what is best and choose it.

In the following example we have two classes that extend the same class. They implement the same getAge() method. If the method changes we have to change both methods, and as seen before this is wrong, because if we change only one method while forgetting the other, we can introduce a bug.

```
class Customer extends Person
{
  ...
  public function getAge()
  {
    return date('Y') - date('Y', $this->getBirthday());
  }
  ...
}

class Vendor extends Person
{
  ...
  public function getAge()
  {
    return date('Y') - date('Y', $this->getBirthday());
  }
  ...
}
```

To delete this duplication we can move the getAge() method in the parent class.

```
class Person
{
```

```
...
public function getAge()
{
    return date('Y') - date('Y', $this->getBirthday());
}
...
}
```

And we remove the method on subclasses.

Refactoring Strategies

Extract method

Pull up field

Form template method

Substitute algorithm

Long Method

Many developers now recognize that the longer a routine is, the more difficult it is to read and maintain. There is a lot of outdated PHP software presenting thousands of code lines in every script. Modifying this code after few months could be an impossible mission. With object-oriented programming, we have learned that the smaller a method is, with the responsibility of the individual classes separated, the simpler the software is to maintain, even after a long time. When we have a lot of methods, it becomes very important to give them meaningful names, so that one can easily remember and understand what each method does, without having to read the code inside.

The most common strategy to refactor this type of software is the **extract method**. We find pieces of code that go great together and put them in an external method. One heuristic method that we can use to correctly separate the code is to follow the comments. Since reading long code is very difficult, diligent programmers often comment on blocks of code that explain what they do. Here, every time we encounter a comment, we can

1. Write a new method in the same class (the name should represent what the code does)

2. Move the block of code under the comment from the routine to the new method

3. Add a comment that explains not what method does but how it does it

We can also create new methods that contain only a single line of code, if the name of the new method explains better what the code does. The key to this strategy is not so much the length of the method, but the semantic distance between what the method does and how it does it. Extracting methods in many ways, the problem that we will face will be to have long lists of parameters to be passed to methods. Later we will see how to shorten this list of parameters. Even flow conditionals and loops may be a sign that we need to extract the code. We must learn to limit the flow conditionals and loops that make reading code very difficult. A strategy for simplifying these blocks is the decomposition conditional. Another strategy might be to redesign part of our code using some patterns. But we will get back to that later.

In the following example we have the `Order` class with a method that is too long.

```
class Order
{
  ...
  public function calculate()
  {
    $details = $this->getOrderDetails();

    foreach($details as $detail)
    {
      if (!$detail->hasVat())
      {
        $vat = $this->getCustomer()->getVat();
      }
      else
      {
        $vat = $detail->getVat();
      }

      $price = $detail->getAmount() * $detail->getPrice();
      $total += $price + ($price/100 * $vat->getValue());
    }

    if ($this->hasDiscount())
    {
      $total = $total - ($total/100 * $this->getDiscount());
    }
    elseif($this->getCustomer()->hasDiscountForMaxAmount()↵
           && $total >= $this->getCustomer()->getMaxAmountForDiscount())
    {
      $total = $total - ($total/100 * $this->getCustomer()->getDiscountForMaxAmount())
    }

    return $total;
  }
  ...
}
```

First, we can simplify this method extracting two methods—one to calculate detail total price and another to calculate the right order discount.

```
class Order
{
  ...
  private function calculateDetailsPrice()
  {
    foreach($this->getOrderDetails() as $detail)
    {
      if (!$detail->hasVat())
      {
        $vat = $this->getCustomer()->getVat();
      }
      else
      {
```

```
      $vat = $detail->getVat();
    }

    $price = $detail->getAmount() * $detail->getPrice();
    $total += $price + ($price/100 * $vat->getValue());
  }
  return $total;

}

private function applyDiscount($total)
{
  if ($this->hasDiscount())
  {
    $total = $total - ($total/100 * $this->getDiscount());
  }
  elseif($this->getCustomer()->hasDiscountForMaxAmount() &&
         $total >= $this->getCustomer()->getMaxAmountForDiscount())
  {
    $total = $total - ($total/100 * $this->getCustomer()->getDiscountForMaxAmount())
  }
  return $total;
}

public function calculate()
{
  return $this->applyDiscount($this->calculateDetailsPrice());
}
...
}
```

If we look carefully at the method calculateDetailsPrice(), we will realize that all code inside the foreach cycle is about order detail object and not order object. So we can extract this code and move it into the OrderDetail class. We can extract two methods—one to retrieve the right vat object and another to calculate detail price.

```
class OrderDetail
{
  ...
  public function getVat()
  {
    if (!$this->hasVat())
    {
      return $this->getOrder()->getCustomer()->getVat();
    }
    return $this->getVat();
  }

  public function calculate()
  {
    $price = $this->getAmount() * $this->getPrice();
    return $price + ($price/100 * $this->getVat()->getValue());
  }
  ...
}
```

```
class Order
{
  ...
  private function calculateDetailsPrice()
  {
    foreach($this->getOrderDetails() as $detail)
    {
      $total += $detail->calculate();
    }
    return $total;
  }
  ...
}
```

Refactoring Strategies
Extract method
Move method

Large Class

A class that tries to do too many things can be easily distinguished by the number of attributes it possesses. When a class has too many attributes, it is very easy to create duplicate code, making it difficult to maintain and read.

The two best strategies are to combine the attributes that go well together, such as attributes with the same prefixes or suffixes, e.g., home_address and office_address, or fax_number and phone_number, and **extract new classes** that include these similar attributes. If the attributes belong strongly to class and can't be merged, but they are used differently in different instances of the same class, we can **extract subclasses** and divide these attributes in these subclasses. Or, if we just have to extract attributes and non-logical behavior, we can use interfaces rather than classes.

In the following example we have a long class Order that has a lot of properties.

```
Class Order
{
  protected $customer_firstname;
  protected $customer_lastname;
  protected $customer_company_name;
  protected $customer_address;
  protected $customer_city;
  protected $customer_country;
  protected $customer_phonenumber;
  protected $customer_faxnumber;
  protected $customer_email;
  protected $customer_$vat;

  protected $order_id;
  protected $order_number;
  protected $order_discount;
  protected $order_total_price;
  protected $order_date;
  protected $order_shipping_date;
```

```
  protected $payment_transaction_id;
  protected $payment_type;
  protected $payment_date;
  protected $payment_method;
  ...

}
```

We also have accessor methods to access to each property. In cases like this, we are giving too much liability to one class only. To reduce the liability and the code length, we can extract new classes and move each property and accessor method to the right new class.

```
class Customer
{
  protected $firstname;
  protected $lastname;
  protected $company_name;
  protected $address;
  protected $city;
  protected $country;
  protected $phonenumber;
  protected $faxnumber;
  protected $email;
  protected $vat;
  protected $payment_method;
  ...

}

class Payment
{
  protected $transaction_id;
  protected $type;
  protected $date;
  protected $method;
  ...
}

class Order
{
  protected $id;
  protected $number;
  protected $discount;
  protected $total_price;
  protected $date;
  protected $shipping_date;
  ...
}
```

Refactoring Strategies

Extract class

Extract subclass

Long Parameter List

With procedural programming we often use lots of long lists of parameters passed to functions. Unfortunately, this method used to be mandatory, since the only alternative was to use global variables, which, we know, are evil. With object-oriented programming, luckily, we no longer need long lists of parameters, for two main reasons:

1. There are objects.

2. A class method knows all private, protected, and public parameters of the class where it's implemented and all protected and public parameters of the inherit class.

Moreover, when we have parameters that can be grouped into a single object we can introduce a **parameter object** and pass it directly to the method rather than individual parameters. Instead, if we are passing the individual attributes of the same object, we can **preserve the whole object** and pass the object directly. If we invoke a method and then pass the result directly to another method, we can **replace the parameter with the method** and call it directly into the later-invoked method.

The only exception for which these strategies can't be applied is when we don't want to create dependency between object and class. In this case we can pass all the attributes separately, but we must be aware of what this means. Before making this decision we have to review the design of our application to understand whether we can improve it to avoid a bad smell.

In the following example we have a User class and a template CSV class that has a method to render a CSV user row.

```
class User
{
  public $first_name:
  public $last_name;
  public $type;
  public $email;
  public $address;
  public $city;
  public $country;
  public $gender;
  ...
}

class UserCsvTemplate
{
  public function render($first_name, $last_name, $type, $email, $address, $city, $country, ↵
$gender)
  {
    echo $first_name, ';', $last_name, ';',
        $type,       ';', $email,     ';',
        $address,    ';', $city,      ';',
        $country,    ';', $gender,    PHP_EOL;
  }
}
```

If we want to render a user CSV row we need to run the following code:

```
$user = new User();
...
$csv_template = new UserCsvTemplate();
```

```
$csv_template->render($user->first_name, $user->last_name, $user->type, $user->email, ↵
$user->address, $user->city, $user->country, $user->gender);
```

The render() method has a very long list of parameters to be passed. Since all the parameters belong to the same object we can pass the entire object directly, preserving it.

```
class UserCsvTemplate
{
  public function render(User $user)
  {
    echo $user->first_name, ';', $user->last_name, ';',
         $user->type,        ';', $user->email,     ';',
         $user->address,     ';', $user->city,      ';',
         $user->country,     ';', $user->gender,  PHP_EOL,
  }
}

$user = new User();
...
$csv_template = new UserCsvTemplate();
$csv_template->render($user);
```

Refactoring Strategies

Replace parameter with method

Preserve whole object

Introduce parameter object

Divergent Change

When we change a certain feature in software that is truly moldable, we should be able to make the change in a single clear point of our system. When this doesn't happen, and, instead, we must change multiple methods of the same class to make different changes, then we have done something wrong.

For example, if we have to modify two methods of the same class to change the database connection, and we have to change four methods to add a new graphical interface to a particular component in the same class, it is probably better to split this class into two classes, so as to isolate the change in a single point. The strategy applied is the **extract class**. We create a new class; we extract the common methods in the new class and let it communicate in some way.

In the following example we have two methods that retrieve their records from the same MySql database.

```
class OrderRepository
{
  public static function retrieveAll()
  {
    $connection = mysql_connect('localhost', 'user', 'user')
                  or throw new Exception('Could not connect: ' . mysql_error());

    mysql_select_db('ecommerce')
                  or throw new Exception('Could not select database');
```

```
    $result = mysql_query('SELECT * FROM order')
                      or throw new Exception('Query failed: ' . mysql_error());
    ...
  }

  public static function retrieveOneById($id)
  {
    $connection = mysql_connect('localhost', 'user', 'user')
                      or throw new Exception('Could not connect: ' . mysql_error());

    mysql_select_db('ecommerce')
                      or throw new Exception('Could not select database');

    $result = mysql_query('SELECT * FROM orde where id = '.$id)
                      or throw new Exception('Query failed: ' . mysql_error());
    ...
  }
}
```

If we want to change the database name, or the database user configuration, we need to change the same line of code in two different methods. If we forget to change one of these, we can introduce a bug. In this case we can extract a new class and instance it inside the method.

```
class Connection
{
  private $connection;

  public function __construct()
  {
    $this->connection = mysql_connect('localhost', 'user', 'user')
                          or throw new Exception('Could not connect: ' . mysql_error());

    mysql_select_db('ecommerce')
      or throw new Exception('Could not select database');
  }
  ...
}

class CustomerRepository
{
  public static function retrieveAll()
  {
    $connection = new Connection();

    $result = mysql_query('SELECT * FROM customer')
                      or throw new Exception('Query failed: ' . mysql_error());
    ...
  }

  public static function retrieveAll()
  {
    $connection = new Connection();

    $result = mysql_query('SELECT * FROM order')
                      or throw new Exception('Query failed: ' . mysql_error());
    ...
  }
}
```

Refactoring Strategies

Extract class

Shotgun Surgery

This bad smell is the perfect opposite of the previous divergent change. In practice, when we have to modify many classes to make a single change, this means that we have a design overhead.

When we have to change two different methods of two different classes, we can move the method in the most representative class. If we instead have to change attributes of different classes, we can move only attributes in the most representative class. Sometimes we might remove all classes and move all attributes within the class that uses it. This strategy takes the name of inline class.

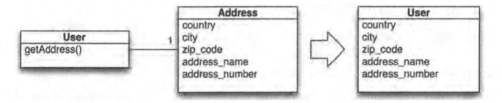

Refactoring Strategies

Move method

Move field

Inline class

Feature Envy

When we write our software, we must never forget that an object is a set of data and processes that compute these data. This thought should help us to identify all the methods that do not process the data in our class, but data of the other classes, invoking only external methods. As you can imagine, these methods are in the wrong position. To resolve this situation we can simply **move the method** from one class to another.

If only a part of the code must be moved, first **extract** it in a new method and then **move** it. If our code actually invokes methods of different classes, it can sometimes be complex to figure out where to move the method. When we are in trouble, the strategy is always the same—extract more methods and move everyone in your class.

```
class Order
{
  public function calculate()
  {
    foreach($this->getOrderDetails() as $detail)
    {
```

```
      $this->total += $this->calcultateOrderDetail($detail);
    }
  }

  public function calcultateOrderDetail($detail)
  {
    return $detail->getAmount() * $detail->getPrice();
  }
}
```

The calculateOrderDetail is a method that doesn't belong to Order class. This method calls only methods of OrderDetail class. We need to move this method to OrderDetail class.

```
class OrderDetail
{
  public function calcultateOrderDetail()
  {
    return $this->getAmount() * $this->getPrice();
  }

}

class Order
{
  public function calculate()
  {
    foreach($this->getOrderDetails() as $detail)
    {
      $this->total += $detail->calcultateOrderDetail();
    }
  }
}
```

Refactoring Strategies

Move method

Extract method

Data Clamps

When our classes start to proliferate groups of attributes that must be changed all at once when one inserts a new feature or change, we have to stop and rewrite that attribute group differently.

The first strategy is to extract these attributes and put them together into a new class, because surely all of these attributes can be represented by another entity. Then declare a new class, extract the attributes in the new class, and add a single attribute in the class that is an instance of the new class. Then we can concentrate on simplifying the parameter list of those methods that use these attributes, preserving the whole object.

Refactoring Strategies
Extract class
Introduce parameter object
Preserve whole object

Primitive Obsession

Many programming languages, including PHP, provide two basic data types—the primitive type and structured type, which we represent with associative arrays in PHP. The structured data is used when none of the system primitives provided can properly represent certain data. A very common example is a record in a database, or a matrix. These data types are often duplicated within our code and, as we have seen before, are not good, because the duplicated code is the first bad smell. In this case the objects are the solution to our problem. The object itself is just the right compromise between primitive data and structured data. In this way we can replace our data with objects. For example, PHP supports integers, strings, and primitive booleans, but not the date data. So to represent our data, we can create a Date custom class, or use the Date class that PHP already makes available to us. There are many other cases where it can be very helpful to use objects instead of structured data, such as when we have to represent currency, or area code. We often resist creating this type of object. But if we strive instead to use them, our code can become much easier to read and less duplicated.

To implement this type of class, the strategy that we can use is to **replace data value with an object**, but if we find type code that is an alias for a structured data, we can **replace it with a class or subclass** it represents. If we have a condition that depends on the type of a given data, we can **replace type code with a subclass** or with a **state/strategy** pattern.

In the following example we retrieve a record from a database, fetching it with array hydration mode.

```
$id = 0;
$db = new PDO('mysql:dbname=mytest', 'root');
$stmt = $db->prepare('SELECT * FROM user WHERe id = :id');
$stmt->bindParam(':id', $id, PDO::PARAM_INT);

$stmt->execute();
$user = $stmt->fetch(PDO::FETCH_ASSOC);
echo $user['firstname'], ' ', $user['lastname'], PHP_EOL;
```

Instead we can define a User class and use it to hydrate query result.

```
class User
{
  protected $firstname;
  protected $lastname;

  public function __toString()
  {
    return $this->firstname. ' '. $this->lastname;
  }
}

...
$stmt->execute();
```

```
$user = $stmt->fetchObject('User');
echo $user, PHP_EOL;
```

Refactoring Strategies

Replace data value with object

Replace type code with class

Replace type code with subclasses

Replace type code with state/strategy

Switch Statements

Another widespread bad smell is the use of repeated and duplicate switches. The switch control structure usually seeks to change the behavior or the state of an object based on one or more parameters. Using switches in this way, we forget that in object-oriented programming this type of behavior has the name "polymorphism" and is a property of objects themselves.

Through the polymorphism property we can remove conditional logic, since the change occurs according to the type of the object itself, not because someone knows how to choose based on the value of a given parameter. The strategy that we implement to remove the switches is as follows:

1. Extract the switch in a method.

2. Move the newly extracted method in a class more accountable to the knowledge of polymorphism.

3. Decide whether to replace the type code executed by the switch with a subclass, or a state/strategy pattern.

4. After setting the structure of inheritance, we can use the replace conditional with the polymorphism strategy.

Sometimes the polymorphism may not be the appropriate solution. In this case we can simply replace the condition code with the methods, and in cases where the condition must return null, we can think of **introducing a NullObject**.

```
class User
{
  ...
  public function initCredentials()
  {
    switch($this->type)
    {
      case 'admin':
        $this->addCredential('admin');
        break;
      case 'premium':
        $this->addCredential('premium');
        break;
      case 'base':
        $this->addCredential('base');
        break;
      default:
```

```
        throw new Exception('Error: type is not valid');
        break;
    }
  }
  ...
}
```

For example, the following switch statement should be removed using the polymorphism strategy.

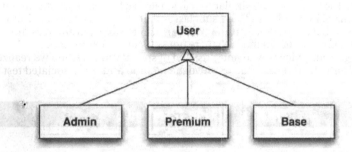

Refactoring Strategies

Extract method

Move method

Replace type code with subclass

Replace type code with state/strategy

Replace conditional with polymorphism

Introducing NullObject

Lazy Class

All classes or subclasses that we make must have a reason to exist. If you think a class is not doing enough and is not very useful, it must be removed, because it costs a lot to maintain. If a subclass is not used in a class, we can **collapse the inheritance hierarchy**. If an attribute is an instance of a class of which we use only a single attribute or a single method, let's make it a **class inline** into the referred class.

Refactoring Strategies

Collapse hierarchy

Inline class

Speculative Generality

Developers often commit the sin of pride, thinking that they can predict the future. How many times have we decided to continue with the amount of code produced because we believed that someday it would be useful, for example, to have one abstract class, or a certain method, or that particular interface, only to find that such a day never arrives? Unfortunately, we must accept that we cannot predict the future. To have a good-smelling code, we must remove all the speculative code, such as code that nobody uses except for a test case. We must think only about what we need today, not tomorrow.

For this bad smell, the strategies are similar to bad smells we have already discussed. In fact, we can use the strategy of **collapse hierarchy** for those subclasses that are not used, or the **inline class** to remove delegations from classes that are not really useful. We can also **remove parameters** from methods that never use them, and rename all the methods that are not sufficiently expressive.

As previously suggested, a nice way to find this kind of speculation is when we realize that the only users of these methods are the test cases. So, remove the method and the associated test cases.

Refactoring Strategies
Collapse hierarchy
Inline class
Remove parameter
Rename method

Temporary Field

In object-oriented programming, all the attributes of a certain class should characterize that object in any context. Often when we implement our code, it happens that some of the attributes are used only in one context and the others in another context, perhaps chosen by a given parameter. This type of behavior is wrong because it introduces a lot of unnecessary conditional logic within our code. Instead we can safely extract a subclass that better characterizes the object in that kind of context.

Therefore, the strategy is to **extract a subclass** and add the attributes that in a certain context do not represent the object. If the condition allows no object if the variable is null, we can **introduce a NullObject** to handle this case.

```
class Customer
{
  protected $company_name;
  protected $first_name;
  protected $last_name;
  protected $is_company;

  public function getFullName()
  {
    if ($this->is_company)
    {
      return $this->getCompanyName();
    }

    return $this->getFirstName() . ' ' . $this->getLastName();
  }
}
```

In the previous class we have a $first_name and $last_name that are temporary properties of our class. They are used only when Customer is not a company, so they are context-dependent. We can remove this double behavior, extracting two subclasses and making Customer an abstract class.

```
abstract class Customer
{
  abstract public function getFullName();
}

class Person extends Customer
{
  protected $first_name;
  protected $last_name;

  public function getFullName()
  {
    return $this->getFirstName(), ' ', $this->getLastName();
  }
}

class Company extends Customer
{
  protected $company_name;

  public function getFullName()
  {
    return $this->getCompanyName();
  }
}
```

Refactoring Strategies

Extract subclass

Introduce NullObject

Data Class

The data classes are all those classes that only have to set and get a set of their attributes, without having some business logic. They are also called setter/getter classes. Usually these classes, when born, publicly expose all their attributes, and this behavior may be too brash. When the class is small and we have it under control, the problem will be minimal, but when these classes grow, if we are not careful, we risk exposing too much. These classes are like children—while they are growing, they must assume some responsibility.

The first suggestion is to set all the attributes of those classes to private or protected, and create a series of getter and setter that may provide public access to these attributes. This strategy is known as **encapsulation field**. When an attribute is a collection of objects or structured data, we must do the same thing because the collection can't be changed all at once—only one item at a time. This strategy is called **encapsulate the collection**. Moreover, if we have attributes that should never be modified outside, we should not **remove setting methods** that modify them. If there is an object that uses the setter on the attributes that should not be changed, extract the external method into our data class and related external object to it, so that the change is internal.

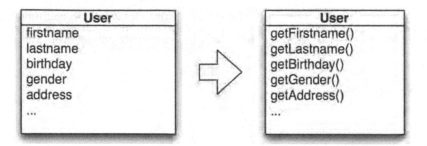

Refactoring Strategies

Encapsulate field

Encapsulate collection

Remove setting method

Comments

When we say that comments are a source of bad smells, hordes of programmers may become angry. In our opinion, as that of Martin Fowler, the point is that a comment is not a bad smell, but when the comment is inline to code and it is used to explain what the code does, this is a bad smell. All method or class comments are important and should be used to explain how something works, but not what it does. To remove this bad smell, you can implement the following strategy whenever you want to write a comment to a block of code:

1. Instead of the comment, write a method where the method name expresses exactly the same concept of the comment.

2. **Extract the block of code** that we wanted to comment in the method.

3. Invoke the method where we wanted to put the comment.

But if we want to write a comment about what a certain call to method does because it isn't clear, rename the method with a more expressive name and reduce the list of parameters passed, **introducing a parameter object** or **preserving the whole object** via parameters or creating objects of any object. If you need to remember some rules required by the system in a certain context, instead of writing the comment, introduce a method that tests the assertion rule.

> *When you feel the need to write a comment, first try to refactor the code so that any comment becomes superfluous.*

—Martin Fowler

Comments may make code even more malodorous. But they can be helpful by letting others know that you are not sure of what has been done or that you do not know what to do in that particular context or piece of code.

```
class Order
{
  ...
  public function calculate()
  {
    foreach($this->getOrderDetails() as $detail)
    {
      // Retrieve vat
      if ($detail->hasVat())
      {
        $detail_vat = $detail->getVat();
      }

      // Calculate details price
      $detail_price = $detail->getAmount() * $detail->getPrice();

      // Calculate details price adding vat value
      $order_total += $detail_price + ($detail_price/100 * $detail_vat->getValue());
    }

    // Retrieve order discount
    if ($this->hasDiscount())
    {
      $order_total = $order_total - ($order_total/100 * $this->getDiscount());
    }

    return $total;
  }
  ...
}
```

In the previous method we can remove the inline comment, extracting some new private methods.

```
class Order
{
  ...
  private function retrieveVat($detail)
  {
    return $detail->hasVat() ? $detail->getVat() : 0;
  }

  private function calculateDetailPrice($detail)
  {
    return $detail->getAmount() * $detail->getPrice();
  }

  private function calculateDeatilPriceAddingVatValue($price, $vat)
  {
    return $price + ($price/100 * $vat->getValue());
  }

  private function calculatePriceOrderWithDiscount($total)
  {
    if ($this->hasDiscount())
    {
      return $total - ($total/100 * $this->getDiscount());
    }
```

```
    return $total;
  }

  public function calculate()
  {
    foreach($this->getOrderDetails() as $detail)
    {
      $detail_vat = $this->retrieveVat($detail);
      $detail_price = $this->calculateDetailPrice($detail);
      $order_price += $this->calculateDeatilPriceAddingVatValue($price, $vat);
    }
    return $this->calculateOrderPriceWithDiscount();
  }
  ...
}
```

Refactoring Strategies

Extract method

Preserve whole object

Introduce parameter object

Procedural Code

PHP is an easy and affordable language for unskilled developers to learn. Unfortunately, this advantage can sometimes become a disadvantage. Writing good code is not enough to know a language. As we have seen, we must have much deeper knowledge about design, patterns, and especially object-oriented programming. Today, PHP is a mature and powerful language that lets you use all the best practices of object-oriented programming. Well, we should use them. The procedural or functional code is surely an easy and affordable way to write code, but when that code involves thousands of duplicate lines, which are difficult to read and maintain, our code loses the ability to grow with our needs and we lose the true value of our software.

There is a strategy called **big refactoring**, which we will see at the end of this book, which turns your application from procedural code to object-oriented code. This is a complex activity but it is worth the effort.

Refactoring Strategies

Big refactoring

■ ■ ■

CHAPTER 3

Introduction to Refactoring

Due to the strong practical nature of refactoring and the essentially empirical nature of human knowledge, we want to provide you with an example of what all this refactoring is about. Refactoring is a practice addressed to some of the main object-oriented development principles, so we think it best for the reader is to see a real example before diving deep into the refactoring techniques list.

In this chapter we'll try to give you an idea of what refactoring is and what could it mean to developers like us.

The Concept: What Refactoring Is

Everyone can understand the following expression:

$(a + b)(a - b) = c$

It means that depending on a and b values as input we get another value injected in c as output. It's a defined process, as well as an algorithm, and it has a well-known and expected outcome. Knowing that's true, we can also write

$a^2 - b^2 = c$

and say it's true, too. We can say that because, in general, we know

$(a + b)(a - b) = a^2 - b^2$

since it's a well-known factoring rule we all study in the early years of school.

The inner meaning we can read between these lines is that given an input, there are many ways to get the same output, or many routes to lead us to our desired result. Among these, we can prefer one more than another not by results—the same by definition—but by other factors such as readability, suppleness, or even just elegance.

That's the main thought behind refactoring: changing the inner structure of software with no change in its external behavior.

The Reason: What's the Goal of Refactoring?

Code has a cost. Always. It has a cost to be created, it has a cost to be maintained, it even has a cost to be executed, though several orders of magnitude less than the first two. That's the reason developers cost much more than CPUs. We have no way (yet?) to code software without use of the human brain.

Considering how we cannot avoid the intrinsic nature of our software costs, we have a strong need to find a way to hugely reduce those costs. That means removing typical pitfalls the human brain falls into. Those pitfalls lie beneath each of the *bad smells* we met in the previous chapter: long lists, big and complicated structures, interleaved dependencies, and similar things; they all deviate a human brain from control towards panic, resulting in an increment of development and maintenance costs.

Architecture and Structure, They Fade Away

One of the most powerful concept in physics is the second law of thermodynamics. It states that the potential for disorder of a system tends to *increase*. A glass, along a sufficient elapse of time, tends to break; biological tissue tends to decompose; ice tends to melt. It never happens by chance that a bunch of broken glasses recompose into a bottle fit to contain water; a dead cell never steps back to life; no ice is created spontaneously from water at 25°C. It means that systems need an external contribution to keep themselves in a given state or to step into a *more ordered* state: broken glasses must be melted to create bottles; cells need lots of energy coming from food to survive; ice is created by means of an A/C supply and a fridge. Everything, if left on its own, tends to decay.

What does that mean for us sitting in front of our nasty and unmaintainable code? It unfortunately means that it will get even nastier and less maintainable if we don't recover its structure in some way. Even the best-designed architecture is exposed to entropy's restless effect: its structure decays if left unattended. We start a project from scratch with the best intentions, and we design the most beautiful architecture ever. Then the code goes into the wild and, even before going into production, we are left with not enough time to redesign our software as long as new features or bugs are discovered. Then disorder creeps in, exposing that beloved good architecture of ours to a progressive decay, leading us to cope with a bad, nasty, uncomfortable, and unmaintainable code base.

We must distinguish between *complexity* and *complicatedness*. The first is something we might even want, since in our software we are likely encoding complex business behavior that is the *core sense* of it. The latter is just an obstacle. We don't want things to get complicated while we try to make our software reach the desired level of complexity.

Reworking Chaos into Well-Designed Code

Refactoring is the best known way to keep code away from disordered states. While the tendency of code is to slowly decay towards chaos, refactoring is exactly the opposite: we actively change the inner structure of our software, bringing it from chaos to a more ordered design through a series of simple stable steps.

No word in the last statement has a secondary role. Apart from the most obvious ones, all of the words have strong consequences in the global meaning. *Actively* means that we are acting on our code, thus providing that *external contribution* the second law of thermodynamics refers to. *Changing* means we have to operate to get a differently-written code at the end of our refactoring steps. *Inner* means we are acting on the inside of our code, without changing its interface and its external behavior. *More* means that *order* is a relative concept, and thus that we could refactor our code indefinitely, while it's our main aim to keep an eye on pragmatic choices. *Series* refers to the potential concatenation between different refactoring techniques we can exploit to achieve a better global result. *Simple* implies that every step must be "*simple, even simplistic*" (quoting Martin Fowler), thus multiplying chances that we won't introduce chaos (errors) while refactoring. *Stable* states our need to go from a stable condition to another stable one with the smallest leap ahead, to keep reversibility and correctness always granted.

Refactoring, then, is a way to oppose the natural tendency of code to become unmaintainable, while using the right techniques to improve the design of our code, improving it *after* having written it.

An Example, at Last

We waited long enough, then! Let's have a look at the next example. Ladies and gentlemen, please welcome the Order class:

```php
class Order
{
  public $gold_customer = false;
  public $silver_customer = false;

  public $items = array();

  protected $first_name;
  protected $last_name;
  protected $customer_address;
  protected $customer_city;
  protected $customer_country;
  protected $shipping_address;

  public function setItem($code, $price, $description, $quantity)
  {
    $this->items[] = array('code' => $code,
                           'price' => $price,
                           'description' => $description,
                           'quantity' => $quantity
                          );
  }

  public function setItems($items)
  {
    $this->items = $items;
  }

  public function listItems()
  {
    return $this->items;
  }

  public function setCustomer($customer)
  {
    list($this->first_name, $this->last_name) = explode(' ', $customer);
  }

  public function getCustomer()
  {
    return $this->first_name.' '.$this->last_name;
  }

  public function setShippingAddress($address)
  {
    $this->shipping_address = $address;
  }

  public function getShippingAddress()
  {
```

```php
    return $this->shipping_address;
}

public function isGoldCustomer()
{
  return $this->gold_customer;
}

public function getTotal()
{
  $total = 0;

  foreach ($this->items as $item)
  {
    $currency = '';

    // we check for the item to be valid
    if (isset($item['price']) && isset($item['quantity']))
    {
      // we detect currency if indicated
      $price = explode(' ', $item['price']);
      if (isset($price[1]))
      {
        $currency = $price[1];
      }
      $price = $price[0];
      $total += $price * $item['quantity'];
    }
  }

  // If the customer is gold we apply 40% discount and...
  if ($this->gold_customer)
  {
    $total = $total * 0.6;

    // ...if amount is over 500 we apply further 20% discount
    if ($total > 500)
    {
      $total = $total * 0.8;
    }
  }
  // If the customer is silver we apply 20% discount and...
  elseif ($this->silver_customer)
  {
    $total = $total * 0.8;

    // ...if amount is over 500 we apply further 10% discount
    if ($total > 500)
    {
      $total = $total * 0.9;
    }
  }
  else
  {
    // if customer subscribed no fidelity program we apply 10% over 500
    if ($total > 500)
    {
```

```
      $total = $total * 0.9;
    }
  }

  if ($currency)
  {
    return round($total, 2).' '.$currency;
  }
  else return round($total, 2);
  }
}
```

This is a simple class meant to describe and manage an order for a simple e-commerce web site. It features a collection of some items bought by a customer whose data are also stored in proper fields. It provides an interface to manage the items list and customer data and to compute the total amount due for the order, including a discount policy based on the total price for the items and the type of affiliation program joined by the customer.

The class is correct, as the next PHPUnit test proves:

```
class OrderTest extends PHPUnit_Framework_TestCase
{

  public function setUp()
  {
    $this->order = new Order();
  }

  public function testGetTotal()
  {
    $items = array(
      '34tr45' => array(
                          'price' => 10,
                          'description' => 'A very good CD by Jane Doe.',
                          'quantity' => 2
                        ),
       '34tr89' => array(
                          'price' => 70,
                          'description' => 'Super compilation.',
                          'quantity' => 1
                        )
    );
    $this->order->setItems($items);

    $this->assertEquals((20 + 70), $this->order->getTotal());
  }

  public function testGetTotalAfterRemovingItem()
  {
    $items = array(
      '34tr45' => array(
                          'price' => '9.99 EUR',
                          'description' => 'A very good CD by Jane Doe.',
                          'quantity' => 2
                        ),
       't667t4' => array(
                          'price' => '69.99 EUR',
```

```php
                        'description' => 'Super compilation.',
                        'quantity' => 1
                        ),
    'jhk987' => array(
                        'price' => '49.99 EUR',
                        'description' => 'Foo singers. Rare edition.',
                        'quantity' => 3
                        ),
  );
  $this->order->setItems($items);
  unset($this->order->items['jhk987']);

  $this->assertEquals((9.99 * 2 + 69.99).' EUR', $this->order->getTotal());
}

public function testListItems()
{
  $this->assertEquals(array(), $this->order->listItems());

  $items = array(
    '34tr45' => array(
                        'price' => 10,
                        'description' => 'A very good CD by Jane Doe.',
                        'quantity' => 2
                        ),
    '34tr89' => array(
                        'price' => 70,
                        'description' => 'Super compilation.',
                        'quantity' => 1
                        ),
  );

  $this->order->setItems($items);
  $this->assertEquals($items, $this->order->listItems());
}

public function testGetCustomer()
{
  $this->order->setCustomer('Jean Pistel');
  $this->assertEquals('Jean Pistel', $this->order->getCustomer());
}

public function testShippingAddress()
{
  $this->order->setShippingAddress('84 Doe Street, London');
  $this->assertEquals('84 Doe Street, London', $this->order->getShippingAddress());
}

public function testDiscountForGoldSilverCustomer()
{
  $this->assertFalse($this->order->isGoldCustomer());

  $items = array(
    '34tr45' => array(
                        'price' => 9.99,
                        'description' => 'A very good CD by Jane Doe.',
```

```
                                'quantity' => 2
                            ),
        '34tr89' => array(
                            'price' => 69.99,
                            'description' => 'Super compilation.',
                            'quantity' => 1
                            ),
    );
    $this->order->setItems($items);

    $this->assertEquals((19.98 + 69.99), $this->order->getTotal());

    $this->order->silver_customer = true;

    $this->assertEquals(71.98, $this->order->getTotal());

    $this->order->gold_customer = true;

    $this->assertEquals(53.98, $this->order->getTotal());
}

public function testDiscountOverOrderTotal()
{
    $items = array(
        '34tr45' => array(
                            'price' => 300,
                            'description' => 'A very good CD by Jane Doe.',
                            'quantity' => 1
                            ),
        '34tr89' => array(
                            'price' => 270,
                            'description' => 'Super compilation.',
                            'quantity' => 1
                            ),
    );
    $this->order->setItems($items);

    $this->assertEquals(570 * 0.9, $this->order->getTotal());


}
```

We will see PHPUnit in better detail later; if you don't get all the details right now, don't worry. We will be using variables and method names suitable to be understood in their ultimate essence.

What you may notice here is that this class shows a lack of compliance with good design principles, violating common good practices like single-responsibility—it cares about the order details, customer details, and discounting policies—and featuring quite long methods, even hard to be extended, mostly due to the wide use of conditional expressions. We will now try to detect and address each of these design defects with a step-by-step incremental strategy.

Look Ma'! No Comments!

We are quite used to reading and hearing suggestions about better and more widespread use of comments to make our code clearer to other developers and to ourselves, after even a small period away from a given portion of source code. We strongly agree with this rule, but we would like to point out that way too often this rule is misinterpreted to justify the use of comments as a substitute for clear and self-explanatory code.

While we advocate the use of code in classes and methods headers[1] we would like to see the smallest number possible of inline comments among lines of code, writing a code that shows the intention of the coder by itself, in a way almost as readable as natural language. It can be a difficult pursuit, but it pays, both in the short and the long run: it provides an easy way to communicate design among developers, as well as from developers to non-technical stakeholders, including the customer, and to ease the acquisition of new domain knowledge.

In our example we have the whole discount calculation made clear by means of comments, and we would like to get a clearer code on its own. We can overcome this defect by extracting commented code into a separated method. So we extract the code commented with

```
// ...if amount is over 500 we apply further 20% discount
```

into a private method with a meaningful name:

```
private function ifAmountIsOver500WeApplyFurther20Discount($total)
{
  if ($total > 500)
  {
    $total = $total * 0.8;
  }
  return $total;
}
```

And we do the same with the code commented with

```
// ...if amount is over 500 we apply further 10% discount
```

extracting it into

```
private function ifAmountIsOver500WeApplyFurther10Discount($total)
{
  if ($total > 500)
  {
    $total = $total * 0.9;
  }
  return $total;
}
```

After these two simple extractions we get a slightly different getTotal() method.

```
public function getTotal()
{
  $total = 0;

  foreach ($this->items as $item)
  {
    $currency = '';

    // we check for the item to be valid
```

---

[1] You may already know PHPDocumentor, a PHP documentation–generator available at http://www.phpdoc.org.

```
  if (isset($item['price']) && isset($item['quantity']))
  {
    // we detect currency if indicated
    $price = explode(' ', $item['price']);
    if (isset($price[1]))
    {
      $currency = $price[1];
    }
    $price = $price[0];
    $total += $price * $item['quantity'];
  }
}

// If the customer is gold we apply 40% discount and...
if ($this->gold_customer)
{
  $total = $total * 0.6;
  $total = $this->ifAmountIsOver500WeApplyFurther20Discount($total);
}
// If the customer is gold we apply 20% discount and...
elseif ($this->silver_customer)
{
  $total = $total * 0.8;
  $total = $this->ifAmountIsOver500WeApplyFurther10Discount($total);
}
else
{
  $total = $this->ifAmountIsOver500WeApplyFurther10Discount($total);
}

if ($currency)
{
  return round($total, 2).' '.$currency;
}
else return round($total, 2);
}
```

We run our test and we still find the class doing what we expect it to do. Though we think we still have a bad design, we have taken a little step towards quality. Let's move on, and we will see our design improve at each step.

Once Is Better than Twice

Now that we got rid of useless comments, the code started speaking for itself. Good. If only the Order class showed less duplicated code it would be a lot nicer!

Code duplication is one of the nastiest things a developer will ever have to cope with. It leads to bugs, hard maintenance, and badly-structured design of our software. Luckily enough we can count on many techniques to remove duplications in the code, and entire sections of this book will be about how to find a way through the complexity of your code to encapsulate every single datum or behavioral aspect of your code in one single and well-defined spot.

In our example we extracted two very similar methods: ifAmountIsOver500WeApplyFurther20Discount() and ifAmountIsOver500WeApplyFurther10Discount(). They encapsulate the very same logic applied to two different discount values. It calls for a very rewarding change. We rename one of those methods to keep its name as close as possible to its meaning and we add a $discount parameter:

```php
private function applyDiscountOverThreshold($total, $discount = 1)
{
  $threshold = 500;
  if ($total > $threshold)
  {
    $total = $total * $discount;
  }
  return $total;
}
```

Then we replace all the references to the two original methods with proper calls to this new method.

```php
$total = $this->applyDiscountOverThreshold($total, 0.8);
```

and

```php
$total = $this->applyDiscountOverThreshold($total, 0.9);
```

Now we can remove the second original method we didn't edit and make the new code more expressive by bringing the common threshold into a class constant, obtaining

```php
class Order
{
  const DISCOUNT_THRESHOLD = 500;
  ...
  private function applyDiscountOverThreshold($total, $discount = 1)
  {
    if ($total > self::DISCOUNT_THRESHOLD)
    {
      $total = $total * $discount;
    }
    return $total;
  }
  ...
}
```

With a similar reasoning we can further reduce code duplication by identifying a frequently-used code pattern like

```php
$total = $total * 0.6;
```

and extracting a method to generalize its use across our class:

```php
private function applyDiscount($total, $discount)
{
  return $total * $discount;
}
```

Let us rewrite our applyDiscountOverThreshold() and getTotal() methods:

```php
private function applyDiscountOverThreshold($total, $discount = 1)
{
  if ($total > self::DISCOUNT_THRESHOLD)
  {
    $total = $this->applyDiscount($total, $discount);
  }
```

```php
    return $total;
}

public function getTotal()
{
  $total = 0;

  foreach ($this->items as $item)
  {
    $currency = '';

    // we check for the item to be valid
    if (isset($item['price']) && isset($item['quantity']))
    {
      // we detect currency if indicated
      $price = explode(' ', $item['price']);
      if (isset($price[1]))
      {
        $currency = $price[1];
      }
      $price = $price[0];
      $total += $price * $item['quantity'];
    }
  }

  // If the customer is gold we apply 40% discount and...
  if ($this->gold_customer)
  {
    $threshold_discount = 0.8;
    $total = $this->applyDiscount($total, 0.6);
  }
  // If the customer is gold we apply 20% discount and...
  elseif ($this->silver_customer)
  {
    $threshold_discount = 0.9;
    $total = $this->applyDiscount($total, 0.8);
  }
  else
  {
    $threshold_discount = 0.9;
  }
  $total = $this->applyDiscountOverThreshold($total, $threshold_discount);

  if ($currency)
  {
    return round($total, 2).' '.$currency;
  }
  else return round($total, 2);
}
```

Goliath Died in the End

We split our code into better self-explanatory single-responsibility methods, but we are still violating the same encapsulation principle at the level of classes. The Order class is still managing the purchase, the customer data, and the discounting policy, and the bad entanglement of these aspects is well represented by the not-so-short if-else block we find in the getTotal() method of our Order class.

We want to attack this bad structure by first extracting customer data management into another new Customer class and then using it as a powerful device to remove stiff conditional logic.

First, we extract the Customer class along with all its related attributes:

```php
class Customer
{
  protected $is_gold = false;
  protected $is_silver = false;

  protected $first_name;
  protected $last_name;
  protected $customer_address;
  protected $customer_city;
  protected $customer_country;

  public function isGold()
  {
    return $this->is_gold;
  }

  public function makeGold()
  {
    $this->is_gold = true;
  }

  public function isSilver()
  {
    return $this->is_silver;
  }

  public function makeSilver()
  {
    $this->is_silver = true;
  }

  public function setName($customer)
  {
    list($this->first_name, $this->last_name) = explode(' ', $customer);
  }

  public function __toString()
  {
    return $this->first_name.' '.$this->last_name;
  }

}
```

Then we add references to this new class in the Order class, changing the constructor and all the methods, using the customer data to empower the needed interaction:

```php
class Order
{
  const DISCOUNT_THRESHOLD = 500;

  public $items = array();
```

```php
protected $customer;
protected $shipping_address;

public function __construct()
{
  $this->customer = new Customer();
}

public function setItem($code, $price, $description, $quantity)
{
  $items[] = array(
                    'code' => $code,
                    'price' => $price,
                    'description' => $description,
                    'quantity' => $quantity
                  );
}

public function setItems($items)
{
  $this->items = $items;
}

public function listItems()
{
  return $this->items;
}

public function getCustomer()
{
  return $this->customer;
}

public function setShippingAddress($address)
{
  $this->shipping_address = $address;
}

public function getShippingAddress()
{
  return $this->shipping_address;
}

private function applyDiscountOverThreshold($total, $discount = 1)
{
  if ($total > self::DISCOUNT_THRESHOLD)
  {
    $total = $this->applyDiscount($total, $discount);
  }
  return $total;
}

private function applyDiscount($total, $discount)
{
  return $total * $discount;
}
```

```php
public function getTotal()
{
  $total = 0;

  foreach ($this->items as $item)
  {
    $currency = '';

    // we check for the item to be valid
    if (isset($item['price']) && isset($item['quantity']))
    {
      // we detect currency if indicated
      $price = explode(' ', $item['price']);
      if (isset($price[1]))
      {
        $currency = $price[1];
      }
      $price = $price[0];
      $total += $price * $item['quantity'];
    }
  }

  // If the customer is gold we apply 40% discount and...
  if ($this->customer->isGold())
  {
    $threshold_discount = 0.8;
    $total = $this->applyDiscount($total, 0.6);
  }
  // If the customer is gold we apply 20% discount and...
  elseif ($this->customer->isSilver())
  {
    $threshold_discount = 0.9;
    $total = $this->applyDiscount($total, 0.8);
  }
  else
  {
    $threshold_discount = 0.9;
  }
  $total = $this->applyDiscountOverThreshold($total, $threshold_discount);

  if ($currency)
  {
    return round($total, 2).' '.$currency;
  }
  else return round($total, 2);
}
```

Notice how we removed the isGoldCustomer() method since we plan to use $this->customer->isGold() as a predicate to determine whether the customer belongs to the Gold affiliation program.

This time we have to edit our unit test as well, to match our newly-set interaction between the Order and Customer classes. Unit tests are such if they isolate a single unit of code—usually a class—and mock any related external behavior, usually belonging to other classes. Though this is the best way to test a well-defined portion of code in our systems, for clarity's sake here we will switch to so-called integration tests, testing the two classes together. Though it is absolutely not our favorite practice, it will be a lot clearer for those not used to unit tests: all in all, we are here to understand and learn step-by-step, not to exhibit brute force. With that disclaimer given, let's have a look at our test changes:

```php
class OrderTest extends PHPUnit_Framework_TestCase
{
    …
    public function testGetCustomer()
    {
        $this->order->getCustomer()->setName('Jean Pistel');
        $this->assertEquals('Jean Pistel', (string)$this->order->getCustomer());
    }
    …
    public function testDiscountForGoldSilverCustomer()
    {
        $this->assertFalse($this->order->getCustomer()->isGold());

        $items = array(
            '34tr45' => array(
                            'price' => 9.99,
                            'description' => 'A very good CD by Jane Doe.',
                            'quantity' => 2
                            ),
            '34tr89' => array(
                            'price' => 69.99,
                            'description' => 'Super compilation.',
                            'quantity' => 1
                            ),
        );
        $this->order->setItems($items);

        $this->assertEquals((19.98 + 69.99), $this->order->getTotal());

        $this->order->getCustomer()->makeSilver();
        $this->assertEquals(71.98, $this->order->getTotal());

        $this->order->getCustomer()->makeGold();
        $this->assertEquals(53.98, $this->order->getTotal());
    }

    public function testDiscountOverOrderTotal()
    {
        $items = array(
            '34tr45' => array(
                            'price' => 300,
                            'description' => 'A very good CD by Jane Doe.',
                            'quantity' => 2
                            ),
            '34tr89' => array(
                            'price' => 270,
                            'description' => 'Super compilation.',
                            'quantity' => 1
                            ),
        );
        $this->order->setItems($items);

        $this->assertEquals(870 * 0.9, $this->order->getTotal());
```

```
    $this->order->getCustomer()->makeSilver();
    $this->assertEquals(870 * 0.8 * 0.9, $this->order->getTotal());

    $this->order->getCustomer()->makeGold();
    $this->assertEquals(870 * 0.6 * 0.8, $this->order->getTotal());
  }
}
```

Now that we decoupled `Customer` and `Order`, we can launch our ultimate assault on the if-else cascading block, where most of the discounting policy is mainly implemented.

Big conditional blocks are a very bad pattern to be used in our software. They are hard to understand if they go over a minimal size, they are error-prone, they incentivize code duplication, and, above all, they are not robust against behavioral extensions: whenever I want to add another case I have to arrange at least a new conditional branch, not to mention complex nested conditional structures.

In our `Order` class, if we were to add a new customer affiliation program, we would need to add another else-if clause after those meant to manage Gold and Silver affiliation programs. Furthermore, the way we structured the `getTotal()` method badly manages the default case, forcing us to maintain a whole else branch just to set the `$threshold_discount`. Last but not least, "Gold" and "Silver" conditional fragments are very similar, feeding our desire to remove that duplication.

A powerful and often suitable solution is to exploit polymorphism. We can encapsulate the concept of *affiliation* in a stand-alone class and then extend it to represent all kinds of affiliation programs. Once encapsulated, that concept becomes a lot easier to use.

We create an abstract `Affiliation` class and a few children:

```
abstract class Affiliation
{
  abstract public function getType();
}

class GoldAffiliation extends Affiliation
{
  public function getType()
  {
    return Customer::GOLD;
  }
}

class SilverAffiliation extends Affiliation
{
  public function getType()
  {
    return Customer::SILVER;
  }
}

class NullAffiliation extends Affiliation
{
  public function getType()
  {
    return null;
  }
}
```

We add needed constants, fields, and methods to the Customer class:

```
class Customer
{
  const GOLD = 'gold';
  const SILVER = 'silver';

  protected $type;
  protected $affiliation;

  ...

  public function __construct()
  {
    $this->affiliation = new NullAffiliation;
  }

  public function isGold()
  {
    return $this->affiliation->getType() == self::GOLD;
  }

  public function makeGold()
  {
    $this->affiliation = new GoldAffiliation();
  }

  public function isSilver()
  {
    return $this->affiliation->getType() == self::SILVER;
  }

  public function makeSilver()
  {
    $this->affiliation = new SilverAffiliation();
  }
  ...
}
```

This is a middle step. We can run our test to check that everything is syntactically right, but still our Order class doesn't rely on polymorphic behavior. We have to equip our Affiliation hierarchy with methods to calculate the proper discount and then make the getTotal method in the Order class reference them.

We start by adding a protected attribute, $threshold_discount, and an abstract calculateDiscount() method to our abstract Affiliation class. By extending this method in each affiliation program, we get the right behavior case-by-case, moving into the subclass method the code coming from the related source conditional fragment:

```
class GoldAffiliation extends Affiliation
{
  ...
  public function calculateDiscount($order, $total)
  {
    $this->threshold_discount = 0.8;
    $total = $order->applyDiscount($total, 0.6);
```

```
    return $order->applyDiscountOverThreshold($total, $this->threshold_discount);
  }
}

class SilverAffiliation extends Affiliation
{
  …
  public function calculateDiscount($order, $total)
  {
    $this->threshold_discount = 0.9;
    $total = $order->applyDiscount($total, 0.8);
    return $order->applyDiscountOverThreshold($total, $this->threshold_discount);
  }
}

class NullAffiliation extends Affiliation
{
  …
  public function calculateDiscount($order, $total)
  {
    $this->threshold_discount = 0.9;
    return $order->applyDiscountOverThreshold($total, $this->threshold_discount);
  }
}
```

This way we can get rid of the whole if-else block used in the getTotal() method to compute discounting policies just by calling

```
$total = $this->customer->getAffiliation()->calculateDiscount($this, $total);
```

Here you get all Customer, Affiliate, and Order classes presented together for you to have a look at them before we come to the conclusion of this chapter:

```
class Customer
{
  protected $type;
  protected $affiliation;

  protected $first_name;
  protected $last_name;
  protected $customer_address;
  protected $customer_city;
  protected $customer_country;

  public function __construct()
  {
    $this->affiliation = new NullAffiliation;
  }

  public function isGold()
  {
    return $this->affiliation->isGold();
  }

  public function makeGold()
  {
    $this->affiliation = new GoldAffiliation();
  }
```

```php
  public function isSilver()
  {
    return $this->affiliation->isSilver();
  }

  public function makeSilver()
  {
    $this->affiliation = new SilverAffiliation();
  }

  public function setName($customer)
  {
    list($this->first_name, $this->last_name) = explode(' ', $customer);
  }

  public function __toString()
  {
    return $this->first_name.' '.$this->last_name;
  }

  public function getAffiliation()
  {
    return $this->affiliation;
  }
}

class GoldAffiliation extends Affiliation
{
  public function getType()
  {
    return Affiliation::GOLD;
  }

  public function calculateDiscount($order, $total)
  {
    $this->threshold_discount = 0.8;
    $total = $order->applyDiscount($total, 0.6);
    return $order->applyDiscountOverThreshold($total, $this->threshold_discount);
  }
}

class SilverAffiliation extends Affiliation
{
  public function getType()
  {
    return Affiliation::SILVER;
  }

  public function calculateDiscount($order, $total)
  {
    $this->threshold_discount = 0.9;
    $total = $order->applyDiscount($total, 0.8);
    return $order->applyDiscountOverThreshold($total, $this->threshold_discount);
  }
}
```

```php
class NullAffiliation extends Affiliation
{
  public function getType()
  {
    return null;
  }

  public function calculateDiscount($order, $total)
  {
    $this->threshold_discount = 0.9;
    return $order->applyDiscountOverThreshold($total, $this->threshold_discount);
  }
}

class Order
{
  const DISCOUNT_THRESHOLD = 500;

  public $items = array();

  protected $customer;
  protected $shipping_address;

  public function __construct()
  {
    $this->customer = new Customer();
  }

  public function setItem($code, $price, $description, $quantity)
  {
    $items[] = array(
                    'code' => $code,
                    'price' => $price,
                    'description' => $description,
                    'quantity' => $quantity
                  );
  }

  public function setItems($items)
  {
    $this->items = $items;
  }

  public function listItems()
  {
    return $this->items;
  }

  public function getCustomer()
  {
    return $this->customer;
  }

  public function setShippingAddress($address)
  {
```

```php
    $this->shipping_address = $address;
  }

  public function getShippingAddress()
  {
    return $this->shipping_address;
  }

  public function applyDiscountOverThreshold($total, $discount = 1)
  {
    if ($total > self::DISCOUNT_THRESHOLD)
    {
      $total = $this->applyDiscount($total, $discount);
    }
    return $total;
  }

  public function applyDiscount($total, $discount)
  {
    return $total * $discount;
  }

  public function getTotal()
  {
    $total = 0;

    foreach ($this->items as $item)
    {
      $currency = '';

      // we check for the item to be valid
      if (isset($item['price']) && isset($item['quantity']))
      {
        // we detect currency if indicated
        $price = explode(' ', $item['price']);
        if (isset($price[1]))
        {
          $currency = $price[1];
        }
        $price = $price[0];
        $total += $price * $item['quantity'];
      }
    }

    $total = $this->customer->getAffiliation()->calculateDiscount($this, $total);

    if ($currency)
    {
      return round($total, 2).' '.$currency;
    }
    else return round($total, 2);
  }
}
```

After we performed this simple series of changes, the `Order` class became

1. Easier to understand. We can even ignore what happens in the `Affiliation` and `Customer` classes to understand that a discount depending on customer *type* will be applied to our order's total amount.

2. Easier to extend. Its behavior is now depending on a *plug-in-like* device. You add a new `Affiliation` subclass and you can get a completely different discount policy *without even needing the* `Order` *class to know it*.

3. Easier to read. We don't rely on comments anymore to figure out how the discount policy is computed. Every method *communicates its role and responsibility* in a clear and effective way. Every class is focused on a single concept, creating a smaller context to cope with when reading, understanding, designing, and writing our code.

Some readers could argue that we still keep lots of code duplication in `Affiliation` subclasses and we still manage the currency in a bad procedural style. We agree. We decided to stop our example here to move on to the next few chapters, but our improvement of the code could go a lot further.

This is not a real-life example and we had to find a trade-off between complexity and clarity. Anyway, in real-life projects, as well, we come to a point when we have to decide whether to stop refactoring a given portion of code, and whether to invest time in improving existing code or developing new features. The right skills to decide this are to be derived from the context with the help of experience. By now what we care about most is that you met your first *refactoring*.

CHAPTER 4

Principles and Rules

Refactoring software is a practice adopted during recent years within agile software development processes. Like all agile practices, refactoring is based on clear principles and rules that must be observed to improve the software production process.

In this chapter we'll see the main principles and rules about software refactoring. We'll see why and when we should do refactoring and also why sometimes we shouldn't do it.

Why Should You Do Refactoring?

There are four important reasons for introducing the refactoring practice in your production process:

- Refactoring improves the design of our software.

- Refactoring makes our software easier.

- Refactoring helps find bugs.

- Refactoring makes the team more productive.

All four reasons are really important in software development. If your team is already very good at producing software with good design, which is simple and free from bugs—and all of this at a satisfactory production rhythm—then refactoring just might improve this excellent process, assuming that your team can always do better.

Refactoring Improves the Design of Our Software

In the last few years software production has changed a lot. The needs are growing, domains are very disparate, customer requirements are often unclear, software must change very quickly, and deadlines are very narrow. With these assumptions it is a struggle for even the best software architects to create a good application design that is always correct throughout the software's life cycle. What we did yesterday may no longer reflect today's needs, or what we knew yesterday may be different than what we understand today. Grasping complex domains is a difficult task for developers, and design software in these domains is difficult too.

Through refactoring, with many small steps, we can change, not the functionalities of our software, but the design of how these features have been implemented, without losing the value already accrued. Day after day we can improve the design of our software, while the software grows; we can bring out the correct design in time, rather than trying to force an early design of the project. Our software will fit like a glove.

Thanks to this ability to embrace change, everything that is technically feasible will be possible. We will never be afraid to change direction; we will always be sure of keeping the produced value.

For example, if we have a Person object that can have only one address, but we want to change its behavior, adding more than one, we can improve its design, first extracting the address class as in Figure 4-1, and then implementing the ability to add other addresses.

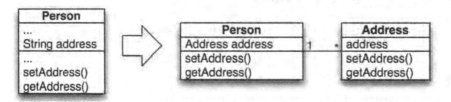

Figure 4-1. Extract class

Refactoring Makes Software Easier to Understand

How many times have you ever wanted to change software after months without working on it, and realized that you forgot everything and no longer know where to start? How often have you been forced to change code written by others, while being afraid to add a single line of code, thinking that even the slightest change could break everything?

When you are faced with code that is hard to read, called "spaghetti code" because it is as tangled as a plate of spaghetti, the desire to throw it away and rewrite it from scratch is always great. There is software that has been unchanged for years and cannot grow because there is no one developer who can modify it, except the one who created it.

The technique of refactoring helps us make software easy to understand, so any developer can get back to working on code after months, without needing to remember everything or being afraid of breaking something by changing only a small line of code. This is because all the methods applied in refactoring are based on the principles of "keep it simple and stupid" (KISS), "don't repeat yourself" (DRY), and "test-driven development" (TDD).

For example, by changing our application from procedural code to object-oriented code through the techniques of big refactoring, we make our code easier to understand and modify, because, in general, reading an object-oriented code with a good design is simpler than reading a functional code.

In general, bad smells make our code difficult, but by removing them we make our code easier.

Keep It Simple and Stupid (KISS)

"Everything should be made as simple as possible, but no simpler."

—Albert Einstein

"Keep it simple and stupid" refers to keeping our code as simple as possible. It doesn't mean "easy," but as "lean" as possible. We have to think only about what we need today and not try to foresee the demands that might come in the future, since, after all, the human mind is not capable of predicting the future. Simple means doing something as well as possible, but in the simplest way.

Don't Repeat Yourself

"Every piece of knowledge must have a single, unambiguous, authoritative representation within a system."

—Andrew Hunt [HUN99]

A duplicate code is difficult to read and maintain, as a code that does the same thing in the same way in many parts of our software, or does the same things but differently. Duplication of code lines or functionalities is the biggest flaw in our software, because we can't change it simply and it could exponentially increase the risk of introducing bugs. Less is better. Our code shouldn't be duplicated, and we must not repeat. Our system must implement functionality in only one point. Only in this way we can maintain and modify our software easily.

Test-Driven Development (TDD)

Test-driven development is a software development technique that consists in the repetition of a short development cycle divided into the following steps:

1. Add a test.
2. Run all tests and see if the new one fails.
3. Write the simplest code that will cause the test to pass.
4. Run tests and see them succeed.
5. Refactor the code.

Once the cycle is finished, you can start again with a new test (TDD). A study found that TDD drives developers to write more tests, debugging less and making a better design for the software they are working on.

Testing software in a unitary and automatic manner means being able to measure change. Unit tests are to software development what standard units of measurement are to physics. Without the ability to measure change, physicists would not be able to perform their experiments. Without unit tests, software engineers would not be able to modify software and discover whether something has changed.

The practice of refactoring is based on TDD, because it is a subset. There can't be refactoring without TDD, and TDD cannot exist without refactoring.

Refactoring Helps You Find Bugs

Finding bugs before they go into production is truly an art. There are excellent programmers who can read hundreds of lines of procedural or object-oriented code and instantly find all the bugs. Unfortunately, not all developers have this skill. For me, finding a bug from hundreds of lines of code is like finding a needle in a haystack.

When we do refactoring, our work is low-level, so we must understand what a piece of code does in order to decide whether we have to change it. In this activity, finding bugs becomes very simple, because when we understand what our code really does, we understand also what the code doesn't do. Repeating this activity every day in every single piece of code greatly increases the chances of finding bugs before they get into production.

When we write tests for our software, we have to understand what the code does to be able to test everything that could easily fail. Thanks to this detailed work, we can find a lot of hidden bugs.

Refactoring Increases Our Productivity

We have seen that refactoring improves the design of our software, as well as its readability, retention, and quality, by reducing the number of bugs. But what can we say about the development speed?

Productivity, in software development, is a measure of how much functioning, corrected, and tested code a developer produces in a unit of time.

It might seem that refactoring slows the production of software, focusing our efforts too much on quality and not enough on delivery dates, a bit as if we had unlimited time. Actually this perception isn't true. When we begin to write code for a new software, at first, may seem faster to write procedural code rather than object-oriented code, to provide a prototype or to meet delivery, but what happens when a customer ask us to change what we did because it doesn't fully meet the requirements? What happens when the customer finds the first bug and we need to fix it? What happens if the customer asks us to add a new feature? After the first delivery, the time we spend in modifying the software, finding and resolving bugs, and adding patches to meet the customer requests becomes uncontrolled and immeasurable, as we can see in Figure 4-2.

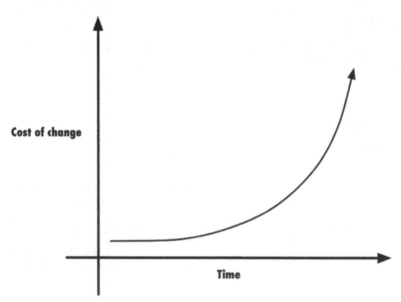

Figure 4-2. Classical cost of change

We can change this strange habit. By giving our software the right quality, creating an appropriate design, decreasing the presence of bugs, and testing our code, we'll pay a small initial price, but then the curve of maintaining complexity will be linear and measurable, as we can see in Figure 4-3. We will never lose the value acquired, and we won't be afraid to embrace change, when needed.

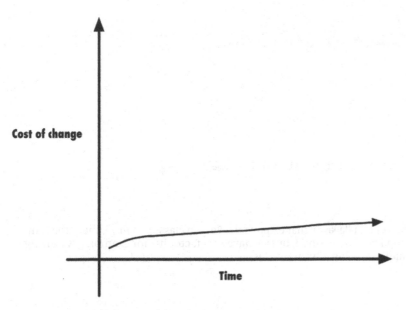

Figure 4-3. Cost of change with refactoring

When Should We Do Refactoring?

When we should do refactoring is a question that developers ask me often. My answer is very simple: "When tests are green." Our primary goal is to provide immediate value to our customers and stakeholders, and our second goal is to provide this value in the best way. It's in the second goal that we can do refactoring. When a test is green, we have given value to the customer. If we realize that we can improve the code, we have to do refactoring.

This rule is very simple, but first, we have to be familiar with the refactoring techniques. To achieve this understanding, we can start with three simple and explicit rules.

The Rule of Three

This rule is the one I enjoy most. It was presented for the first time by Martin Fowler in his book *Refactoring: Improving the Design of Existing Code*[FOW01].

As we have seen, one of the worst enemies of clean code is code duplication. The first rule seeks to mitigate the copy-and-paste action. It says that if there are problems in our software that are solved with the same piece of code or portions of such codes, we can duplicate this piece of code at most twice. The third time, however, we have to do refactoring and remove the duplication.

By applying this simple rule, you'll see hundreds of lines disappear from your software and you'll begin to understand the behavior and communication of your objects, if you didn't before. Try it now.

For example, we have two classes, Student and Teacher, that extend the Person class:

```
class Student extends Person
{
  ...
```

```
  public function __toString()
  {
    return ucfirst($this->lastname).' '.ucfirst($this->firstname);
  }
  ...
}

class Teacher extends Person
{
  ...
  public function __toString()
  {
    return ucfirst($this->lastname).' '.ucfirst($this->firstname);
  }
  ...
}
```

If we need to add a new class called `Manager` that extends the `Person` class, and implement the same `toString()` method, we can't duplicate the method, but we have to refactor it—for example, by moving the method in the super class and removing it from subclasses.

```
class Person
{
  ...
  public function __toString()
  {
    return ucfirst($this->lastname).' '.ucfirst($this->firstname);
  }
  ...
}
```

Refactoring When You Add Functionality

Another magic moment—or tragic, depending on the code with which we are working—is when we add functionalities to our software. Regardless of whether the software has a perfect design, when we add functionality, especially if the code wasn't written by us, we must first understand what the software does. If we realize that the software design isn't appropriate to accommodate new features, we have to do refactoring to change and improve it to receive the long-awaited new features. Through this practice, the design of our code evolves constantly, perfectly incorporating the proper behavior of the implemented features.

For example, as we saw in Figure 4-1, we did refactoring of our code before adding a new functionality.

Refactoring When You Need to Fix a Bug

When the customer or a beta tester reports a bug, our job is to fix it. To accomplish this arduous task, the first thing we do is find out what our software does during the process in which the bug happens. Before starting to debug, it's advisable to try to reproduce the bug locally. Write a test that fails, and once you have the red test, begin the inspection. Once we fix the bug, we can be sure it will not recur, because next time the test will notify us of the error before going into production.

If during debugging tasks we find that the bug is due to a wrong block of code or a wrong design, first we have to fix the bug in the easiest way. Then, when the test is green, we can start doing refactoring.

In most cases, the proliferation of bugs is due to an untested code, which is code with an incorrect design. If you cannot test your code, don't blame the testing framework. Rather, ask whether your design is correct.

When You Shouldn't Do Refactoring

From my experience I can tell you that there are no contraindications for doing refactoring, so my advice is to do it always and often. It should become an activity of your daily production process. If we put refactoring in our toolbox, our code will always be fragrant.

However, if we aren't a refactoring expert and we have to refactor very complex code that is untested and full of bugs, written by someone else, in this case we should strongly consider rewriting it from scratch. The risk of rewriting software, however, is to miss the value that the software already has for our customers and users who currently use it. Before rewriting the software from scratch, you need to interview all users to figure out what features they use and how, so you can implement all features including those hidden.

Some Simple Rules

The rules to follow when refactoring are few but strict. They must be observed to avoid the risk of decreasing the software's value and wasting time.

- Test before refactoring.
- Make small and simple changes.
- Never change functionality.
- Follow the bad smells.
- Follow refactoring techniques step-by-step.

Test Before Refactoring

The first rule, and, in my opinion, the most important, means that we cannot do refactoring in a piece of our code if that piece of code is not tested. The refactoring work does not have to change the behavior of code, but it should improve code executing the same behavior. In writing a test, we cage the behavior, making sure, first, that it is correct, and that the refactoring work will be finished only when the tests become green again.

If we're applying refactoring techniques that introduce new units in our code, remember to write new tests for these new units before creating them.

Just by performing the tests, we are able to measure whether the behavior of the software has changed, and fix it, if needed. We have to see the test as the main tool in our toolbox, which gives us instant feedback if something goes wrong. Our minds are often unable to remember how units communicate within the system, and often a simple change can affect the whole system. But the test may notify us of the malfunction before it is put into production. In this way we entrust the responsibility for reporting errors to an external, automatic, and repeatable tool, which will always work in the same way, instead of our minds, which often fail.

Small and Simple Changes

Refactoring is a low-level task. When we perform it, we are constantly working with the heart of our software system. It's a bit like performing surgery to improve something in your body that no longer works well—it is always a very delicate activity.

That is why we always have to create as much value as possible and be able to go back, if we are going the wrong way. Sometimes the changes we make can create more problems than benefits. For example, we can pursue a design that does not fit our needs, and we have to go back quickly because our changes are incorrect. To be able to go back easily, we must make small and clear steps, verifying that at each step, tests are still green. Thus we ensure the highest value, and we can more easily go back, when needed.

The refactoring process is an iterative process that consists of the following steps:

1. Find the piece of code to change.

2. Write a unit test if you didn't.

3. Do a small step to improve.

4. Run the test and fix the code until the test is not green.

5. Go back to step 3.

Sometimes you may be tempted to iterate too many times, trying to find the perfect code. The code is almost never perfect, but there is a code right now. This is what we pursue, because if it goes wrong tomorrow, we can do refactoring.

We must learn when to stop—we can't iterate the process of refactoring an infinite number of times, because there is always a delivery date that we must respect.

Sometimes it can seem like the value of the software is not increasing with these small steps. You always need to remember that the activity of refactoring is an everyday activity that gives results over time, because the whole value is made up of small changes.

Never Change Functionality

All the refactoring techniques are conservative techniques that aim to improve our code in performing the procedures it already runs. Refactoring does not need to add new functionalities, but to modify the existing code to better accommodate new features. When we add new features to our software, we can't begin with development and refactoring while we are adding the features. We can do refactoring only before or after. If we immediately realize that the design of our software is incorrect, we must modify it immediately. If we realize late that the design is incorrect, we can add the features and then do refactoring of the code, making it more suited to the features just included.

If you want to do a proper refactoring and, at the same time, maintain the most value for your customer, try to follow this rule. Otherwise, you could spend some bad nights trying to find bugs.

Follow the Bad Smells

In Chapter 2 we learned how to recognize bad smells. Refactoring assumes that there are some bad smells; if there aren't, we can't do refactoring. I have seen some developers do refactoring to improve design, simply because the finished design was unexpected.

When design emerges through TDD techniques, sometimes it happens that the design implemented is different from the one expected. In this case, doing refactoring won't increase value. If the code is correct, the test is green, the customer has accepted the functionalities implemented, and there are no bad smells, there isn't a reason to do refactoring. The only important thing is that the code must be tested in order to change it, as soon as we realize that we want to change it.

When we're not sure if our code has any bad smells, never mind—simply test the code and move on. If things should be changed, they will be obvious, and at that point you will have no doubts about what to do.

Metaphorically speaking, we must use smell rather than sight. Sometimes, our eyes can deceive us in refactoring. Just follow the smell—if there isn't one, we can move on with our work.

Follow Refactoring Techniques Step-by-Step

In the next chapters, we will see a catalogue of the main refactoring techniques created by Martin Fowler [FOW01]. Each technique will be accompanied by practical reasons, a step-by-step mechanism, and some examples. The rule is to follow all the steps as described.

We must learn to recognize bad smells and to identify which techniques to apply. Once we have identified the technique, we need to follow the steps of the mechanism, because these steps are small enough that we can go back easily if needed and not get lost in the difficult art of refactoring.

The goal is to become autonomous and know the technique by memory. Then refactoring will be automated and applied in our daily coding.

Summary

In this chapter we have seen the principles and rules behind the application of refactoring techniques. If we respect the principles and follow the rules, we can learn and perform all the techniques of refactoring in the best way.

In the next chapters, we deepen our knowledge of test-driven development and learn about some tools that can simplify the execution of refactoring techniques.

CHAPTER 5

■ ■ ■

Test-First Development

Refactoring is a powerful tool, enabling you to improve the design of your software. It means taking your working code and changing it, sometimes deeply, to make it perform the same tasks it performed before changing it. Somehow this could sound quite pointless: why be at risk of losing a piece of working code just to improve its design? Shouldn't the functionality of working code be valued more than its structure?

Any wise programmer should ask herself questions like these at the first mention of refactoring. We have already called attention many times to the importance of preserving our existing code base and why this should be our main goal. Then how can we change it without introducing errors? How should I explore new ways to arrange my software? Is it possible for me to refactor my code protected by a strong and soft safety net? Yes, it is, because automated tests are at hand, one of the most powerful tools ever in the history of software development.

Building Value One-Way

You have been coding thousands and thousands of lines of code for years, and you have spent thousands of hours debugging that code, but how often did you stop and think about how unproductive debugging your code is? Yes, we really mean it: debugging is not productive. Debugging is just a way to finally deliver what you were already supposed to have delivered.

Even the best of our customers is willing to pay to get some technical value to invest in her business. In a healthy environment the customer should also try to maximize her return on investment (ROI) by getting the most value for the lowest expense, taking into consideration any short-term goal together with longer-term ones. In the same healthy environment we should support these needs by trying to maximize our ROI by reducing costs, not by delivering lower quality.

Debugging is a step back from a healthy developer-customer system because debugging is always a cost. Even on a fixed price contract featuring a warranty option on bugged features, the customer will pay a cost for debugging, because a dollar lost now is not paid back by the same dollar next week. If debugging were considered a standard practice in the automotive market, we would be buying cars incapable of bringing us home 60–70% of the time, attached to warranties providing us with ones that actually function. It can happen, we know, but I bet you wouldn't be pleased to see it happen 60–70% of the time. Those numbers are considered low in the software industry indeed!

Obviously this way of conceiving software development has its roots in the reality of the software industry and engineering, and no one should be faulted for debugging code if a defect is found. What we would like to advocate here is a way to model your software development process, being aware of the fact that during the last 20 years many techniques arose to reduce or even erase the need for debugging, making the development of software a one-way process, from customer requirements to implementation with few or no features bouncing between being done or in progress.

Chaos in a Cage

We have more than one kind of automatic test to rely upon. In this book we will focus on unit tests and functional tests. Unit tests are meant to be closer to the developer's point of view, while functional tests are meant to test software correctness and conformity in fulfilling customer requirements from a user point of view. We will see those two kinds of tests in better detail in the following chapter, but we want to make clear here that both together constitute a way to defend your code from chaotic evolution and attack the complexity every developer inherently has to cope with.

Before we go on, let us introduce you to unit tests and functional tests.

Unit Tests

Unit tests confirm that a single unit of code computes the correct output when passed a well-defined input. The developer writes a test that automatically passes on a meaningful set of different inputs and checks whether the output is right. A unit test is meant to test only a single unit of code, thus any interaction between that code and some external actor providing a service or some data should be simulated in a safe way, so that a developer knows which few lines of code are wrong whenever a unit test fails. If anything like a database or a web service is needed by the code we are testing, it must be simulated with a fake version to avoid tainting our testing scope.

What does a unit test look like? It depends on the testing framework you use, but a wide range of frameworks sticks to the xUnit de facto standard. When writing this book, we opted for PHPUnit and, while we will describe its use in detail in the next chapter, we want you to have a first look right now. The following test is nothing more than a test class—yes, a class itself!—testing the Sale class to return the right price after a given state is set:

```
class SaleTest extends PHPUnit_Framework_TestCase
{
  public function testGetPrice()
  {
    $sale = new Sale();
    $sale->amount = 10;
    $this->assertEquals(100, $sale->getPrice());
  }
}
```

With a complete suite of tests like that, a development team can prevent chaos from creeping into its design at a very low level, testing a single object's behavior and—as too often overlooked—mutual interaction between objects.

Functional Tests

Functional tests are a powerful way to *use* our software on the end-user's behalf and to verify its behavior's correctness. They describe the interaction of the user with the machine we are building our software upon, reproducing every click and drag-and-drop relentlessly. This kind of test relies on the whole system to run with no isolation of units coming into play. Every testing action involves the user interface, the controller, the model, its logic, and real data as if it were a real person using the software we are testing.

What does a functional test look like? It depends a lot on the testing framework you decide to use. Unlike unit tests, at the time of writing this book, no shared standard has emerged yet, nor does some widely adopted technology seem to pave the way towards convergence to a common rule. For the purpose of explaining functional tests in this book we chose Selenium RC, a tool that is part of the

Selenium project that provides you with an API to use a browser in many programming languages, PHP included. It is obviously focused on web applications, but we think this is an advantage here, since most of the PHP applications are built for the web environment. A typical Selenium RC test in PHP looks like this:

```php
class Example extends PHPUnit_Extensions_SeleniumTestCase
{
  function setUp()
  {
    $this->setBrowser("*firefox");
    $this->setBrowserUrl("http://www.google.com/");
  }

  function testMyTestCase()
  {
    $this->open("/");
    $this->type("q", "selenium rc");
    $this->click("btnG");
    $this->waitForPageToLoad("30000");
    $this->assertTrue($this->isTextPresent("Results * for selenium rc"));
  }
}
```

Functional tests like this are obviously several magnitudes slower than the unit tests, but in the right amount they can provide many valuable tests, even reaching corners of our software that are hardly testable without these tools.

You Don't Know What You've Got 'til It's Gone

What's the value brought in by a complete unit and functional test suite covering the most hidden spot of our application and the most complex synergy between two classes? While we could be tempted to see those tests as just a bug-ratio reduction tool, there's a lot more in them. Analyzing the way a web software project typically makes people closely relate to each other and the way bugs affect those relationships, we will be able to see much more value in using automated tests. The following sections will show you how automated tests can bring in value that goes beyond strictly technical issues, addressing many typical concerns often overlooked by usual project management by strongly empowering the team to be successful.

Trust Me: Communication

Among the ways automated tests address chaos is that they provide better communication among team members and between the team and the customer. Software is hard to keep tidy. It is such a chaotic beast that we cannot even be sure we understand the customer's requirements until the day we deliver it, unless we use some unambiguous way to agree on what has to be done. In the manufacturing industry, each product is described by a well-defined list of tests to distinguish acceptable products from bad ones. Automated software tests represent the same type of constraint: unit tests state *how* the system is supposed to do its job, while functional tests state *what* the system is expected to do.

Functional tests are a perfect tool to supplement or even replace traditional customer requirements documents. Every detail emerging from conversations among the customer, the interaction designers, and the development team should be frozen into some functional test, not to be forgotten, overlooked, misunderstood, or left untested.

Unit tests then define how those detailed requirements become working software. Every requirement is not considered fulfilled until every design detail of its implementation is well covered by a proper set of unit tests. This way unit tests become a conversation place for developers to agree upon the structure of the software they are all committed to, improving the spread of implicit knowledge about the project.

If you are new to automated tests and used to traditional documenting processes, you may think that good old ways to write documentation always worked, and so learning a brand-new way would be just a waste of time. We won't argue about the value of well-written documentation—though we could argue about the effort required for keeping it up to date. What we strongly oppose, though, is thinking there's some real alternative to writing tests to find out whether your software is doing what it's supposed to do. Writing those tests before the implementation of the working code would be a way to get even more value from your test suite, enabling their use as documentation.

Listen to What You Say, and Write It Down

Every time a programmer implements a feature requested by the customer he looks for a quick way to check when it's done, so he can start working on the next task. This is how code is developed by everyone, everywhere, anytime; it couldn't be different. Whenever we do something to reach a planned goal we have to find a way to know when the goal is reached, no matter the issue with which we are coping. That said, once we have found a way to test the effectiveness of our work, why not capture that test and reuse it freely?

The best thing about automated tests is that they are cheap, they are coded by developers (the only ones to know which details deserve to be tested first and how), and they can be run at will. This causes teams using automated tests to run them as often as possible since they provide a complete and *objective* status about the quality of their code. No one we introduced to automated tests ever went back, not once in years. This is because we always need something to report our progress instantaneously.

Feedback is also an issue in the customer-developer relationship: the customer has the right to understand and be sure that everything he asked for is going to be delivered, and he also has the right to information that is as close to real time as possible. The money invested by the customer in development deserves our respect, and letting him know how well the investment is going is a minimum requirement. Functional tests are the tool to give the customer almost real-time feedback about the project's progress rate. As far as every requirement is expressed in a functional test, the more functional tests pass, the closer we are to the end of the project.

The most important strategic team commitment about testing should be to keep them quick. Non-automated tests or tests taking too long will be run with less frequency. This will naturally tend to cause more new functionalities to be tested at once, to reduce testing overhead. This strategy will bring failure more often on a larger code changeset, making it harder to spot the problem, and raising the bug rate again.

Pleasant Constraints

Refactoring is a technique that involves changing critically large portions of already-working code. This can be very dangerous, because of the unintended consequences and side effects. Thousands of details spread across hundreds of thousands of lines of code must all be correct, with hundreds of components communicating with each other in a hard-to-predict way. As the codebase grows larger, we are exposed to an exponentially larger risk.

Even if you are not using refactoring, you should be aware that usually in the software industry half of the development occurs after the initial release. That means that the software needs to be safely changed anyway and that those changes must be cheap. Many common techniques make changes safer: encapsulation, layering, external components, web services, and open sourcing. But the most effective way to ease changes preventing disasters is an automated test suite that tests the code the developers intend to change and the system behavior the customer is going to get in return.

An up-to-date test suite will not only snipe emerging bugs, keeping the system close to its quality requirements, but will also greatly reduce the scope to look within to fix the bug. The developer's duty then becomes to write those tests, freezing requirements in a formal language, making sure they are correct, complete, version-controlled, maintained, and considered part of the released product. Even if they end up constituting a large portion of the overall codebase, they will be many times worth the effort they will require to be created and maintained.

As more functional tests add up with time, they become an ever-growing repository of requirements that will never be forgotten, not even once through the whole system lifespan. This is great news for development and testing teams that have to run through the whole system every time a change is made, in order to be sure no regression has been introduced by the change itself. This is great news for the customer, too, because quality assurance teams can be very skilled and proficient, but they are human—sooner or later they will be wrong. Automated tests don't get distracted, bored, annoyed, angry, or tired. They just perform their duty.

Create Trust

Communication, feedback, and safety nets all together deliver a fourth crucial value in the life of a team: trust. Communication is the root of trust. Proven working software builds the customer's trust in the team. An unambiguous design specification increases the team members' trust in each other. A widely applied test suite may communicate many times a day how good the team is performing, improving the manager's trust in the team. A software project in which trust is not increasing day by day, minute by minute, is a dead project. Defensive behaviors will start creeping in and people will begin to cheat. There is no way to squeeze value out of a cheating team, since defensive behavior will not create business value—just like debugging won't.

A winning project is one devoted to building value, not one that incentivizes barriers. Any tool, technique, or mindset capable of raising trust among the whole team to the highest level is always worth its cost. Automated tests are one of those tools.

Test-Driven Development

At least a brief acknowledgment should be given to a discipline based on a test-first programming approach, unit tests, and refactoring: test-driven development (TDD).

This set of techniques is a way to *discover* the best design for our systems in an amazingly effective way to combine top-down and bottom-up thinking. On one hand, it empowers developers to think of the main tasks and responsibilities without worrying about the interactions going on at lower levels; on the other hand it requires us to develop the simplest actors and interactions that solve our problem. The main *mantra* of test-driven development is *Red, Green, Refactor*. What does it all mean?

Red: We write a failing test expressing in a well-defined way what we want our unit of code to do.

Green: We write the minimal amount of code needed to make the test pass.

Refactor: We refactor the code we wrote to improve its design without breaking tests. In case we need to create new tests and new units of code to accommodate the newly improved design, we apply TDD to those components, too.

While we consider this theme to be too crucial to be reductively explained in a single chapter of this book, it is also true that very few written resources exist on this subject. This is mostly due to the inherently non-theoretic nature of this discipline, making it very hard to define and explain it by means of a book. No wonder Kent Beck's main book on TDD [TDD] is based on a series of examples to make TDD clear to the reader.

TDD, by the way, represents the state-of-the-art use of automated tests as a tool for not only checking and anticipating the correctness of code, but also guiding its design.

Summary

In this chapter, we discovered the technical and strategic value of automated tests, learned about several kinds of automated tests, and scratched the surface of test-driven development. We also learned there is a way to inject value in our software, making it constantly grow by reducing its wandering across chaotic states. The next chapter will unveil what tools we can rely upon while taming the beast of software complexity.

CHAPTER 6

■ ■ ■

Refactoring Tools

Without tools helping us with refactoring, doing a good job could be very difficult. We need a test framework to perform all refactoring activities and some automated tools to increase our productivity.

In this chapter we will see which features we should have in our integrated development environment (IDE) for our refactoring activities, and we'll see how to write unit tests with the PHPUnit testing framework and functional tests with Selenium. We'll see also how integrate the two tools through an extension of PHPUnit to completely automate the execution of our build test.

PHP IDE

In the PHP programming world there are several Integrated Development Environments (IDE). Each of us surely has a favorite. Refactoring activities can be done with a text editor like "vi" but if we have an IDE that supports the automation of some refactoring activities, certainly it could increase our productivity in this kind of job.

Our intention isn't to promote one IDE rather than another, so we will stay neutral, considering only the features that an IDE should have to support us in some refactoring activities.

Refactoring Activities

When you refactor a very large application, there are some costly operations that can be easily automated using the right IDE:

- Renaming parameters, methods, and classes
- Moving parameters, methods, and classes
- Encapsulating the parameters of a class
- Making override methods
- Safely removing

Rename

"Rename" means the ability of an IDE to automatically rename a parameter of a class, a method of a class, or the class itself, wherever it is invoked or used in our code.

Move

"Move" refers to the ability of an IDE to automatically move a class parameter or method within a hierarchy, or from a class to another linked.

Encapsulate Field

"Encapsulate field" refers to the ability of an IDE to automatically create getter and setter methods for the public properties of a certain class in order to be able to change the visibility.

Override

"Override" means the ability of an IDE to automatically create override methods from a parent class in child classes.

Safely Remove

"Safely remove" means the ability of an IDE to delete a file from a project virtually and not physically, so that you can restore it in case there are errors caused by the absence of this file.

Cross-Platform Open-Source IDE

There is a lot of open-source and closed-source software that has these features, but to be neutral, we want to talk only about two IDEs that are open-source and multi-platform. These two applications have some of the features mentioned, and the developers are working to integrate all of them in future releases. The first software is NetBeans, a very complete IDE that was made to develop Java applications. It is sponsored by Oracle, and the latest version supports PHP language and some refactoring activities.[1]

The other is PHP Development Tools (PDT), a module for the Eclipse open-source software, developed by the open-source community, Zend, and IBM, which incorporates many features for development with PHP and refactoring activities.[2]

For more information on this software and its refactoring tools, we recommend the official documentation.

Unit Tests with PHPUnit

PHPUnit is a framework of the xUnit family that allows testing units of PHP code. Through the available tools we can test classes, methods, and functions, run the tests from the console, and create reports to analyze the results.

What Is It?

The PHPUnit framework is the complete port of JUnit 3.8.1, a Java testing framework, to PHP5. Through this framework, the following is also possible:[3]

---

[1] NetBeans, NetBeans IDE 6.8 Release Information, http://netbeans.org/community/releases/68/

[2] Eclipse, PHP Development Tools Project, www.eclipse.org/pdt.

[3] PHPUnit, Features, www.phpunit.de/wiki/Features, 11/13/2008

- Testing the database

- Using the mock object to test the behavior of classes that depend on other classes

- Organizing your own tests in suites and groups

- Filtering the tests to be run

- Performing custom operations at the end and beginning of each test

- Logging the tests running in various formats (XML, JSON, TAP, GraphViz, etc.)

- Creating functional tests for Selenium RC

- Integrating testing with third-party software (Apache Maven, Bamboo, Bitten, CruiseControl, Parabuild, etc.)

The minimum requirements[4] to use PHPUnit are

- PHP 5.1.4 or later (5.2 is recommended)

- DOM, PCRE, and SPL extensions

Installation

The latest version of PHPUnit, at the time of publication, is 5.1.4. This version requires PHP 5.1.4 or later, and the 5.3.2 version (or later) is strongly recommended.

We can install the framework with the PEAR distribution system or do it manually, downloading the source code from the official repository.

PEAR Installation

Before we install PHPUnit via PEAR it is necessary to record two new channels with the following command:

```
$ pear channel-discover pear.phpunit.de
$ pear channel-discover pear.symfony-project.com
```

This should be done only the first time. Once registered, the new channels will always be set in our environment. Then execute the following command to install the framework:

```
$ pear install phpunit/PHPUnit
```

When the installation is completed, we find the folder PHPUnit in the PEAR directory. We will also have available the "phpunit" command that we can run from our shell.

Manual Installation

The PEAR installer isn't the only way to install PHPUnit. We can also install the PHPUnit framework manually, following these steps:

1. Download the latest release archive from http://pear.phpunit.de/get/.

---

[4] PHPUnit, Requirement, www.phpunit.de/wiki/Requirements, 07/17/200

2. Extract it to a directory that is listed in the include_path of your `php.ini` configuration file.

3. Go into the PHPUnit directory and rename the `phpunit.php` file in phpunit.

4. Open the file phpunit, just renamed, and replace the `@php_bin@` string with your command line PHP interpreter path (usually /usr/bin/php).

5. Copy the `phpunit` file into one of the filesystem paths included in the environment PATH variable (usually /usr/local/bin) and make it executable (chmod +x phpunit).

6. Go again into the PHPUnit directory and replace the `@php_bin@` string in the `Util/PHP.php` file with your command line PHP interpreter path (usually /usr/bin/php).

7. Run the "phpunit" command and check that it works well.

How to Write Unit Tests

Unit tests, as the name implies, are used to test the code unit, which is the smallest part of our code that can be tested. In PHP, by units we mean the classes and the functions. A unit test should test a single-unit independent piece of code, decoupled from its dependencies.

A PHPUnit test corresponds to a single class that extends the class `PHPUnit_Framework_TestCase`. The methods of this class are the tests of our code. The name of the methods that represent our tests must begin with the prefix "test," or have the `@test` annotation in the method comment.

The class we extend gives us all the assertion methods needed to write our tests easily. For example, we can check if a result of a certain method is equal to a given string, or if it is true or false, in a very simple manner.

In the next example, we create a unit test to verify some array properties.

```php
<?php
class ArrayTest extends PHPUnit_Framework_TestCase
{
  public function testArray()
  {
    $empty_array = array();
    $array = array(
                    'fruit' => 'apple',
                    'color' => 'red',
                    'name' => 'james',
                    'boolean' => false
                  );

    // Check array items number
    $this->assertEquals(0, count($empty_array));
    $this->assertEquals(4, count($array));

    // Check array values
    $this->assertEquals('apple', $array['fruit']);
    $this->assertEquals('red', $array['color']);
    $this->assertEquals('james', $array['name']);
    $this->assertEquals(false, $array['boolean']);
    $this->assertFalse($array['boolean']);
```

```
    // Check array keys
    $this->assertArrayHasKey('fruit', $array);
    $this->assertArrayHasKey('color', $array);
    $this->assertArrayHasKey('name', $array);
    $this->assertArrayHasKey('boolean', $array);

    // Check array value
    $this->assertContains('apple', $array);
    $this->assertContains('red', $array);
    $this->assertContains('james', $array);
    $this->assertContains(false, $array);
  }
}
?>
```

Testing arrays seems easy enough. To create a more complex unit test we test the unit of the class Person.

```php
<?php
class Person
{
  public $firstname;
  public $lastname;
  public $address;
  public $country;
  public $city;

  public function __toString()
  {
    return $this->firstname.' '.$this->lastname;
  }

  public function fromArray($array)
  {
    $this->firstname = isset($array['firstname']) ? $array['firstname'] : $this->firstname;
    $this->lastname  = isset($array['lastname']) ? $array['lastname'] : $this->lastname;
    $this->address   = isset($array['address']) ? $array['address'] : $this->address;
    $this->country   = isset($array['country']) ? $array['country'] : $this->country;
    $this->city      = isset($array['city']) ? $array['city'] : $this->city;
  }

  public function toArray()
  {
    $array = array();
    $array['firstname'] = $this->firstname;
    $array['lastname']  = $this->lastname;
    $array['address']   = $this->address;
    $array['country']   = $this->country;
    $array['city']      = $this->city;

    return $array;
  }
}

?>
```

We write a `PersonTest` class test where we test each method and each class attribute.

```php
<?php

include_once('Person.php');

class PersonTest extends PHPUnit_Framework_TestCase
{
  /**
   * Initialize a Person instance
   */
  public function setUp()
  {
    $this->person = new Person();
    $this->person->firstname = 'James';
    $this->person->lastname = 'Doe';
    $this->person->address = '56 Rupert St';
    $this->person->city = 'London';
    $this->person->country = 'UK';
  }

  /**
   * Test Person attributes
   */
  public function testAttributes()
  {
    $this->assertEquals('James', $this->person->firstname);
    $this->assertEquals('Doe', $this->person->lastname);
    $this->assertEquals('56 Rupert St', $this->person->address);
    $this->assertEquals('London', $this->person->city);
    $this->assertEquals('UK', $this->person->country);

    $this->assertClassHasAttribute('firstname', 'Person');
    $this->assertClassHasAttribute('lastname', 'Person');
    $this->assertClassHasAttribute('address', 'Person');
    $this->assertClassHasAttribute('city', 'Person');
    $this->assertClassHasAttribute('country', 'Person');
  }

  /**
   * Test for Person::__toString() method
   */
  public function testToString()
  {
    $this->assertEquals('James Doe', (string) $this->person);
  }

  /**
   * Test for Person::fromArray() method
   */
  public function testFromArray()
  {
    $array = array('firstname' => 'John', 'lastname' => 'Marshall');

    $this->person->fromArray($array);
    $this->assertEquals('John', $this->person->firstname);
    $this->assertEquals('Marshall', $this->person->lastname);
    $this->assertEquals('56 Rupert St', $this->person->address);
```

```php
    $this->assertEquals('London', $this->person->city);
    $this->assertEquals('UK', $this->person->country);

}

/**
 * Test for Person::toArray() method
 * @test
 */
public function toArray()
{
    $array = $this->person->toArray();
    $this->assertEquals(5, count($array));
    $this->assertEquals('James', $array['firstname']);
    $this->assertEquals('Doe', $array['lastname']);
    $this->assertEquals('56 Rupert St', $array['address']);
    $this->assertEquals('London', $array['city']);
    $this->assertEquals('UK', $array['country']);
}
}

?>
```

The framework provides two methods—setUp() and tearDown()–that are executed for each test execution. The setUp() method is run at the beginning of each method, and tearDown() is run at the end of each method. We can use these two methods to initialize and destroy our fixtures. In this way we can isolate the execution of each test.

A test method can accept arbitrary attributes as arguments. This content is provided by a data provider method, which can be defined by the notation @dataProvider in the method comment. The method must be public and should return an array of arrays or an object that implements the Iterator interface. The test will be executed many times for the values of the data provider array.

```php
<?php

class MaxTest extends PHPUnit_Framework_TestCase
{
    /**
     * @dataProvider provider
     */
    public function testMax($a, $b, $result)
    {
        $this->assertEquals($result, max($a, $b));
    }

    public function provider()
    {
        return array(
            array(1, 10, 10),
            array(100, 20, 100),
            array(1, 2, 2),
            array(12.4, 12.55, 12.55),
        );
    }
}

?>
```

Sometimes we have to test that a class method throws an exception. To test the exceptions just use the annotation @expectedException, with the value of the exception we expect, in the remarks of the method.

```php
<?php

class ExceptionTest extends PHPUnit_Framework_TestCase
{
    /**
     * @expectedException InvalidArgumentException
     */
    public function testException()
    {
    }
}

?>
```

How to Run Tests

PHPUnit provides a shell script to run our tests and to provide immediate feedback of results. During installation we copied the script "phpunit" in our executable path and we made it executable. To execute the tests we run the script phpunit from the shell and pass a folder path where our test files are, or the direct test file path to run.

For example, we have all the tests previously presented in the same folder Test.

```
|- Test
|   |- ArrayTest.php
|   |- ExceptionTest.php
|   |- MaxTest.php
|   |- PersonTest.php
```

In this case, we can go inside the folder and run the following command:

```
$ phpunit .
PHPUnit 3.4.1 by Sebastian Bergmann.

.........

Time: 0 seconds

OK (9 tests, 41 assertions)
```

PHPUnit will automatically find all test files inside the directory executing all test methods. If some of our tests fail, PHPUnit will notice which tests failed, with an "F" character instead of a "." char, and with an error message above with an execution stack trace.

```
$ phpunit .
PHPUnit 3.4.1 by Sebastian Bergmann.

.F......F

Time: 0 seconds
```

```
There were 2 failures:

1) MaxTest::testMax with data set #1 (100, 20, 20)
Failed asserting that <integer:100> matches expected <integer:20>.

/Users/cphp/Dropbox/Progetti/Libri/Apress/ProPHPRefactoring/drafts/chapter05 -
Tools/code/MaxTest.php:10

2) ArrayTest::testArray
Failed asserting that two strings are equal.
--- Expected
+++ Actual
@@ @@
-banana
+apple

/Users/cphp/Dropbox/Progetti/Libri/Apress/ProPHPRefactoring/drafts/chapter05 -
Tools/code/arrayTest.php:15

FAILURES!
Tests: 9, Assertions: 29, Failures: 2.
```

How to Organize Our Tests

The easiest way to organize our test suite is to order our test files in folders and subfolders. PHPUnit is able to recursively traverse the filesystem and find all our test files.

For example, we have a directory of classes grouped by packages.

```
Src
|- Component
|  |- Autoloader
|  |  |- Autoloader.php
|  |  |- Exception.php
|  |- Cli
|  |  |- Application.php
|  |  |- Cli.php
|  |  |- Exception.php
|  |  |- Task.php
|  |- Deploy
|  |  |- Deploy.php
|  |  |- Exception.php
|  |  |- History.php
|  |  |- Repository.php
|  |- FileSystem
|  |  |- FileSystem.php
|  |  |- Interface.php
|  |  |- Local.php
|  |- Net
|  |  |- Connection.php
|  |  |- Local.php
|  |  |- Ssh2.php
|  |- Util
|  |  |- Rsync.php
|  |  |- Time.php
```

We can arrange the relative test suites as follows:

```
Test
|- Component
|  |- Autoloader
|  |  |- AutoloaderTest.php
|  |  |- ExceptionTest.php
|  |- Cli
|  |  |- ApplicationTest.php
|  |  |- CliTest.php
|  |  |- ExceptionTest.php
|  |  |- TaskTest.php
|  |- Deploy
|  |  |- DeployTest.php
|  |  |- ExceptionTest.php
|  |  |- HistoryTest.php
|  |  |- RepositoryTest.php
|  |- FileSystem
|  |  |- FileSystemTest.php
|  |  |- InterfaceTest.php
|  |  |- LocalTest.php
|  |- Net
|  |  |- ConnectionTest.php
|  |  |- LocalTest.php
|  |  |- Ssh2Test.php
|  |- Util
|  |  |- RsyncTest.php
|  |  |- TimeTest.php
```

Running the PHPUnit command and passing as a parameter the folder Test, the script will find all the tests in the folder and its subfolders and will run them.

$ phpunit Tests
```
PHPUnit 3.4.2 by Sebastian Bergmann.

.......................................................... 60 / 81
....................

Time: 0 seconds
```

OK (81 tests, 212 assertions)

The problem of organizing the test suite through the filesytem is that we can't decide in which order to run them.
A more elegant and effective way to organize the test suite is through the class
PHPUnit_Framework_TestSuite. This class allows you to create a hierarchy of ordered tests. We can create a suite class for each package, and a generic file suite that includes all other package suites, so you can run all tests or just test for a certain package.
Returning to the preceding example, we could have a suite class for each package.

```
Test
|- Component
|  |- Autoloader
|  |  |- ...
|  |  |- AutoloaderSuite.php
|  |- Cli
```

```
|  |  |- ...
|  |  |- CliSuite.php
|  |- Deploy
|  |  |- ...
|  |  |- DeploySuite.php
|  |- FileSystem
|  |  |- ...
|  |  |- FileSystemSuite.php
|  |- Net
|  |  |- ...
|  |  |- NetSuite.php
|  |- Util
|  |  |- ...
|  |  |- UtilSuite.php
|  |- ComponentSuite.php
```

The ComponentSuite class is the class that includes the suite test of each package.

```php
<?php

include_once('Autoloader/AutoloaderSuite.php');
include_once('Cli/CliSuite.php');
include_once('Deploy/DeploySuite.php');
include_once('FileSystem/FileSystemSuite.php');
include_once('Net/NetSuite.php');
include_once('Util/UtilSuite.php');

class ComponentSuite
{
  public static function suite()
  {
    $suite = new PHPUnit_Framework_TestSuite('Component');
    $suite->addTest(AutoloaderSuite::suite());
    $suite->addTest(CliSuite::suite());
    $suite->addTest(DeploySuite::suite());
    $suite->addTest(FileSystemSuite::suite());
    $suite->addTest(NetSuite::suite());
    $suite->addTest(UtilSuite::suite());

    return $suite;
  }
}

?>
```

The internal class suites, instead, collect test class files for each package, for example:

```php
<?php

include_once('AutoloaderTest.php');
include_once('ExceptionTest.php');

class AutoloaderSuite
{
  public static function suite()
  {
```

```
   $suite = new PHPUnit_Framework_TestSuite('Autoloader');
   $suite->addTestSuite('AutoloaderTest');
   $suite->addTestSuite('ExceptionTest');

   return $suite;
 }
}

?>
```

The AutoloaderTest class and ExceptionTest class are the test classes that extend PHPUnit_Framework_TestCase. In this way, deciding when to add a class test, we can decide the execution order. To execute all tests, we have to run the following command:

$ phpunit ComponentSuite
```
PHPUnit 3.4.2 by Sebastian Bergmann.

.......................................................... 60 / 81
....................

Time: 0 seconds
```

OK (81 tests, 212 assertions)

To run the tests of Autoload Package, we will run

$ phpunit Autoload/AutoloadSuite
```
PHPUnit 3.4.2 by Sebastian Bergmann.

....

Time: 0 seconds
```

OK (4 tests, 20 assertions)

Test Doubles

"Sometimes it is just plain hard to test the system under test (SUT) because it depends on other components that cannot be used in the test environment. This could be because they aren't available, they will not return the results needed for the test, or executing them would have undesirable side effects. In other cases, our test strategy requires us to have more control or visibility of the internal behavior of the SUT.

When we are writing a test in which we cannot (or choose not to) use a real depended-on component (DOC), we can replace it with a Test Double. The Test Double doesn't have to behave exactly like the real DOC; it merely has to provide the same API as the real one so that the SUT thinks it is the real one!"

—Gerard Meszaros [MES07]

When we do refactoring, we should tests interdependent classes; dependent classes due to poor design or to real domain dependencies. Since the test should be individual and independent, testing interdependent classes may create side effects due to their dependencies. For example, a test may fail not because it changes the class tested, but because it has changed its dependent class.

When the system under test depends on external components, we introduce test doubles. Through this technique we can simulate the behavior of dependent classes without really using them, like a film director using stuntmen, rather than the real actors, for difficult roles.

PHPUnit provides tools to create a Stub Object and a Mock Object. Meszaros [MES07] defines a Stub Object as a real component on which the system under test depends so that the test has a control point for the indirect inputs of the system underneath. This allows the test to force the system under test down paths it might not otherwise execute.

Conversely, he defines a Mock Object as an observation point that is used to verify the indirect outputs of the system under test as it is exercised. Typically, the Mock Object also includes the functionality of a Test Stub in that it must return values to the system under test if it hasn't already failed the tests, but the emphasis is on the verification of the indirect outputs. Therefore, a Mock Object is a lot more than just a Test Stub plus assertions; it is used in a fundamentally different way.

Stub Object

For example, if we want to simulate the following class in one of our tests, because our system under test depends on it, we can use a stub object instead of it.

```php
<?php

class Foo
{
  public function bar()
  {
    // do something
  }
}

?>
```

We can replace the Foo class with a stub object calling the method getMock() of the PHPUnit_Framework_TestCase super class.

```php
<?php

class StubTest extends PHPUnit_Framework_TestCase
{
  public function testStub()
  {
    // Create a stub for the Foo class
    $stub = $this->getMock('Foo', array('bar'));

    // Configure the stub
    $stub->
      expects($this->any())->
      method('bar')->
      will($this->returnValue('something'));

    // Test that calling $stub->doSomething() will now return 'something'
```

```
    $this->assertEquals('something', $stub->bar());
  }
}

?>
```

Thus PHPUnit generates on the fly a class Foo, which returns a static value "something" whenever its bar() method is invoked, without putting at stake the original class Foo. The stub class can be fully configured and can return static values, objects, callbacks, exceptions, or arguments passed to the method.

Mock Object

If we want to create a Mock Object with PHPUnit, we use the same method getMock(), but we can configure the returned object verifying that a certain method is called, when it is called, and how often.

In the next example we want to test the Order class that depends on the Item class. When I call the getTotal() method of the Order class I want to verify that also the getTotal() method of the Item class is called and how often, without introducing a real instance of the Item class.

```php
<?php
class Order
{
  public function addItem(Item $item)
  {
    $this->items[] = $item;
  }

  public function getTotal()
  {
    $total = 0;
    foreach($this->items as $item)
    {
      $total += $item->getTotal(true);
    }
    return $total;
  }
}

class Item
{
  public $quantity;
  public $price;

  public function getTotal()
  {
    return $quantity*$price;
  }
}

class OrderTest extends PHPUnit_Framework_TestCase
{
  public function testGetTotal()
  {
    $item = $this->getMock('Item', array('getTotal'));
```

```
    $item->expects($this->once())->
        method('getTotal')->
        with($this->equalTo(true))->
        will($this->returnValue(10));

    $order = new Order();
    $order->addItem($item);
    $this->assertEquals(10, $order->getTotal());
    }
}

?>
```

Without putting at stake the real Item class on which the Order class depends, we test that by adding an item to order, the getTotal() method of the Item class is called once and that the right argument is passed. We also configure the methods to return a static value, so we can test that the getTotal() method of the Order class returns the right result. If the getTotal() method is called twice instead of once, the test fails, throwing an exception.

PHPUnit Conclusion

PHPUnit is a very powerful and complete framework that provides many other features to support our software development process:

- Code coverage analysis

- Behavior-driven development

- Mock per web services e-file system

- Agile documentation

- Skeleton generator

- Logging

To explore all the functionality of PHPUnit you can consult the online documentation at www.phpunit.de/manual/3.4/en/index.html. PHPUnit is an open-source project developed by Sebastian Bergmann and licensed under BSD-style as free software.

Functional Test with Selenium

Selenium provides a set of components to automate the creation of functional tests of web applications.

What Is It?

"Selenium is a portable software testing framework for web applications. Selenium provides a record/playback tool for authoring tests without learning a test scripting language."

—Wikipedia[5]

---

[5]   Wikipedia, Selenium (software), http://en.wikipedia.org/wiki/Selenium_IDE, 04/22/2010

Selenium provides a set of components to automate the creation of functional tests of web applications. With Selenium you can automate the navigation of a web site by creating assertions for testing the presence of certain elements in the DOM. Selenium can test Javascript routines also. One of the main strengths of this tool is that you can run tests on multiple browsers, like Internet Explorer, Firefox, Safari, or Chrome. This way you can test the cross-browser compatibility of web applications.

Selenium provides three main components:

- Selenium IDE
- Selenium RC
- Selenium Grid

Selenium IDE

Selenium IDE is an integrated development environment to make test cases with Selenium. It is a Firefox extension and provides simple tools to build and run individual test cases or entire test suites.

Through Selenium IDE we can record the user's entire browsing sessions, which may be automatically run later. When recording by right-clicking any part of the page, Selenium IDE provides a context menu through which you can choose to add various command assertions to the test, such as how to verify the presence of a certain text or DOM element. Through the IDE, when you finish recording, you can also change all the commands automatically created to make them more specific or better for that type of testing.

Suites created with Selenium IDE can be run through the IDE itself, or through the server Selenium Remote Control.

Selenium RC

Selenium Remote Control (RC) is the Selenium server written in Java. Through this server, you can schedule and automate the execution of tests written with Selenium IDE. We can use it, for example, to integrate the test suites into a Continuous Integration System.

Besides automating the tests, server provides an API and libraries in various programming languages, including PHP, to integrate the execution of the test with other testing frameworks. PHPUnit integrates the execution of Selenium functional tests through Selenium RC.

Selenium Grid

Selenium Grid is a component that lets you scale the performance of Selenium functional tests. With this component it is possible to parallelize the execution of tests in various browsers and operating systems, across multiple instances of Selenium RC.

Installation

Selenium IDE is a plug-in for Firefox, the open-source browser developed by the Mozilla Foundation. The minimum requirement to install the plug-in is version 1.5 to 3.6.* of Firefox installed on your computer.

To install the plug-in you can:

1. Open Firefox.
2. Go to `http://release.seleniumhq.org/selenium-ide`.
3. Enter the latest release folder.

4. Click on the `selenium-ide-*.xpi` file.

5. Confirm the installation.

Once the add-on is installed, we find a new link, "Selenium IDE," in the Tools menu.

To install Selenium RC you must download the package from `http://seleniumhq.org/download` and uncompress the package. Since the server is written in Java you must have Java Virtual Machine version 1.5 or later installed on your machine. Assuming you downloaded the package on a Linux OS and uncompressed it in the path "`/usr/local/selenium-rc`," to start the server you can run the following shell command:

```
$ java -jar /usr/local/selenium-rc/selenium-server-1.0.*/selenium-server.jar
```

For other operating systems follow the online documentation at `http://seleniumhq.org/docs/05_selenium_rc.html#installation`.

How to Record and Run Functional Tests

To write a functional test with Selenium IDE, open Firefox and click on the submenu "Selenium IDE" of the Tools menu. The IDE is opened in a contextual window already recording. From now on, all the navigation actions we perform with the browser will be registered from the IDE. To stop recording, simply click the red record button in the upper-right corner of IDE window. To resume the recording, click it once again.

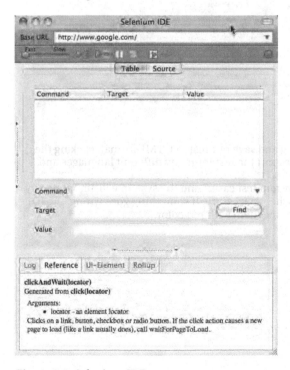

Figure 6-1. Selenium IDE.

As we navigate the page and the IDE is recording, we can check the presence of text or DOM elements on the web page. Clicking any component of the page will open a contextual menu with suggestions for various commands to be used to add assertions to our tests.

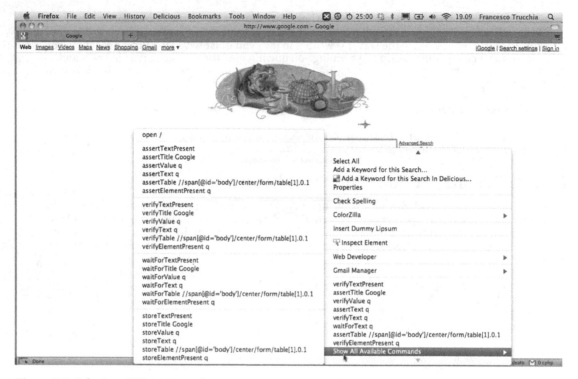

Figure 6-2. Selenium IDE contextual menu.

When we finish the test session, we stop recording and save our test in HTML format, clicking the menu File -> Save Test Case As. Once saved, you can export the test for many different languages and testing frameworks, including PHPUnit for PHP.

To run the test you must click the button "Play current test case," and the system will automatically run the same navigation session, checking elements where necessary. If something goes wrong, the IDE will notice us the number of failed tests and will underline them with red color.

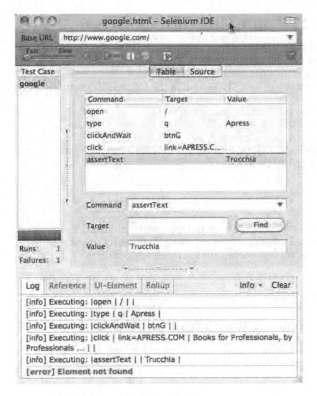

Figure 6-3. Selenium IDE failed error.

The IDE allows you to add additional tests or modify those already entered, suggesting the commands we want to use. Selenium uses XPath to identify elements within the page. Almost all commands take as a first argument the position of elements that can be provided with the ID or the XPath address.

For the complete list of commands and for more information, please read the official documentation at http://seleniumhq.org/docs/03_selenium_ide.html.

How to Organize Selenium Tests

In large applications, it's useful to create more functional tests, divided according to some criteria relating to the application type, such as functional modules in the case of an intranet, or sections of content in the case of web sites. Selenium IDE allows us to organize our tests in suites. A suite is the description of a set of functional tests, so you can automatically run an entire group of related functional tests.

To create a suite with Selenium IDE, first we create more functional tests, save them to disk, and then save the test suite by clicking the File menu and then the "Save test suite as" button.

Now when we open the IDE, we can load the entire group of tests created by simply opening the suite. To run the full set of tests we need to click the button "Play Entire test suite."

Both test suites and single functional tests are saved in a simple HTML format, which can be changed through our preferred IDE or text editor if needed.

Automated Test Execution with Selenium RC

With Selenium IDE it is impossible to automate testing in a Continuous Integration System, as the test execution takes place manually. To do this we can use the Selenium RC server. Through the server you can run a test suite by shell command and create a report file with the tests results.

To run a scheduled execution of our test suite it is sufficient to schedule the following command:

```
$ java -jar selenium-server.jar -htmlSuite "*firefox" "http://www.google.com"
"/absolute/path/to/my/HTMLSuite.html" "/absolute/path/to/my/results.html"
```

With this command we run the HTMLSuite.html suite in the Firefox browser with the base path www.google.com and the results are saved in the file results.html.

Selenium Conclusion

In this section we introduce the reader to the basics of writing functional tests with Selenium. For further study, refer to the official documentation, http://seleniumhq.org/docs. We will use this kind of test in the next chapter, where we will talk about "Big Refactoring" techniques for web applications.

The Best of Two Worlds

The PHPUnit testing framework integrates itself very easily with the functional testing framework Selenium through the Selenium RC server.

Selenium RC and PHPUnit

The Selenium RC server provides a set of APIs to communicate with the server with different languages. Thanks to this feature, an extension for PHPUnit to run Selenium tests into PHPUnit was created.

The integration of two frameworks allows a single framework to write unit tests and functional tests, making the maintenance of the tests very simple, and extending the basic functionality of PHPUnit.

Selenium Functional Test with PHPUnit

To write a functional test with PHPUnit Selenium, simply create a new class test that extends the class PHPUnit_Extensions_SeleniumTestCase.

```php
<?php

require_once 'PHPUnit/Extensions/SeleniumTestCase.php';

class ApressWebTest extends PHPUnit_Extensions_SeleniumTestCase
{
  protected function setUp()
  {
    $this->setBrowser('*firefox');
    $this->setBrowserUrl('http://www.apress.com/');
  }

  public function testTitle()
  {
```

```php
    $this->open('/');
    $this->assertTitle('APRESS.COM | Books for Professionals, by Professionals ...');
  }
}

?>
```

The `PHPUnit_Extensions_SeleniumTestCase` class provides all the interfaces to navigate the web pages through the browser set in the `setUp()` method, and all methods to verify the existence of elements or text within pages that we are viewing.

In each test we must implement the method `setUp()`, used to configure the browsing session. The methods we can use to configure the session are listed in Table 5-1.

Table 6-1. Methods to configure session.

Method	Meaning
void setBrowser(string $browser)	Set the browser to be used by the Selenium RC server.
void setBrowserUrl(string $browserUrl)	Set the base URL for the tests.
void setHost(string $host)	Set the hostname for the connection to the Selenium RC server.
void setPort(int $port)	Set the port for the connection to the Selenium RC server.
void setTimeout(int $timeout)	Set the timeout for the connection to the Selenium RC server.
void setSleep(int $seconds)	Set the number of seconds the Selenium RC client should sleep between sending action commands to the Selenium RC server.

PHPUnit can also capture a screenshot when a test fails. This feature is very useful for understanding what went wrong. To activate it you must configure the test class arguments `$captureScreenshotOnFailure`, `$screenshotPath`, and `$screenshotUrl`.

```php
<?php

require_once 'PHPUnit/Extensions/SeleniumTestCase.php';

class ApressWebTest extends PHPUnit_Extensions_SeleniumTestCase
{
  protected $captureScreenshotOnFailure = TRUE;
  protected $screenshotPath = '/var/www/localhost/htdocs/screenshots';
  protected $screenshotUrl = 'http://localhost/screenshots';

  protected function setUp()
  {
    $this->setBrowser('*firefox');
    $this->setBrowserUrl('http://www.apress.com/');
  }
```

```
  public function testTitle()
  {
    $this->open('http://www.apress.com/');
    $this->assertTitle('APRESS.COM | Books for Professionals, by Professionals ...');
  }
}

?>
```

In our tests, we can use all the commands available for Selenium to navigate, make assertions, or check elements inside our web page, because PHPUnit implements a magic method that is a proxy to all of Selenium RC API. Consult the official documentation of Selenium for a complete list of commands to run: http://seleniumhq.org/docs/04_selenese_commands.html.

Writing functional tests manually is quite a complex task with complex DOM, so we can write our tests simply with the Selenium IDE recorder feature and then export them through the IDE itself in PHPUnit format. To do it, you can click the File menu of Selenium IDE and then the "Export Test case As" -> PHPUnit button.

Running functional tests written for Selenium is as simple as running unit tests. First we check that the Selenium RC server is running; if it isn't, let's start with this command:

```
$ java -jar selenium-server.jar
```

Then run the command shell "phpunit," passing as the first argument the folder where our tests are, or the path of the test file to run.

Summary

In this chapter we have seen the basic tools needed to do refactoring work. There are IDEs that will help us to automate tedious and repetitive tasks through their refactoring features. We also presented two important test frameworks, one to test our unit of code, named PHPUnit, and the other to test web functionalities in an agnostic way, named Selenium; they will help us to write regression tests and not lose the value of our software.

CHAPTER 7

■ ■ ■

Structuring Behavior

A big problem in taming the beast of old legacy code often arises from a method's length. Methods can be too long, too short, overused, or underused. Long methods are hard to keep in mind at once with all their meaning, while short ones can be not meaningful enough. Misused methods can compromise a clean structure by adding unwanted complexity.

In both cases we have to refactor our code to improve its readability, its logical structure, and to keep undesired complexity out of our way. Most of the refactoring techniques we'll see in this book are based on the collection of refactoring methods published by Martin Fowler [FOW01]. For each method we'll see the reason for it, typical use scenarios, refactoring mechanics, and some real-world examples to see how each method works. Here we will learn how to move code back and forth from a stand-alone method and inline code, as well as how to use or get rid of temporary variables to obtain a clear and reusable code. The refactoring techniques in this chapter are among the ones you'll use most frequently, since they also often represent a middle step toward other refactoring.

Extract Method

Problem: "You have a portion of code you can group together."

Solution: "Turn that code into a method named to explain the purpose of the method."

Motivation

The "Extract Method" is a common refactoring meant to communicate meaning to the reader. If you have an excerpt of code that is too long to be clear or you feel the temptation to add comments to explain its purpose, this is the refactoring technique that will help you.

According to Martin Fowler [FOW01], short and well-named methods are preferable, for three reasons at least. First, small methods implicitly carry a smaller behavior, which is likely to be more focused on a given task. These fine-grained methods are easier to use across the whole application. Second, as higher-level methods composed by smaller ones, they are more readable, reducing the need for comments. Third, small methods can be overridden more easily, since they expose a more task-focused interface with fewer side effects.

Fowler also gives us a good example of pragmatic attitude, explaining what the right method length should be: if clarity gets improved, extract the code, even when the method name is longer than the method body.

Mechanics

- Create a new method, and name it after what it does, not how it does it. If you don't manage to find such an expressive name, don't extract the code.

- Copy the extracted code from the source method into the new method.

- Look for any variables that are local in the scope of the source method. These must be turned into local variables and parameters in the new method scope.

- Declare as temporary variables any temporary variables used only within the extracted code.

- Spot any local-scope variables modified by the extracted code. If one variable is modified, try to treat the extracted code as a query and return the result to the external variable to be modified. If there is more than one variable like this you can still try to treat the extracted code as a query using a few workarounds made possible by PHP language constructs, like returning an array and using the list() function to redistribute the values among old-scope variables. You may also need to use other refactoring techniques like "Split Temporary Variable" or "Replace Temp With Query," which you'll learn about later in this chapter.

- Pass local scope variables that are read from extracted code into the new method as parameters.

- Replace the extracted code in the source method with a call to the target method.

- Remove any declaration of temporary variables moved inside the target method.

- Run tests.

Example: No Local Variables

The extract method can be really easy. Consider the following class method:

```php
class Customer
{
  public $orders = array();
  public $name;

  public function printOwing()
  {
    echo '<h2>Customer owes</h2>';
    echo '<h3>Amount based on orders updated yesterday</h3>';

    // calculate oustanding
    $outstanding = 0;
    foreach ($this->orders as $order)
    {
      $outstanding += $order['amount'];
    }

    // print details
    echo "<div>Name: {$this->name}</div>";
    echo "<div>Amount: $outstanding</div>";
  }
}
```

Customer class is tested by the following unit test:

```
class CustomerTest extends PHPUnit_Framework_TestCase
{
  public function testPrintOwing()
  {
    $customer = new Customer();
    $customer->name = 'Edmundo';
    $customer->orders = array(
      array('amount' => 110),
      array('amount' => 300),
      array('amount' => 150)
    );

    ob_start();
    $customer->printOwing();
    $output = ob_get_contents();
    ob_end_clean();

    $this->assertRegExp('/<h2>Customer owes<\/h2><h3>Amount based on orders updated ↵
yesterday<\/h3>/', $output);
    $this->assertRegExp('/Name: Edmundo/', $output);
    $this->assertRegExp('/Amount: \$560/', $output);
  }
}
```

The code printing the header is very easy to extract, just a matter of cutting and pasting:

```
class Customer
{
  public $orders = array();
  public $name;

  public function printOwing()
  {
    $this->printHeader();

    // calculate oustanding
    $outstanding = 0;
    foreach ($this->orders as $order)
    {
      $outstanding += $order['amount'];
    }

    // print details
    echo "<div>Name: {$this->name}</div>";
    echo "<div>Amount: $outstanding</div>";
  }

  public function printHeader()
  {
    echo '<h2>Customer owes</h2>';
    echo '<h3>Amount based on orders updated yesterday</h3>';
  }
}
```

Example: Using Local Variables

We saw an example that's too easy. Local variables are there more often than not, and scope issues require extra work to be correctly managed. In some cases they can even prevent us from doing refactoring at all.

Let's see an easy one: when local variables are read-only we can just pass them as parameters to a newly-written method. In our example we can make this step with the new `printDetails($outstanding)` method:

```php
class Customer
{
  public $orders = array();
  public $name;

  public function printOwing()
  {
    $this->printHeader();

    // calculate oustanding
    $outstanding = 0;
    foreach ($this->orders as $order)
    {
      $outstanding += $order['amount'];
    }

    $this->printDetails($outstanding);
  }

  public function printDetails($outstanding)
  {
    echo "<div>Name: {$this->name}</div>";
    echo "<div>Amount: $$outstanding</div>";
  }

  public function printHeader()
  {
    echo '<h2>Customer owes</h2>';
    echo '<h3>Amount based on orders updated yesterday</h3>';
  }
}
```

It also works if the local variable is an object and you have to invoke a modifying method: you just pass the object in as a parameter.

Example: Reassigning a Local Variable

In the previous example, if we want to extract the calculation we have to cope with the return value of the calculation itself. Let's have a look at the code:

```php
public function printOwing()
{
  $this->printHeader();

  // calculate outstanding
```

```
  $outstanding = 0;
  foreach ($this->orders as $order)
  {
    $outstanding += $order['amount'];
  }

  $this->printDetails($outstanding);
}
```

As we may see, $outstanding is calculated in the original method but passed as a parameter to the printDetails() method. If we move the calculation of $outstanding into a target method by the extract method, we'll have to store the calculation result in some temporary variable in the source method scope.

```
class Customer
{
  public $orders = array();
  public $name;

  public function printOwing()
  {
    $this->printHeader();

    $outstanding = $this->getOutstanding();

    $this->printDetails($outstanding);
  }

  public function getOutstanding()
  {
    $outstanding = 0;
    foreach ($this->orders as $order)
    {
      $outstanding += $order['amount'];
    }

    return $outstanding;
  }
  [...]
}
```

We may notice how the $outstanding variable is now initialized within the target method. This is possible only since the variable has a fixed initialization value. In the next example we will learn how to cope with non-static initializations. The code here shows the updated test.

```
class CustomerTest extends PHPUnit_Framework_TestCase
{
  public function testPrintOwing()
  {
    $customer = new Customer();
    $customer->name = 'Edmundo';
    $customer->orders = array(
      array('amount' => 110),
      array('amount' => 300),
      array('amount' => 150)
    );
```

```
    ob_start();
    $customer->printOwing();
    $output = ob_get_contents();
    ob_end_clean();

    $this->assertRegExp('/<h2>Customer owes<\/h2><h3>Amount based on orders updated ↵
yesterday<\/h3>/', $output);
    $this->assertRegExp('/Name: Edmundo/', $output);
    $this->assertRegExp('/Amount: \$560/', $output);

    ob_start();
    $customer->printOwing(110);
    $output = ob_get_contents();
    ob_end_clean();

    $this->assertRegExp('/Amount: \$670/', $output);
  }
}
```

This is followed by the refactored class methods.

```
[...]
public function printOwing($previous_outstanding = 0)
{
  $this->printHeader();

  $outstanding = $this->getOutstanding($previous_outstanding);

  $this->printDetails($outstanding);
}

public function getOutstanding($previous_outstanding)
{
  $outstanding = $previous_outstanding;
  foreach ($this->orders as $order)
  {
    $outstanding += $order['amount'];
  }

  return $outstanding;
}
[...]
```

What about many temporary variables? How can we cope with the need to assign many local variables? In PHP we can return an array and then distribute it with the list() construct.

Let's assume we have to retrieve more details about our customer: outstanding owed amount and the number of critical orders over $120. These are the new tests.

```
class CustomerTest extends PHPUnit_Framework_TestCase
{
  public function testPrintOwing()
  {
    $customer = new Customer();
    $customer->name = 'Edmundo';
    $customer->orders = array(
```

```
        array('amount' => 110),
        array('amount' => 300),
        array('amount' => 150)
    );

    ob_start();
    $customer->printOwing();
    $output = ob_get_contents();
    ob_end_clean();

    $this->assertRegExp('/<h2>Customer owes<\/h2><h3>Amount based on orders updated ↵
yesterday<\/h3>/', $output);
    $this->assertRegExp('/Name: Edmundo/', $output);
    $this->assertRegExp('/Amount: \$560/', $output);
    $this->assertRegExp('/Critical active orders: 2/', $output);

    ob_start();
    $customer->printOwing(110);
    $output = ob_get_contents();
    ob_end_clean();

    $this->assertRegExp('/Amount: \$670/', $output);
    $this->assertRegExp('/Critical active orders: 2/', $output);
  }
}
```

In the class we have to pass two parameters to the printDetails() method, and both are calculated in the same foreach() loop.

```
class Customer
{
  public $orders = array();
  public $name;

  public function printOwing($previous_outstanding = 0)
  {
    $this->printHeader();

    list($outstanding, $critical) = $this->getOutstanding($previous_outstanding);

    $this->printDetails($outstanding, $critical);
  }

  public function getOutstanding($previous_outstanding)
  {
    $outstanding = $previous_outstanding;
    $critical = 0;
    foreach ($this->orders as $order)
    {
      $outstanding += $order['amount'];
      if ($order['amount'] > 120)
      {
        $critical++;
      }
    }
```

```
    return array($outstanding, $critical);
  }

  public function printDetails($outstanding, $critical)
  {
    echo "<div>Name: {$this->name}</div>";
    echo "<div>Amount: $outstanding</div>";
    echo "<div>Critical active orders: $critical</div>";
  }

  public function printHeader()
  {
    echo '<h2>Customer owes</h2>';
    echo '<h3>Amount based on orders updated yesterday</h3>';
  }
}
```

Though we just provided a solution, we prefer to use single return values as much as possible. To honor this preference and, when impossible to make a clean extraction at all, we can reduce the presence of temps by using "Replace Temp with Query" or choosing to work around the issue by means of other refactoring techniques like "Replace Method with Method Object."

Inline Method

Problem: "Code in a method is no more than its name."

Solution: "Move the called code into the body of the caller and remove the called method."

Motivation

Since indirection is good except when not needed, it is sometimes useful to get rid of a method in case it's short to the point of being as simple and clear as its name. This can happen after a previous refactoring of the method body, bringing you to a clearer and shorter version of it.

Another possible use of this refactoring technique is as a middle step towards other bigger refactoring, to bring the whole involved behavior into a single point and then refactor it again.

Mechanics

- Check that the method is not overridden by any subclasses.

- Find all calls to the method.

- Replace calls with the method body.

- Run tests.

- Remove the definition.

Example

We have a very small class Person and its unit test.

```
class Person
{
  public $firstname;
  public $lastname;

  public function getCompleteName()
  {
    return $this->getFirstName().' '.$this->getLastName();
  }

  public function getFirstName()
  {
    return $this->firstname;
  }

  public function getLastName()
  {
    return $this->lastname;
  }
}

class PersonTest extends PHPUnit_Framework_TestCase
{
  public function testGetCompleteName()
  {
    $person = new Person();
    $person->firstname = 'Edmundo';
    $person->lastname = 'Caipirinha';

    $this->assertEquals('Edmundo Caipirinha', $person->getCompleteName());
  }
}
```

Doing this refactoring is as easy as writing the following code.

```
class Person
{
  public $firstname;
  public $lastname;

  public function getCompleteName()
  {
    return $this->firstname.' '.$this->lastname;
  }
}
```

You may have noted already that we performed the same refactoring twice in this case, one for the firstname property and one for the lastname.

93

Inline Temp

Problem: "A simple expression is assigned once to a temporary variable now in the way of other refactorings."

Solution: "Replace references to temporary variables with the simple expression."

Motivation

If a temp is assigned the value of a method call you can decide to inline it. Usually you should inline it if it's preventing you from performing other refactoring techniques like "Extract Method" or as part of "Replace Temp with Query."

Mechanics

- Find all references to the temp.

- Check that the temp is assigned only once.

- Replace each reference to the temp with the right-hand side expression.

- Test after each replace.

- Remove the temp declaration, if any, and the temp assignment.

- Run tests.

Example

We have a simple Chater class and its unit test.

```php
class Charter
{
  public $travellers;

  public function isOverbooked()
  {
    $overbooked = sizeof($this->travellers) > 120;
    return $overbooked;
  }
}

class CharterTest extends PHPUnit_Framework_TestCase
{
  public function testIsOverbooked()
  {
    $charter = new Charter();
    $charter->travellers = range(0, 125);

    $this->assertTrue($charter->isOverbooked());
  }
}
```

We want to apply "Inline Temp" in isOverbooked() method. To do this, we remove $overbooked variable and directly return the condition value.

```
class Charter
{
  public $travellers;

  public function isOverbooked()
  {
    return sizeof($this->travellers) > 120;
  }
}
```

Replace Temp with Query

Problem: "You are using a temporary variable to store and hold an expression result."

Solution: "Extract a new method and replace all references to the temp with a method call."

Motivation

Local variables encourage a procedural coding style, since they are accessible only in the scope of the method in which they are used. By replacing the temp with a query method, you can make the same information available from any other method in the class. That will strongly contribute to cleaner code and a better structure.

"Replace Temp with Query" is often used before "Extract Method," and its stand-alone use is possible only when temps are assigned once and when the assigned right-hand side expression is side-effect free.

Mechanics

- Look for a temp that is assigned once.
- Extract the right-hand side of the assignment to a private method.
- Run tests.
- Perform "Inline Temp" on the temp.
- Run tests.

Obviously the *private* access modifier is initially suitable for the method. As soon as we find another use for the method we can easily weaken its protection.

If the temp to be replaced is used in a loop as an accumulator, the entire loop can be extracted into a method, making things a lot cleaner. If more than one temp is used in the loop, extract it to a method as many times as needed so that you can replace each temp with a query. As Martin Fowler says, any concern about performance should be let slide at the moment of refactoring. At optimization time, the better structure you'll have got by means of refactoring will make you able to optimize wherever needed.

Example

We first consider the following Product class:

```
class Product
{
  private $price = 5;
  public $quantity;

  public function getPrice()
  {
    $base_price = $this->price * $this->quantity;

    $discount = ($base_price > 1000) ? .90 : 1;

    return $base_price * $discount;
  }
}
```

The ProductTest PHPUnit class tests all product discount rules.

```
class ProductTest extends PHPUnit_Framework_TestCase
{
  public function testGetPrice()
  {
    $product = new Product();

    $product->quantity = 200;
    $this->assertEquals(1000, $product->getPrice());

    $product->quantity = 300;
    $this->assertEquals(1350, $product->getPrice());
  }
}
```

Our aim is to replace both $base_price and $discount temps. Let's move step by step—one temp first, then the second one.

The $base_price temp is assigned only once, so we can move forward to the extraction of the right-hand expression in a new private method.

```
public function getPrice()
  {
    $base_price = $this->getBasePrice();

    $discount = ($base_price > 1000) ? .90 : 1;

    return $base_price * $discount;
  }

  private function getBasePrice()
  {
    return $this->price * $this->quantity;
  }
```

Tests are still green, so I can perform "Inline Temp."

```php
public function getPrice()
{
    $discount = ($this->getBasePrice() > 1000) ? .90 : 1;

    return $this->getBasePrice() * $discount;
}

private function getBasePrice()
{
    return $this->price * $this->quantity;
}
```

Tests are steady on green, with one temp gone. Good! Now let's replace $discount temp in a similar way. First, do the method extraction:

```php
public function getPrice()
{
    $discount = $this->getDiscount();

    return $this->getBasePrice() * $discount;
}

private function getDiscount()
{
    return ($this->getBasePrice() > 1000) ? .90 : 1;
}
```

Then, after a brief test run to ensure everything's right, perform "Inline Temp" to get the refactoring complete.

```php
class Product
{
    private $price = 5;
    public $quantity;

    public function getPrice()
    {
        return $this->getBasePrice() * $this->getDiscount();
    }

    private function getDiscount()
    {
        return ($this->getBasePrice() > 1000) ? .90 : 1;
    }

    private function getBasePrice()
    {
        return $this->price * $this->quantity;
    }
}
```

Please note how hard it would have been to extract `getDiscount()` if not replacing `$base_price` with a query. The `$base_price` temp couldn't exist in both `getPrice()` and `getDiscount()` scopes, leading to bad code duplication.

Introduce Explaining Variable

Problem: "You have a complicated expression."

Solution: "Put the expression or part of it in a temporary variable with a clear name."

Motivation

"Introduce Explaining Variable" is a very common refactoring technique used to overcome the natural tendency of expressions to become hard to read and understand. When one expression gets too complex, temporary variables are useful to break down the expression into easier chunks.

Mechanics

- Declare a temporary variable.

- Assign the result of part of the expression to it.

- Run tests.

- Re-iterate over other parts of the expression.

Example

We have a simple `Product` class, where the only behavior is to calculate its price.

```
class Product
{
  private $price = 5;
  public $quantity;

  /**
   * Returns total price applying 10% discount
   * on each item over 150th
   */
  public function getPrice()
  {
    return $this->price * $this->quantity -
      max($this->quantity - 150, 0) * $this->price * 0.1;
  }
}
```

We need to add a comment to the `getPrice()` method to make it understandable by another reader. While comments are a good means to clarify *what* a method is supposed to do, it's always better to write self-explaining code as far as it makes sense. Introducing a couple of temps can help a lot to get a more readable code. First we check our tests are green:

```
class ProductTest extends PHPUnit_Framework_TestCase
{
  public function testGetPrice()
  {
    $product = new Product();

    $product->quantity = 200;
    $this->assertEquals(975, $product->getPrice());
  }
}
```

Then we move to refactoring the first part of the expression:

```
public function getPrice()
{
  $base_price = $this->price * $this->quantity;

  return $base_price -
    max($this->quantity - 150, 0) * $this->price * 0.1;
}
```

After confirming that our test is green, we complete our refactoring with this:

```
public function getPrice()
{
  $base_price = $this->price * $this->quantity;
  $discount = max($this->quantity - 150, 0) * $this->price * 0.1;

  return $base_price - $discount;
}
```

This final getPrice() method lets tests complete with a perfectly green bar.

Split Temporary Variable

Problem: "A temporary variable is assigned more than once."

Solution: "Declare and assign a separate temp for each assignment."

Motivation

Except for loop and collecting variables, each temporary variable should be assigned once. A temp being assigned more than once is a clue of a violated single responsibility principle. While we could be easily convinced already of this principle's validity at a higher level—one class, one responsibility—we should follow this principle at a variable level too, as long as it makes sense. Using a temp for two different things is very confusing for the reader, and any variable with more than one single responsibility should be split into as many temps as the responsibilities it holds.

Mechanics

- Check that the temp is not being used as a collecting variable (e.g., $i = $i + someMethod()).

- Change the name of a temp at its declaration, if any, and its first assignment.

- Change all references of the temp up to its second assignment.

- Declare the temp at its second assignment, as a good practice.

- Run tests.

- Repeat for each following assignment.

Example

In the Employee class we write the method named getBalance() to compute the net difference between incomes and expenses, after applying small modifiers to each transaction as a bonus or a penalty. Here is the test:

```
class EmployeeTest extends PHPUnit_Framework_TestCase
{
  public function testGetBalance()
  {
    $employee = new Employee();
    $employee->payments = array(100, 100, 100, 100);
    $employee->expenses = array(50, 50, 50, 50);

    $this->assertEquals(200.00, $employee->getBalance());
  }
}
```

Here is the class code:

```
class Employee
{
  public $payments = array();
  public $expenses = array();

  public function getBalance()
  {
    $balance = 0;

    $modifier = 1.1;

    foreach ($this->payments as $payment)
    {
      $balance += $payment * $modifier;
    }

    $modifier = 1.2;

    foreach ($this->expenses as $expense)
    {
```

```
    $balance -= $expense * $modifier;
  }

  return round($balance, 2);
  }
}
```

We can see the temp variable $balance being assigned more than once here. It's OK since its purpose is to accumulate each transaction value to contain the balance value at the end of the method and to be returned.

Instead, the $modifier temp is quite obscure. Easy as it may be, would you have gotten at a very first glance what those modifiers mean if they were not introduced to you as bonuses and penalties? We can rename them to get a better method structure. Applying proposed mechanics, at the first round, we get this getBalance() method:

```
public function getBalance()
{
  $balance = 0;

  $bonus = 1.1;

  foreach ($this->payments as $payment)
  {
    $balance += $payment * $bonus;
  }

  $modifier = 1.2;

  foreach ($this->expenses as $expense)
  {
    $balance -= $expense * $modifier;
  }

  return round($balance, 2);
}
```

While performing the second round we end with this:

```
public function getBalance()
{
  $balance = 0;

  $bonus = 1.1;

  foreach ($this->payments as $payment)
  {
    $balance += $payment * $bonus;
  }

  $penalty = 1.2;

  foreach ($this->expenses as $expense)
  {
    $balance -= $expense * $penalty;
  }
```

```
    return round($balance, 2);
}
```

This keeps our tests strictly green.

Replace Method with Method Object

Problem: "You have a long method and you can't apply 'Extract Method'."

Solution: "Create a new class, instantiate an object, and create a method. Then refactor it."

Motivation

Sometimes local temps make method decomposition too hard, forcing us to keep very long methods. Since we all love writing good short methods (don't we?), we can perform "Replace Method with Method Object" and turn all those local temps into fields on the method object, and then refactor this new object to decompose the original behavior.

Mechanics

- Create a new class named as the method.

- Give the new class an attribute for the original object and for each temp or parameter in the source method.

- Write a constructor to accept source object and parameters.

- Create a `compute()` method in the new class.

- Copy the body of the old method into the new one, using the object field in every invocation of original object methods and adding `$this->` prefix in temps and parameters references.

- Replace the old method with the object instance creation and a `compute()` method call.

- Decompose `compute()` as much as needed considering that all temps are now object fields.

Example

Consider this not-so-meaningful class:

```
class Account
{
  private $state = 3;

  public function getTripleState()
  {
    return $this->state * 3;
  }
```

```php
  public function foo($first_param, $second_param)
  {
    $temporary_1 = $first_param * $second_param;
    $temporary_2 = $first_param * $this->getTripleState();

    if (($temporary_1 - $temporary2) % 2)
    {
      return $first_param - 2;
    }

    return $second_param + 4;
  }
}
```

Consider also this associated test:

```php
class AccountTest extends PHPUnit_Framework_TestCase
{
  public function testFoo()
  {
    $employee = new Account();

    $this->assertEquals(24, $employee->foo(10, 20));
    $this->assertEquals(9, $employee->foo(11, 17));
  }
}
```

We apply the first steps of "Replace Method with Method Object," and we get the following class:

```php
class foo
{
  private
    $account,
    $temporary_1,
    $temporary_2,
    $first_param,
    $second_param;

  public function __construct($account, $first_param, $second_param)
  {
    $this->account = $account;
    $this->first_param = $first_param;
    $this->second_param = $second_param;
  }
}
```

We can now move the method from the source object to the new one.

```php
class foo
{
  [...]
  public function compute()
  {
    $this->temporary_1 = $this->first_param * $this->second_param; ↵
$this->temporary_2 = $this->first_param * $this->account->getTripleState();
```

```
    if (($this->temporary_1 - $this->temporary2) % 2)
    {
      return $this->first_param - 2;
    }

    return $this->second_param + 4;
  }
}
```

In the source class we just replace the old method body like this:

```
public function foo($first_param, $second_param)
{
  $foo = new foo($this, $first_param, $second_param);
  return $foo->compute();
}
```

That's all. The best has yet to come, though, because at this point we can start extracting methods without bothering about arguments, like in the example here:

```
public function compute()
{
  $this->setup();

  if (($this->temporary_1 - $this->temporary2) % 2)
  {
    return $this->first_param - 2;
  }

  return $this->second_param + 4;
}

public function setup()
{
  $this->temporary_1 = $this->first_param * $this->second_param;
  $this->temporary_2 = $this->first_param * $this->account->getTripleState();
}
```

Substitute Algorithm

Problem: "You want to replace an algorithm with another."

Solution: "Replace the body of the method with the new algorithm."

Motivation

Sometimes the only way to make things simpler is to replace the code you have with another one. This may happen when you gain deeper insight into the business domain or when a newly-introduced library does what you already coded to do.

Sometimes when you want to change code to alter behavior just a little bit, it's better to substitute the algorithm first to have a simpler base to start from.

"Substitute Algorithm" is a radical refactoring you should perform after decomposing your methods as much as possible, to keep the problem down to a tractable size.

Mechanics

- Prepare your alternative algorithm.

- Run tests.

- Use both old and new algorithms to run tests and ease debugging.

Example

A very simple example shows the importance of tests in refactoring. We have the BalanceTest unit test.

```php
class BalanceTest extends PHPUnit_Framework_TestCase
{
  public function testGetAmount()
  {
    $balance = new Balance();
    $balance->transactions = array(50, -20, 10, 500);

    $this->assertEquals(540, $balance->getAmount());
  }
}
```

The Balance class satisfy the previous test, as long as we get a green test result.

```php
class Balance
{
  public $transactions = array();

  public function getAmount()
  {
    $amount = 0;

    foreach ($this->transactions as $transaction)
    {
      $amount += $transaction;
    }

    return $amount;
  }
}
```

If we "Substitute Algorithm", we can run our tests, and we see that our substitution worked.

```php
public function getAmount()
{
  return array_sum($this->transactions);
}
```

Summary

The most common refactoring techniques in our day-to-day activities are about composing methods to make the right bricks for our code-building. Problems often come from methods that are too long to be used in a well-structured architecture, since they convey way too much behavior and hold too much information. The most important refactoring technique we saw in this chapter is "Extract Method," since it directly faces that complexity with a *divide et impera* strategy. By the way, all the other refactoring techniques shown in this chapter are very useful to package your code in a meaningful way, and they will prove their usefulness often.

CHAPTER 8

■ ■ ■

Changing Class Responsibilities

Software design is certainly one of the most discussed and most difficult activities in software engineering. Designing correct and complete architecture before development is virtually impossible. The real design emerges only when you implement a certain feature; reasoning in micro is easier than reasoning in macro, and requirements can change any time during the developing phase. For this reason, we will discuss emergent design, which means software design that emerges during development. This process entails renegotiating class responsibilities, properties, behaviors, and interactions.

In short, design must evolve along with application. The techniques we'll see in this chapter help us to develop a simple and correct design, and, using them, we can design today's code and not try to predict a design that will serve us tomorrow. Automated tests will support us in our daily refactoring, ensuring the value of the features already developed and helping to design new ones.

In this chapter we'll see a collection of some refactoring methods created by Martin Fowler [FOW01]. For each method we'll see the motivation and proper situation for its use, the mechanism that will explain how we can apply a method to our existing code, and some examples showing how a method works in the real world.

Move Method

Problem: "A class method is used by more methods of another class than the class on which it is defined."

Solution: "Create a new method with the same body in the class it uses most. Either turn the old method into a simple delegation, or remove it altogether."

Motivation

The "move method" technique is probably the most famous and most useful refactoring of the moving refactoring methods. It is concerned with properly distributing the responsibilities between the classes, responsibilities that are not always easy to identify in the first implementation. The move method helps us to balance these responsibilities between classes, simplifying them and making them easier to manage.

When you move an attribute from one class to another we must also move the methods that use this attribute. It is not always easy to understand if we have to move a method. When we're not sure, try first to move other methods and delay the decision. Let us trust our instincts—if we are not sure, after all, we can always move it back again.

Mechanics

- Write a unit test for our class. This test will ensure that we don't lose value already acquired with refactoring.

- Identify the method to move. Usually the best candidates are those methods that deal with activities that should be delegated to another class using, for example, many properties of this class and not of the class where they are defined.

- Observe the attributes used inside the method. If it uses only some attributes of the class, we have to move them also. If attributes are also used by other methods, we must understand whether to move these methods. If these attributes strongly characterize the class where they are defined, we cannot move them. We have to pass them as parameters to the method we are moving.

- Check that the method doesn't extend the methods of a super class or it will be extended by some subclass. Where it does so, we must check whether we can move the method.

- Write a unit test for the destination class.

- Add a test that designs and tests the behavior of the new moving method.

- Define the method in the target class. Often we can also change the method name by giving it a name that better represents what it does.

- Copy the method code from the class source to the destination class. Adjust the code so that everything is working fine in this new position. If the method uses attributes of the class source, we must understand whether these attributes can be moved in class destination or passed as parameters. If the method includes some exceptions, we have to decide whether to move these exceptions too or keep them in the source class. As for parameters, we can understand how to move based on domain exceptions.

- Run a unit test for the destination class and fix the tests until all are fixed.

- Change the source method and let it be a delegated method.

- Run a unit test for the source class. Fix all tests until they are fixed. Probably, if we use a mock class for the destination class, we have to adjust the mock class code also, so that tests could run.

- Decide whether to remove the source completely or keep it as a delegated method. If the method has public visibility and is called in many parts of our software, it is easier to keep it. If we have good code coverage with our tests, we can be bold and delete it. Tests will show where we have to replace the call.

Example

We must refactor the getActiveInterest() method in the BankAccount class.

```
class BankAccount
{
  private $balance = 0;
  private $active_interest = 0.01;
  private $type;
```

```php
    public function __construct(BankAccountType $type)
    {
      $this->type = $type;
    }

    public function getBalance()
    {
      return $this->balance;
    }

    public function deposits($money_amount)
    {
      $this->balance += $money_amount;
      $this->calculateBalance();
    }

    public function getActiveInterest()
    {
      if ($this->type->isBusiness())
      {
        $interest_constant = 5;
        $active_interest = $this->active_interest * $interest_constant;
      }

      return $active_interest;
    }

    public function calculateBalance()
    {
      if ($this->balance > 0)
      {
        $this->balance += $this->balance * $this->getActiveInterest();
      }
    }
}
```

We need to introduce other business account types with different interest constants. The method getActiveInterest() will not let you change the constant interest, which is hard-coded inside and assigned to the $interest_constant variable. What we should do is move the getActiveInterest() method in the BankAccountType class, so we could add more BankAccountType classes with different constant interests. First we need to identify which attribute must stay in our class and which can be moved in the BankAccountType class. The $active_interest attribute must stay in the BankAccount class; others can be moved in the BankAccountType class.

First, we write a unit test for the getActiveInterest() method of the BankAccount class.

```php
class BankAccountTest extends PHPUnit_Framework_TestCase
{
  public function testgetActiveInterest()
  {
    $bank_account_type = new BankAccountType();
    $bank_account_type->setBusiness(true);
    $account = new BankAccount($bank_account_type);
    $account->deposits(100);

    $this->assertEquals(105, $account->getBalance());
  }
}
```

We run a test and all tests run.

```
# phpunit BankAccountTest.php
PHPUnit 3.4.1 by Sebastian Bergmann.

.

Time: 0 seconds

OK (1 test, 1 assertion)
```

Then we can copy the getActiveInterest() method from the BankAccount class to the BankAccountType class.

```
class BankAccountType
{
  ...
  public function getActiveInterest()
  {
    if ($this->type->isBusiness())
    {
      $interest_constant = 5;
      $this->active_interest = $this->active_interest * $interest_constant;
    }

    return $this->active_interest;
  }
  ...
}
```

Remove the $type property, because it doesn't exist any more in the BankAccountType class, being itself the instance of the $type attribute in the BankAccount class. Then we pass the $active_interest property as a parameter to the method and we change the call into the method from property name to variable name.

```
class BankAccountType
{
  ...
  public function getActiveInterest($active_interest)
  {
    if ($this->isBusiness())
    {
      $interest_constant = 5;
      $active_interest = $active_interest * $interest_constant;
    }

    return $active_interest;
  }
  ...
}
```

The method name does not explain what the method does; in fact, the method doesn't return the active interest, but it modifies them according to a constant. So rename the method calcActiveInterest().

```php
class BankAccountType
{
  ...
  public function calcActiveInterest($active_interest)
  {
    if ($this->isBusiness())
    {
      $interest_constant = 5;
      $active_interest = $active_interest * $interest_constant;
    }

    return $active_interest;
  }
  ...
}
```

With this transaction, we have moved the getActiveInterest() method in the BankAccountType class now responsible for choosing constant interest. The next step is to remove the code from the getActiveInterest() method of the BankAccount class and add a direct call to the calcActiveInterest() method of the BankAccountType class, passing the $active_interest property as a parameter.

```php
class BankAccount
{
  ...
  public function getActiveInterest()
  {
    return $this->type->calcActiveInterest($this->active_interest);
  }
  ...
}
```

Ok, much better. At this point, we can run the BankAccountTest test again to see if something went wrong.

We might also remove the getActiveInterest() method, which has become only a proxy method. Before deleting it, we have to replace all calls to the proxy method with the method call of the BankAccountType object. In our case the only method that calls getActiveInterest() is the calculateBalance() method. Replacing the call, we get the following result:

```php
<?php

class BankAccount
{
  ...
  public function calculateBalance()
  {
    if ($this->balance > 0)
    {
      $this->balance += $this->balance * $this->type->calcActiveInterest($this->active_interest);
    }
  }
  ...
}

?>
```

We run our test for the last time and we see that all tests run.

```
# phpunit BankAccountTest.php
PHPUnit 3.4.1 by Sebastian Bergmann.

.

Time: 0 seconds

OK (1 test, 1 assertion)
```

Now we can remove the entire method getActiveInterest(), which is now useless.

Move Property (or Field)

Problem: "A class property describes a feature of another class instead of a feature of the class where it is declared."

Solution: "Create a new field in the right class, and change all the clients' calls from the old class property to the new class property."

Motivation

Move field is the name given to this refactoring method by Martin Fowler. In PHP the right name of the field class is property. So we will always call field as property (http://www.php.net/manual/en/language.oop5.basic.php).

The move property is one of the best refactoring methods of moving features between object categories, because it is very important to characterize the class in the right way. While we're designing or implementing a class, often we incorrectly declare properties, introducing some properties that don't describe the class where they are declared. Often they describe other connected classes. Other times it may be that a property is correctly defined in its class today, but tomorrow a new feature will arise and the property will no longer describe the class correctly.

We absolutely need to move these properties between classes. One of the most important practices of the object-oriented programming paradigm is defining simple classes where all their properties are always properties of the class. If we have a property that never describes a class feature or a property that only sometimes describes a class feature, this is wrong; we need to move this attribute to a better place.

Mechanics

- Write unit tests for the source and target classes where we want to move property.

- Define a new property in the target class with the same name of the source class property we want to move.

- Add the accessory methods to the new property in the target class.

- Run tests for the target class and fix it until all errors are fixed.

- Understand how to reference to the new object instead of the property. If there is a method or a property that already does it, we can use it. If we don't have this possibility, we can add a new property to store the object.

- Remove the property, just moved, from the source class.

- Change the property call in the source class with the right accessory methods of the target class.

- Run a test for the source class and fix it until all errors are fixed.

Example

We need to move $active_interest from the BankAccount class to the BankAccountType class.

```
class BankAccount
{
  ...
  private $active_interest = 0.01;
  ...

  public function calculateActiveInterests()
  {
    if ($this->balance > 0)
    {
      $this->balance += $this->balance * $this->type->calcActiveInterest($this->active_interest);
    }
  }
}
```

We need it because we want to add a new feature: an active interest that is dependent on bank account type. $active_interest isn't an attribute of the BankAccountType class, so we can't change it for a different bank account type. We could do it only by introducing a lot of "ifs," but we know that "if" is undesirable because it makes our code difficult to maintain, read, and manage.

We want the $active_interest property to depend on the BankAccountType class, which means that the $active_interest attribute describes the BankAccountType class, not the BankAccount class. So we have to move this field from the BankAccount class to the BankAccountType class.

To do this, first of all, we need to declare the same attribute in the target class with all accessory methods.

```
class BankAccountType
{
  ...
  private $active_interest = 0.01;
  ...

  public function setActiveInterest($active_interest)
  {
    $this->active_interest = $active_interest;
  }

  public function getActiveInterest()
  {
    return $this->active_interest;
  }
}
```

Then we have to change the BankAccount class code where there are $active_interest property calls with the getActiveInterest() method of BankAccountType and remove its declaration.

113

```
class BankAccount
{
  public function calculateActiveInterests()
  {
    if ($this->balance > 0)
    {
      $this->balance += $this->balance * $this->type->calcActiveInterest($this->type->↵
getActiveInterest());
    }
  }
}
```

If we have accessory methods for the class property we are moving, we need to modify them to self-encapsulate the new call.

```
class BankAccount
{
  ...
  private $active_interest = 0.01;
  ...

  public function calculateActiveInterests()
  {
    if ($this->balance > 0)
    {
      $this->balance += $this->balance * $this->type->calcActiveInterest($this->↵
getActiveInterest());
    }
  }

  public function setActiveInterest($value)
  {
    return $this->active_interest = $value;
  }

  public function getActiveInterest()
  {
    return $this->active_interest;
  }
}
```

In this case we use accessory methods to access the field we want to move. We have to change the $active_interest call into accessory methods with the new call to target class accessory methods.

```
class BankAccount
{
  public function calculateActiveInterests()
  {
    if ($this->balance > 0)
    {
      $this->balance += $this->balance * $this->type->calcActiveInterest($this->↵
getActiveInterest());
    }
  }

  public function setActiveInterest($value)
```

```
  {
    return $this->type->setActiveInterest($value);
  }

  public function getActiveInterest()
  {
    return $this->type->getActiveInterest();
  }
}
```

This step is small, so that we don't go too fast with our refactoring. After this step we can also remove the source accessory methods and change all the calls to these methods with the target accessory methods.

Extract Class

Problem: "We have one class that has responsibilities for more classes than one."

Solution: "Create a new class, and move the properties and methods that don't belong to the origin class into the new class."

Motivation

One of the best object programming practices is to have small classes that are highly empowered for a single feature. This is because maintaining small classes with small methods and a few smaller properties is much easier than maintaining very large classes with multiple responsibilities.

Following the best practice sometime isn't simple, and that is why every day we are working with classes with more than 500 lines of code, with many properties and methods that are very long. This happens because during the development of any software, our classes grow, and when we add new responsibilities to the class, they seem, at first, to be too minimal to delegate to a new class, and later they seem too large to move. We must not fall into this trap. When class responsibilities are too much and the class does actions that should be done by two classes, we have to take a deep breath, and create a new class. With an automatic test, we can ensure the maintenance of the initial value.

When we have methods and/or properties with similar prefixes and/or suffixes, we can extract them in a new class. When we have groups of properties that we always change together when we should change only one, because there are big dependencies, we can extract them in a new class. When it seems that some properties and methods are concerned with the same features that do not always represent the class, we can extract them in a new class.

Mechanics

Follow this mechanism to extract a new class:

- Create a new unit test for the source class.

- Decide which properties and/or methods to extract.

- Create a new test for the new class and for each new method you are moving. If class or method names aren't meaningful, give them better names.

- Create the new class.

- In the old class constructor, store an instance of the new class in an existent property or in a new one.

- Use the "move field" method to move each property in the new class.

- Run new and old class tests. Fix it until all errors are fixed.

- Use the "move method" to move each method in the new class.

- Run new and old class tests. Fix it until all errors are fixed.

- Decide how to expose the new class through the old class. Decide whether to modify the new class through the old class, or only to access it without modifying it.

Example

We want to extract a new class for the following Book class, decoupling author features to book features:

```php
class Book
{
  ...
  private $author_firstname;
  private $author_lastname;
  ...

  public function getAuthor()
  {
    return $this->author_firstname . ' ' . $this->author_lastname;
  }

  public function setAuthorFirstname($firstname)
  {
    $this->author_firstname = $firstname;
  }

  public function getAuthorFirstname()
  {
    return $this->author_firstname;
  }

  public function setAuthorLastname($lastname)
  {
    $this->author_lastname = $lastname;
  }

  public function getAuthorLastname()
  {
    return $this->author_lastname;
  }

  ...
}
```

Following the mechanism, first of all we write the unit test for the Book class, because we don't want to change and lose the original class behavior.

```php
class BookTest extends PHPUnit_Framework_TestCase
{
```

```
...

  public function testAuthorInfo()
  {
    $book = new Book();
    $book->setAuthorFirstname('Francesco');
    $book->setAuthorLastname('Trucchia');

    $this->assertEquals('Francesco Trucchia', $book->getAuthor());
    $this->assertEquals('Francesco', $book->getAuthorFirstname());
    $this->assertEquals('Trucchia', $book->getAuthorLastname());
  }

  ...
}
```

We run the BookTest test and it works fine.

```
PHPUnit 3.4.1 by Sebastian Bergmann.

.

Time: 0 seconds

OK (1 test, 3 assertions)
```

As stated before, we want to extract the author properties and methods from the Book class. To do it we create a new test for our new Author class. Doing a test first, we can better design the Author interfaces.

```
class AuthorTest extends PHPUnit_Framework_TestCase
{
  ...

  public function testInfo()
  {
    $author = new Author();
    $author->setAuthorFirstname('Francesco');
    $author->setAuthorLastname('Trucchia');

    $this->assertEquals('Francesco', $author->getAuthorFirstname());
    $this->assertEquals('Trucchia', $author->getAuthorLastname());
  }

  ...
}
```

We run the AuthorTest test and it fails because the Author class does not exist. So we create the new class Author.

```
class Author
{

}
```

Now for $author_firstname and $author_lastname properties of the Book class we use the "move field" method to extract them in the Author class. So we copy the properties in the new class and use the encapsulate field practice to create the accessory methods.

```
class Author
{
  var $author_firstname;
  var $author_lastname;

  public function setAuthorFirstname($firstname)
  {
    $this->author_firstname = $firstname;
  }

  public function getAuthorFirstname()
  {
    return $this->author_firstname;
  }

  public function setAuthorLastname($lastname)
  {
    $this->author_lastname = $lastname;
  }

  public function getAuthorLastname()
  {
    return $this->author_lastname;
  }
}
```

We run AuthorTest and it works fine.

```
PHPUnit 3.4.1 by Sebastian Bergmann.

.

Time: 0 seconds

OK (1 test, 2 assertions)
```

We remove properties moved from the old class, introduce a new property, $author, on the Book class that stores an instance of the new class Author, and, at the end, we change all code where the Book methods use properties just removed with accessory methods of the Author class.

```
class Book
{
  ...
  private $author;
  ...

  public function __construct()
  {
    $this->author = new Author();
  }

  public function getAuthor()
```

```
  {
    return $this->author->getAuthorFirstname() . ' ' . $this->author->getAuthorLastname();
  }

  public function setAuthorFirstname($firstname)
  {
    $this->author->setAuthorFirstname($firstname);
  }

  public function getAuthorFirstname()
  {
    return $this->author->getAuthorFirstname();
  }

  public function setAuthorLastname($lastname)
  {
    $this->author->setAuthorLastname($lastname);
  }

  public function getAuthorLastname()
  {
    return $this->author->getAuthorLastname();
  }
  ...
}
```

We run BookTest and it works fine.

If we want to give direct access to the Author class through the Book class we can change the getAuthor() method of the Book class to return the Author object.

```
class Book
{
  ...
  public function getAuthor()
  {
    return $this->author;
  }
  ...
}
```

We run BookTest and it fails, because the interface is not more consistent with the previous behavior. Now getAuthor() returns an object instead of a string.

```
PHPUnit 3.4.1 by Sebastian Bergmann.

F

Time: 0 seconds

There was 1 failure:

1) BookTest::testAuthorInfo
Failed asserting that
Author Object
(
    [author_firstname] => Francesco
```

```
    [author_lastname] => Trucchia
)
 matches expected <string:Francesco Trucchia>.
```

/Users/cphp/Dropbox/Progetti/Libri/Apress/ProPHPRefactoring/chapters/code/test/BookTest.php:15

```
FAILURES!
Tests: 1, Assertions: 1, Failures: 1.
```

In PHP5 there is a magic method, __toString(), which allows a class to decide how it will react when it is converted to a string (http://www.php.net/manual/en/language.oop5.magic.php#language.oop5.magic.tostring). We can move the original getAuthor() method to this magic method in the Author class.

```php
class Author
{
  ...
  public function __toString()
  {
    return $this->getAuthorFirstname() . ' ' . $this->getAuthorLastname();
  }
  ...
}
```

Now we have to change our test, forcing the typecasting to string when we call the getAuthor() method of the Book class.

```php
class BookTest extends PHPUnit_Framework_TestCase
{
  ...
  public function testAuthorInfo()
  {
    ...
    $this->assertEquals('Francesco Trucchia', (string)$book->getAuthor());
    ...
  }
  ...
}
```

We run BookTest and it works fine.

```
PHPUnit 3.4.1 by Sebastian Bergmann.


.

Time: 0 seconds

OK (1 test, 3 assertions)
```

Later we can also redirect clients' calls using accessory Book methods to access Author properties directly to the new Author accessory methods, removing the Author accessory method from the Book class. In this way we greatly simplify Book class interfaces.

Inline Class

Problem: "A class isn't doing very much."

Solution: "Move all its features into another class and delete it."

Motivation

The `Inline` class is the opposite refactoring of the `Extract` class. Sometimes `Extract` class refactoring delegates responsibility to a class that remains too small for exists. Having a lot of code to maintain is a bad smell, so if we have some classes that don't do enough to be a class, we need to remove with this refactoring.

For example, if a class is used only by another class and this class has only a property and some accessory methods, maybe this class could be removed and made inline to the absorbing class that uses it.

Mechanics

- Find the absorbing class to which to move all properties and methods of the class to remove.

- Write unit tests for the absorbing class. It needs to declare all public methods from the source class to the absorbing class, so add tests for these new methods.

- Declare a public method into the absorbing class referenced to the source class.

- Run tests. Fix them if they are broken.

- Change all clients' calls to the source class with calls to the absorbing class's new methods.

- Run all suite tests. Fix them until all errors are fixed.

- Use move field and move method refactoring to move all properties and methods from the source class to the absorbing class.

- Run tests. Fix them until all errors are fixed.

Example

We start from the `Book` and `Author` classes.

```
class Book
{
    ...
    protected $author;
    ...
    public function __construct()
    {
        $this->author = new Author();
    }

    public function getAuthor()
```

```
  {
    return $this->author;
  }
  …
}
class Author
{
  protected $fullname;

  public function __toString()
  {
    return $this->fullname;
  }

  public function setFullname($fullname)
  {
    $this->fullname = $fullname;
  }

  public function getFullname()
  {
    return $this->fullname;
  }
}
```

The Author class is too small and has too few properties, so we can remove it and move all properties and methods to the Book class, which is the only class that uses it.

First we write a functional test for the Book class. We improve the Book tests also, testing the public methods we need to declare in the Book class to reference to the author.

```
class BookTest extends PHPUnit_Framework_TestCase
{
  public function testAuthor()
  {
    $book = new Book();
    $book->setAuthorFullname('Francesco Trucchia');

    $this->assertEquals('Francesco Trucchia', $book->getAuthorFullname());
    $this->assertEquals('Francesco Trucchia', (string)$book->getAuthor());
  }
}
```

While we are writing tests, we decide to rename accessory public methods of Author properties because the original names are not meaningful. Now we declare these methods in the Book class.

```
class Book
{
  …
  public function getAuthorFullname()
  {
    return $this->author->getFullname();
  }

  public function setAuthorFullname($fullname)
```

```
  {
    $this->author->setFullname($fullname);
  }
  ...
}
```

We run our tests, and if everything works fine we can change all clients' calls to author objects from the Book class with the new public methods.

```
PHPUnit 3.4.1 by Sebastian Bergmann.

.

Time: 0 seconds

OK (1 test, 2 assertions)
```

Ok, so we can change clients' calls, as in the following example:

```
// We change this call
$book = new Book();
$book->getAuthor()->setFullname('Francesco Trucchia');
echo $book->getAuthor()->getFullname();

// to this call
$book = new Book();
$book->setAuthorFullname('Francesco Trucchia');
echo $book->getAuthorFullname();
```

At the end, with move field and move method refactoring, we can move all properties and methods from the Author class to the Book class, and then we can remove the Author class safely. Do not forget to remove the associated unit tests also.

Our finished Book class will be

```
class Book
{
  protected $author_fullname;

  public function getAuthor()
  {
    return $this->author_fullname;
  }

  public function getAuthorFullname()
  {
    return $this->author_fullname;
  }

  public function setAuthorFullname($fullname)
  {
    $this->author_fullname = $fullname;
  }
}
```

Hide Delegate

Problem: "A client is calling a delegate class of an object."

Solution: "Create methods on the server to hide the delegate."

Motivation

Inline class refactoring is used to implement encapsulation between objects. Encapsulation is "the process of compartmentalizing the elements of an abstraction that constitute its structure and behavior; encapsulation serves to separate the contractual interface of an abstraction and its implementation." [http://en.wikipedia.org/wiki/Encapsulation_(computer_science)]

Encapsulation, in practice, means that objects need to know as little as possible of the other parts of the system. In this way, when the behavior of parts of the system changes, there are few items to change.

The first example of encapsulation is about classes properties. Everyone knows that the classes properties should be hidden, especially in PHP, where all properties are public by default. This is because the less that is known outside the class about its properties, the easier it will be to change it.

With more experience, we realize that this same principle can be applied to parts of more complex systems.

If a client object directly calls a method of a property of a server object, and if that method or the property changes, the client call will have to change also. If I have a lot of these calls from different objects in different parts of the system, we can easily understand that maintenance will be very difficult. To overcome this problem, many times we prefer to encapsulate the delegate class in the class server, so the client object directly calls a method of server class and not that of his property. With encapsulation, if the property or its interfaces change, it will be enough to change only the class server.

Mechanics

- Detect the delegate class to hide.

- Write a unit test for the server class and add a test for each method you need to declare to hide delegate methods.

- Declare methods to hide delegate methods from the client.

- Run tests and fix until all errors are fixed.

- Change all calls from clients to delegate methods class.

- Run all suite tests.

- Remove accessory methods to the delegate class from the server class.

Example

I have two classes, `Project` and `User`. `User` can be assigned to a project, and a `Project` has a manager.

```
class Project
{
  protected $manager;

  public function getManager()
```

```
    {
        return $this->manager;
    }

    public function setManager(User $manager)
    {
        $this->manager = $manager;
    }
}

class User
{
    protected $project;

    public function setProject(Project $project)
    {
        $this->project = $project;
    }

    public function getProject(Project $project)
    {
        return $this->project;
    }
}
```

If we want to know who is the project manager of a user, we need to use the following code:

```
$romei = new User();
$trucchia = new User();
$project = new Project();

$project->setManager($romei);
$trucchia->setProject($project);
$trucchia->getProject()->getManager();
```

We want to hide the access to the project object from the User class, and we want to directly know who is the project manager of a user.

First of all we write a unit test for the User class, and we add tests for all public methods of the Project class.

```
class UserTest extends PHPUnit_Framework_TestCase
{
    public function testProjectManager()
    {

        $trucchia = new User();
        $romei = new User();

        $project = new Project();
        $project->setManager($romei);

        $trucchia->setProject($project);

        $this->assertEquals($romei, $trucchia->getProject()->getManager());
        $this->assertEquals($romei, $trucchia->getManager());
```

```
    $trucchia->setManager($trucchia);

    $this->assertEquals($trucchia, $trucchia->getManager());
  }
}
```

Now we declare delegate methods in the server class User for each method into the delegate class Project.

```
class User
{
  protected $project;

  public function setProject(Project $project)
  {
    $this->project = $project;
  }

  public function getProject()
  {
    return $this->project;
  }

  public function getManager()
  {
    return $this->project->getManager();
  }

  public function setManager(User $manager)
  {
    $this->project->setManager($manager);
  }
}
```

We run tests and everything works fine.

We change all clients calls to Project objects through User objects, and then we remove the accessory methods getProject() to the Project class, so clients can no longer call the methods of the Project class through the User class. We need to also fix our unit test removing the Project direct call.

This is our User class after we removed the getProject() method. The User class must no longer display the interface to access the project property to its clients, in keeping with our refactoring goal.

```
class User
{
  protected $project;

  public function setProject(Project $project)
  {
    $this->project = $project;
  }

  public function getManager()
  {
    return $this->project->getManager();
  }
```

```
  public function setManager(User $manager)
  {
    $this->project->setManager($manager);
  }
}
```

With its relative tests:

```
class UserTest extends PHPUnit_Framework_TestCase
{
  public function testProjectManager()
  {
    $trucchia = new User();
    $romei = new User();

    $project = new Project();
    $project->setManager($romei);

    $trucchia->setProject($project);
    $this->assertEquals($romei, $trucchia->getManager());

    $trucchia->setManager($trucchia);
    $this->assertEquals($trucchia, $trucchia->getManager());
  }
}
```

Remove the Middle Man

Problem: "A class is doing too much simple delegation."

Solution: "Get the client to call the delegate directly."

Motivation

In the previous section we saw how, through encapsulation, it is possible to hide direct access to attribute methods of a server class. The encapsulation is an object-oriented programming property that is very useful when we are sure that we want to hide our object properties interface, but in others it may be very restrictive and can complicate our code uselessly. For example, if the methods of the class, whose attribute is instance in the server class, change often, we will often change the code in server class methods, or we'll frequently have to add or remove methods to access the attribute properties.

When this job becomes too arduous, we can directly access attribute methods through the server class, which in this case would be the man in the middle. For this reason this refactoring is named "remove middle man," and it is the opposite of "hide delegate" refactoring.

Mechanism

We need to add a new method in the server class through which we can directly access to attribute. In this way, clients can call attribute methods directly without using the delegate methods of the server class. Once you change all the calls you can remove delegate methods in the server class.

• Write a test for the method that will access the delegate class.

- Add the new method in the server class.
- Run the test and fix it until all errors are fixed.
- Change all clients calls to go directly to the attribute through the new method.
- Remove all delegate methods by the server class.
- Correct server class tests, removing those tests relating to the methods just removed.
- Run all test suites and fix the code until all errors are fixed.

Example

Starting from the example in the previous section, regarding "hide delegate" refactoring, we can go backwards to figure out how to remove object encapsulation.

We have User and Project classes:

```
Class User
{
  protected $project;

  public function setProject(Project $project)
  {
    $this->project = $project;
  }

  public function getManager()
  {
    return $this->project->getManager();
  }

  public function setManager(User $manager)
  {
    $this->project->setManager($manager);
  }
}

Class Project
{
  protected $manager;

  public function getManager()
  {
    return $this->manager;
  }

  public function setManager(User $manager)
  {
    $this->manager = $manager;
  }
}
```

The User class forbids us to go directly to the Project class, encapsulating its methods within their own. Instead the design of my code is changing, and now I need to have direct access to all public methods of the Project class through the User class.

In practice, now, we can access Project class methods only through the User class and, for example, if we want to know who the project manager is of a project to which we are assigned, we can call

```
echo $user->getManager();
```

Instead we would like to have direct access to Project class methods, as follows:

```
echo $user->getProject()->getManager();
```

Following the refactoring mechanism, we first need to write a new test for the User class to test the new method that we will create to directly access the Project class properties.

```
class UserTest extends PHPUnit_Framework_TestCase
{
  public function testProjectManager()
  {
    $trucchia = new User();
    $romei = new User();

    $trucchia->setProject(new Project());
    $trucchia->getProject()->setManager($romei);

    $this->assertEquals($romei, $trucchia->getProject()->getManager());
  }
}
```

In this test, we add a test for the getProject() method that does not exist yet in the User class, and we will need it to directly access to $project properties and all its methods.

Now we can add the new method:

```
Class User
{
  protected $project;

  public function setProject(Project $project)
  {
    $this->project = $project;
  }

  public function getProject()
  {
    return $this->project;
  }

  public function getManager()
  {
    return $this->project->getManager();
  }

  public function setManager(User $manager)
  {
    $this->project->setManager($manager);
  }
}
```

Run the test that was previously prepared and make sure everything is correct. Now we can change all clients calls to delegate methods in the User class. For example, we can finally change the call

```
echo $user->getManager();
```

to

```
echo $user->getProject()->getManager();
```

Once we change all the calls, we run all test suites to be sure we haven't broken anything. If this happens, we correct our test until all is correct.

Finally, we can remove all delegate methods on the User class, because now no one will use them.

```
Class User
{
  protected $project;

  public function setProject(Project $project)
  {
    $this->project = $project;
  }

  public function getProject()
  {
    return $this->project;
  }
}
```

We run the test suite one last time and adjust the code if some tests are red.

Introduce Foreign Method

Problem: "A server class you are using needs an additional method, but you can't modify the class."

Solution: "Create a method in the client class with an instance of the server class as its first argument."

Motivation

While we are using a class included in the PHP core or from third-party libraries, such as Zend Framework, Symfony, or another, we realize that we need a functionality that the class does not implement. Damn! Why did the author not think about this essential feature? Finding complete classes is very difficult because the domains in which we use the same class can be really different, and it is almost unthinkable that a single class is perfectly adaptable to all.

At this point we need to introduce some business logic related to the server class in our class. If it happens one time, have patience, but if we begin to need the same functionality in other places, we have to wrap the functionality in a method, introducing a foreign method. This refactoring is a workaround for all those times that we cannot change the classes we are using, because obviously the best thing would be to add the method in an outer class. Being an outside virtual method, we must remember that it absolutely mustn't have visibility of the properties of our class; all parameters must be passed in the call and the first parameter must be an instance of the server class.

Method visibility should be private, because it doesn't represent the class where it is implementing. Therefore the method is not testable.

Mechanism

- Write a test for the client class.
- Run tests and all must run.
- Create the foreign method in the client class.
- The first parameter of the method must be an instance of the server.
- Comment method as "Foreign method: should be in server class."
- Run tests and all must run.

Example

We have some code that needs to check the deadlines in a billing period. To control these deadlines we need to know what is the next day of a certain date. Starting from the Bill class,

```
Class Bill
{
  protected $previous_end;
  protected $new_start;

  public function setPreviousEnd($date)
  {
    $this->previous_end = new DateTime($date);
    $this->new_start = clone $this->previous_end;
    $this->new_start->modify('+1 day');
  }

  public function getNewStart($format = 'm-d-Y')
  {
    return $this->new_start->format($format);
  }

  public function getPreviousEnd($format = 'm-d-Y')
  {
    return $this->previous_end->format($format);
  }
}
```

We want to introduce a foreign method, which should be implemented in the DateTime class, called nextDay(), which must calculate the next day.

First of all, we write the test in the Bill class:

```
class BillTest extends PHPUnit_Framework_TestCase
{
  public function testNewStart()
  {
    $bill = new Bill();
    $bill->setPreviousEnd('tomorrow');
```

131

```
    $this->assertEquals(date('m-d-Y', strtotime('+2 days')), $bill->getNewStart());
    $this->assertEquals(date('m-d-Y', strtotime('tomorrow')), $bill->getPreviousEnd());
  }
}
```

We include all the code inside the nextDay() method, passing the instance of DateTime as the first parameter and returning the new date incremented by one day.

```
Class Bill
{
  protected $previous_end;
  protected $new_start;

  public function setPreviousEnd($date)
  {
    $this->previous_end = new DateTime($date);
    $this->new_start = self::nextDay($this->previous_end);
  }

  public function getNewStart($format = 'm-d-Y')
  {
    return $this->new_start->format($format);
  }

  public function getPreviousEnd($format = 'm-d-Y')
  {
    return $this->previous_end->format($format);
  }

  /**
   * Foreign method: should stay in DateTime class
   */
  private static function nextDay(DateTime $date)
  {
    $next_day = clone $date;
    return $next_day->modify('+1 day');
  }
}
```

We run all tests and all must run, because we simply added an internal interface.

Summary

In this chapter we learned how to change the responsibilities of our classes if they do not fit our software. We learned how to move the methods and properties of classes in other classes if they do not represent them. We learned how to hide or reveal access to delegated classes. We also learned how to extract new classes from a class that is too empowered and delete unnecessary classes. In the next chapter, we'll discuss how to better organize data.

■ ■ ■

CHAPTER 9

Dealing with Data Rationalization

Encapsulation means the hiding of data and behavior from a client. It is a key object-oriented concept and, in some ways, the key to object-oriented programming. Since our goal is to make each part as independent as possible from anything external, classes and methods should receive as much information as is needed to satisfy the task they are meant for.

Anyone interested in good object-oriented development cares about encapsulation and is likely concerned with hiding or exposing the best data structure in their object, depending on the needed architecture. In this chapter we'll learn how to unlock or prevent access to data with proper interfaces, how to couple the data with the behavior processing them and how to manage type-oriented code in the proper way, leading to a better organized structure.

Self-Encapsulate Field

Problem: "Accessing a field directly can lead to bad maintainability and errors."

Solution: "Create getter and setter methods."

Motivation

The most important scenario that will make you need this refactoring is when a super class directly accessing an attribute is extended by a subclass needing to override the access to that attribute with added logic. With a self-encapsulated attribute you are free to manage logic all along the hierarchy.

Mechanics

1. Create getting and setting methods for the attribute.

2. Find and replace all references to the attribute with a getter or setter method call.

3. Make the attribute private.

4. Run tests.

Example

This is a very easy refactoring. Let's see the class and the unit test:

```php
class Sale
{
  public $product_price = 10;
  public $amount;

  public function getPrice()
  {
    return $this->amount * $this->product_price;
  }
}
class SaleTest extends PHPUnit_Framework_TestCase
{
  public function testGetPrice()
  {
    $sale = new Sale();
    $sale->amount = 10;
    $this->assertEquals(100, $sale->getPrice());
  }
}
```

Now we apply the refactoring steps and obtain the refactored class, still passing tests.

```php
class Sale
{
  protected $product_price = 10;
  public $amount;

  public function getProductPrice()
  {
    return $this->product_price;
  }

  public function getPrice()
  {
    return $this->amount * $this->getProductPrice();
  }
}
```

The benefit becomes clearer if we have to extend the Sale class in DiscountedSale.

```php
class DiscountedSale extends Sale
{
  public function getProductPrice()
  {
    return $this->product_price * 0.9;
  }
}
```

This passes the following test:

```
public function testExtendedGetPrice()
{
  $sale = new DiscountedSale();
  $sale->amount = 10;
  $this->assertEquals(90, $sale->getPrice());
}
```

Replace Data Value with Object

Problem: "Some data needs additional behavior."

Solution: "Turn the data into an object."

Motivation

You start developing a class trying to keep things simple, and you just represent data with simple data types. As the software grows, though, some of the simple data attributes you wrote need to get more complex. A simple username is just a string at the very beginning, but as you add firstname, lastname, address, e-mail, etc. this data set gets a sense of its own and likely starts showing the need to acquire independence and get some encapsulated behavior. Turning this data into an object solves the problem.

Mechanics

- Create the class to hold the value, featuring a getter and a constructor that accept the attribute as an argument.
- If you want, you can add a type hint in the signature of all methods accepting the attribute as a parameter.
- Make the getter in the source class call the getter in the new class.
- If the source class's constructor uses the attribute, make it use the new class constructor.
- Change the setter method in the source class to create a new instance of the new class.
- Run tests.

Example

We have the Order class with its private attribute $customer.

```
class Order
{
  private $customer;

  public function __construct($customer)
```

```
  {
    $this->setCustomer($customer);
  }

  public function setCustomer($customer)
  {
    $this->customer = $customer;
  }

  public function getCustomer()
  {
    return $this->customer;
  }
}
```

We can write a very simple test to check this class's behavior.

```
class OrderTest extends PHPUnit_Framework_TestCase
{
  public function testGetCustomer()
  {
    $order = new Order('Edwin Moses');
    $this->assertEquals('Edwin Moses', $order->getCustomer());
  }
}
```

After verifying that the test is OK, start refactoring the class. First, we create the Customer class:

```
class Customer
{
  private $name;

  public function __construct($name)
  {
    $this->name = $name;
  }

  public function getName()
  {
    return $this->name;
  }
}
```

Thereafter we change Order's setter to create an instance of Customer and the getter to reference Customer's name getter:

```
class Order
{
  private $customer;

  public function __construct($customer)
  {
    $this->setCustomer($customer);
  }
```

```php
  public function getCustomer()
  {
    return $this->customer->getName();
  }

  public function setCustomer($customer)
  {
    $this->customer = new Customer($customer);
  }
}
```

As you may have noticed already we created a `Customer` object for each `Order`, and we didn't reference a unique `Customer` object shared among many `Order` objects. This is because we are treating the customer as a value object. If you want to give the customer her own identity, the next refactoring technique "Change Value to Reference" addresses this need.

Change Value to Reference

Problem: "You have many equal instances of a class that you want to replace with a single object."

Solution: "Turn the object attribute into a reference object."

Motivation

Objects can be often grouped in two well-defined categories: *reference objects* and *value objects*.

Reference objects are those standing for a given object in the real world. They are defined by identity, and that identity is checked when testing for those objects to be equal. In domain-driven design [Evans] they are called *entities*. User accounts in a system or a purchase order are typical examples.

Value objects have no identity. The intention of a value object is to represent something by its attributes only. Two value objects are identical if they have identical attributes. However, not having any value other than by virtue of their attributes, they can be freely copied around. Dates, money, and RGB colors are usually represented as value objects.

The decision to change a value to a reference comes after having a small initial value grow in complexity as long as development goes on. At some point you want to add some mutable data to that value and have the same changes shared across objects using that value: you then change value to reference.

Mechanics

- Use "Replace Constructor with Factory Method."

- Run tests.

- Decide what object is responsible for providing access to the objects.

- Determine whether the objects are referenced with a Proxy/Flyweight pattern [GOF] or created when needed. If you rely on preloaded objects, make sure they get loaded before they are needed.

- Change the factory method to return the reference object.

- Run tests.

Example

We'll be using "Replace Data Value with Object" as a starting point for this example. We have a
`Customer` class:

```
class Customer
{
  private $name;

  public function __construct($name)
  {
    $this->name = $name;
  }

  public function getName()
  {
    return $this->name;
  }
}
```

This is used to create customer instances as value objects in an `Order` class:

```
class Order
{
  private $customer;

  public function __construct($customer)
  {
    $this->setCustomer($customer);
  }

  public function getCustomer()
  {
    return $this->customer->getName();
  }

  public function setCustomer($customer)
  {
    $this->customer = new Customer($customer);
  }
}
```

We follow with a test checking its correctness:

```
class OrderTest extends PHPUnit_Framework_TestCase
{
  public function testGetCustomer()
  {
    $order = new Order('Edwin Moses');
    $this->assertEquals('Edwin Moses', $order->getCustomer());
  }
}
```

We can now use "Replace Constructor with Factory Method."

```
class Customer
[...]
public static function getInstance($name)
{
  return new Customer($name);
}

private function __construct($name)
{
  $this->name = $name;
}
[...]
```

And replace the call to the Customer constructor in the Order setter method with the factory method:

```
public function setCustomer($customer)
{
  $this->customer = Customer::getInstance($customer);
}
```

The factory method also facilitates testing the classes. In the real world, the Customer factory method would probably talk with the DB mapper or with an identity map to retrieve new or preloaded instances of the Customer class. In our case we simplify the reading using a Customer stub class to test the Order class. Our stub preloads a small set of Customer instances and the factory method will be changed to retrieve one of those preloaded instances.

```
class Customer
{
  private $name;

  private static $customers;

  public static function loadCustomers()
  {
    self::$customers = array(
      'Edwin Moses' => new Customer('Edwin Moses'),
      'John Foo'    => new Customer('John Foo')
    );
  }

  public static function getInstance($name)
  {
    return self::$customers[$name];
  }

  private function __construct($name)
  {
    $this->name = $name;
  }

  public function getName()
  {
```

```
    return $this->name;
  }
}
```

Add this setup method in our unit test:

```
class OrderTest extends PHPUnit_Framework_TestCase
{
  […]
  public function setUp()
  {
  Customer::loadCustomers();
  }
  […]
}
```

Change Reference to Value

Problem: "A reference object is immutable and hard to manage."

Solution: "Turn it into a value object."

Motivation

The definition of a value object is in its consistent and not mutable state. This means that any time you call a method on a value object you will always get the same output in return. This property makes value objects interchangeable, thus many clients invoking a query on a reference object and getting the same result can easily be linked to many different objects representing the same value. On the other hand, if in changing a value you don't have to ensure every other object using that value must be updated, again there is no problem in using a value object.

If working with a reference becomes awkward for any reason and it can be represented by many value objects, then you can make things simpler with "Change Reference to Value."

Mechanics

- Check that the candidate object is (or can become) immutable. If the candidate object can mutate its state, don't perform this refactoring.

- Remove any existing factory methods and make the constructor public.

- Run tests.

Replace Array with Object

Problem: "You have an array containing elements meaning different things."

Solution: "Replace the array with an object featuring an attribute for each array element."

Motivation

Since the very beginning of computer science, arrays were meant to store collections of homogenous data. As the years passed, modern languages let us freely aggregate several types of data. PHP arrays are very flexible and provide a single construct to represent arrays, hashes, structs, and records (a few well-known examples in other languages). By the way, classes can sometimes be more expressive, and, above all, they provide the fittest ground to make behavior grow. As soon as this data is processed by very dedicated code, this is likely to be encapsulated in a class along with that data. Replacing arrays with objects, then, is the way to go.

Mechanics

- Create a new class to move data into. Create a public field in it to host the array.
- Make all users of the array use the new class.
- Run tests.
- Add meaningful setters and getters for an array element and make users of that array element call those accessors. Run tests and repeat for each array element.
- Make array fields private.
- Run tests.
- For each array element create a related field in the class and change related accessors accordingly. Run tests and repeat for each array element.
- Delete the array.

Example

We consider a simple `Order` class using some data about the customer:

```php
class Order{
  private $customer;

  public function __construct($customer_data)
  {
    $this->customer = $customer_data;
  }

  public function getShippingAddress()
  {
    return $this->customer[0].', '.$this->customer[1];
  }
}
```

This is tested with the following:

```php
class OrderTest extends PHPUnit_Framework_TestCase
{
  public function testGetCustomer()
  {
```

```
    $order = new Order(array('Gerardo Rossi', 'BeckerStrasse 12, Utopia'));
    $this->assertEquals('Gerardo Rossi, BeckerStrasse 12, Utopia', $order->getShippingAddress());
  }
}
```

We can then apply the refactoring steps. First we create a new class with a public array field and make the Order class use it:

```
class Customer
{
  public $data;
}

class Order
{
  private $customer;

  public function __construct($customer_data)
  {
    $this->customer = new Customer;
    $this->customer->data = $customer_data;
  }

  public function getShippingAddress()
  {
    return $this->customer->data[0].', '.$this->customer->data[1];
  }
}
```

At this point, tests are strictly green. Then we create accessors for the two fields:

```
class Customer
{
  private $data;

  public function getName()
  {
    return $this->data[0];
  }

  public function getAddress()
  {
    return $this->data[1];
  }
}

class Order
{
  public function __construct($customer_data)
  {
    $this->customer = new Customer;
    $this->customer->setName($customer_data[0]);
    $this->customer->setAddress($customer_data[1]);
  }
  public function getShippingAddress()
  {
```

```
    return $this->customer->getName().', '.$this->customer->getAddress();
  }
}
```

Now we've set the $data field private in the `Customer` class. Last we turn the array elements into `Customer` class fields and get rid of the array:

```
class Customer
{
  private $name, $address;

  public function getName()
  {
    return $this->name;
  }

  public function getAddress()
  {
    return $this->address;
  }

  public function setName($name)
  {
    $this->name = $name;
  }

  public function setAddress($address)
  {
    $this->address = $address;
  }
}
```

Tests continue to show that everything was changed within safe boundaries.

Change Unidirectional Association to Bidirectional

Problem: "You have two classes needing each other's features, but there is only a one-way link."

Solution: "Add a backward link and change the setter and getter methods to update both sets."

Motivation

You have a class attribute referring to another class. As development goes on you find that an instance of the referred class needs to get the object referring to it. The referred class features no reference to the referring class, so we have to set up a two-way reference.

Mechanics

- Add an attribute for the back link.
- Decide which class will control the association.

- Create any needed helper method on the non-controlling side of the association.
- If the existing setter is on the controlling side, modify it to update the back link.
- If the existing setter is on the controlled side, create a controlling method on the controlling side and call it from the existing setter method.

Example

This time we have to unit test more than a class—we have to test a relationship, and it would require building correct stubs for both sides of the association. It would not be hard and, indeed, we could just arrange the right stub set in minutes, but for the sake of clarity here we will see another kind of test: integration tests. They are based on more than one real class and will be useful here to keep the example concise.

Please note how a simple dependency like the one we are about to model and test makes things lots harder to code and test, giving us strong clues about how harmful dependencies can be for our architecture.

Let's now dive into the "Change Unidirectional Association to Bidirectional" technique. Let's start from a simple version of the one Customer–many Orders relationship:

```
class Customer
{
  private $name;

  public function __construct($name)
  {
    $this->name = $name;
  }

  public function getName()
  {
    return $this->name;
  }
}

class Order
{
  private $customer;

  public function __construct($customer)
  {
    $this->setCustomer($customer);
  }

  public function getCustomer()
  {
    return $this->customer;
  }

  public function setCustomer(Customer $customer)
  {
    $this->customer = $customer;
  }
}
```

This is tested by:

```
class OrderTest extends PHPUnit_Framework_TestCase
{
  public function setUp()
  {
    $this->customer = new Customer('Edwin Moses');
  }

  public function testGetCustomer()
  {
    $order = new Order($this->customer);
    $this->assertEquals($this->customer, $order->getCustomer());
  }
}
```

Following the refactoring steps, we add an attribute to the Customer class to hold the back link to its Order objects, and we also add a couple of helper methods here, having decided the Order class will be controlling the association:

```
class Customer
{
  private $name;
  private $orders = array();

  public function __construct($name)
  {
    $this->name = $name;
  }

  public function getName()
  {
    return $this->name;
  }

  public function getOrders()
  {
    return $this->orders;
  }

  public function setOrders($orders)
  {
    $this->orders = $orders;
  }
}
```

Now we have to change the setter method in the Order class.

```
public function setCustomer(Customer $customer)
{
  if (!is_null($this->customer))
  {
    $this->customer->setOrders(array_diff($this->customer->getOrders(), array($this)));
  }
  $this->customer = $customer;
```

```
    $this->customer->setOrders(array_merge($this->customer->getOrders(), array($this)));
}
```

Then create a test for the `Customer` class:

```
class CustomerTest extends PHPUnit_Framework_TestCase
{
  public function testGetOrders()
  {
    $customer = new Customer('Edwin Moses');
    $order1 = new Order($customer);
    $order2 = new Order($customer);

    $this->assertEquals(array($order1, $order2), $customer->getOrders());
  }
}
```

After running both tests, they should be green now.

Change Bidirectional Association to Unidirectional

Problem: "Two classes reference each other but one class no longer needs other class's features."

Solution: "Make the two-way association one-way."

Motivation

Bidirectional associations are sometimes needed but they always introduce complexity. This complexity comes in the form of maintaining the two-way links and avoiding errors while writing the code to manage them.

Bidirectional associations also force an interdependency between two classes, leading to a more coupled system that is harder to maintain or change without cascading and unpredictable side effects.

Thus bidirectional associations should be used only when needed. If a bidirectional association is no longer providing its benefit, make it unidirectional.

Mechanics

- Check if the link attribute you want to remove is removal-safe. You must look at getter methods and methods using those accessors.

- If the client needs the getter, use the "Self-Encapsulate Field" technique, and perform "Substitute Algorithm" on the getter. Also consider adding the object as an argument to all methods that use the field you are about to remove.

- Run tests.

- When no attribute reader is left, remove all updates to the attribute and remove the attribute. If the attribute is assigned many times, use the "Self-Encapsulate Field" technique to use a single setter, then empty its body. At this point remove the setter, all setter calls, and the attribute.

- Run tests.

Example

The hardest step while performing this refactoring is the first step: being sure the bidirectional association is not needed anymore. If a reference to the object that the reference we are killing points to is still needed by some method, we can opt to pass that object as an argument of that method.

Let's consider an example where the Order can be discounted on a per-Customer basis.

```php
class OrderTest extends PHPUnit_Framework_TestCase
{
  public function setUp()
  {
    $this->customer = new Customer('Edwin Moses');
  }

  public function testGetCustomer()
  {
    $order = new Order();
    $this->customer->addOrder($order);
    $this->assertEquals($this->customer, $order->getCustomer());
  }
}
```

This integration test is satisfied by these two classes:

```php
class Customer
{
  private $name;
  private $orders = array();
  public $discount;

  public function __construct($name)
  {
    $this->name = $name;
  }

  public function getName()
  {
    return $this->name;
  }

  public function addOrder(Order $order)
  {
    $order->setCustomer($this);
  }

  public function getOrders()
  {
    return $this->orders;
  }

  public function setOrders($orders)
  {
    $this->orders = $orders;
  }
}

class Order
{
```

```php
  private $customer;
  private $price = 100;

  public function getCustomer()
  {
    return $this->customer;
  }

  public function setCustomer(Customer $customer)
  {
    if (!is_null($this->customer))
    {
      $this->customer->setOrders(array_diff($this->customer->getOrders(), array($this)));
    }
    $this->customer = $customer;
    $this->customer->setOrders(array_merge($this->customer->getOrders(), array($this)));
  }

  public function getDiscountedPrice()
  {
    return $this->price * $this->customer->discount;
  }
}
```

We want to remove the reference to Customer in the Order class. We need that reference in the getDiscountedPrice() method, so we decide to pass it as an argument:

```php
public function getDiscountedPrice($customer)
{
  return $this->price * $customer->discount;
}
```

We change the test accordingly, modifying testGetDiscountedPrice():

```php
public function testGetDiscountedPrice()
{
  $this->customer->discount = 0.7;
  $order = new Order();
  $this->customer->addOrder($order);
  $this->assertEquals(70, $order->getDiscountedPrice($this->customer));
}
```

Now it will pass green.

We can then remove the testGetCustomer() method from the test and remove the getter from the Order class. The tests are still green.

Now we want to remove the setter method, but it's still used in the addOrder() method in the Customer class. We perform "Substitute Algorithm" on it:

```php
public function addOrder(Order $order)
{
  $this->orders[] = $order;
}
```

We are now free to remove the setCustomer() method from the Order class along with the $customer attribute, keeping tests green.

```php
class Order
{
  private $price = 100;

  public function getDiscountedPrice($customer)
  {
    return $this->price * $customer->discount;
  }
}
```

Replace Magic Number with Symbolic Constant

Problem: "You have a literal meaningful number."

Solution: "Create a meaningful constant and replace the number with it."

Motivation

Magic numbers are those usually-not-obvious numbers with special values. The gravitational constant and pi are good examples of magic numbers in the fields of physics and mathematics.

Hardcoding magic numbers leads to less maintainable code. First, they are harder to change, and second, it's a lot harder to read the code and understand it. Declaring constants in a PHP class is easy, and they are cheap enough from a performance point of view, providing a great improvement in maintainability and readability.

Mechanics

- Declare a constant and set it to the magic number's value.

- Find and replace all occurrences of the magic number.

- Run tests.

Example

This a very simple case to exemplify. Let's have a look at a class called Circle that stores its radius providing a method to compute its circumference.

```php
class Circle
{
  public $radius;

  public function getCircumference()
  {
    return $this->radius * 2 * 3.1416;
  }
}
```

This is tested by:

```php
class CircleTest extends PHPUnit_Framework_TestCase
{
  public function testGetCircumference()
  {
    $circle = new Circle();
    $circle->radius = 2;
    $this->assertEquals(12.5664, $circle->getCircumference());
  }
}
```

We apply the simple steps just described and we get:

```php
class Circle
{
  const PI = 3.1416;

  public $radius;

  public function getCircumference()
  {
    return $this->radius * 2 * self::PI;
  }
}
```

And it still passes the test.

Encapsulate Field

Problem: "A class exposes a public attribute."

Solution: "Make the attribute private and add accessor methods."

Motivation

As we have already seen in "Self-Encapsulate Field," accessing a field directly from within a class can be a choice subject to many arguments. The issue becomes even worse as we face this situation regarding some public field used by some foreign client. Encapsulation is one of the fundamentals of object-oriented programming: never make your data public. Making an attribute public means that other objects can edit the attribute with the owning object not knowing this, then making its state unknown.

This leads to distributed logic that harms the modularity of the software. Data and behavior should go together in a close relationship because it is easier to change the code in just one place rather than across the whole application.

The technique "Encapsulate Field" hides the data and adds the accessors, paving the way for one or more uses of "Move Method" to bring scattered logic into one place.

Mechanics

- Create getter and setter methods.

- Find all client references to the attribute. Change attribute readings with getter calls and attribute assignments with setter calls. If the attribute is an object and the client uses a modifier on it, then keep the call to the modifier.

- Run tests after each change.

- Declare the attribute as private.

- Run tests.

Example

We start from where we left with the technique "Replace Magic Number with Symbolic Constant," and we apply the steps to refactor the Circle class, beginning with adding the radius setter:

```
public function setRadius($radius)
{
   $this->radius = $radius;
}
```

fixing the test to make it green again:

```
public function testGetCircumference()
{
   $circle = new Circle();
   $circle->setRadius(2);
   $this->assertEquals(12.5664, $circle->getCircumference());
}
```

Green tests allow us to make the $radius attribute private:

```
class Circle
{
   const PI = 3.1416;

   private $radius;

   public function setRadius($radius)
   {
      $this->radius = $radius;
   }

   public function getCircumference()
   {
      return $this->radius * 2 * self::PI;
   }
}
```

Replacing Type Code with Subclasses

Problem: "You have an immutable type code affecting the class behavior."

Solution: "Replace the type code with subclasses."

Motivation

Quite often we have to write conditional code based on the value of a type code. Switches and if-then-else constructs are the spots to look for this kind of behavior, where we test the value of the type code to execute different code depending on that value. This conditional code needs to be refactored with the technique "Replace Conditional with Polymorphism." For this refactoring to be performed we need the type code to be replaced by a class hierarchy that will structure the polymorphic behavior, featuring a subclass for each type code.

The simplest way to create this structure is to use the technique "Replace Type Code with Subclasses." You take the class featuring the type code and extend it once for each type code. As long as the type code is immutable and the parent class is not already subclassed for another reason, you can apply this refactoring. If one of these conditions is not verified then you should perform "Replace Type Code with State/Strategy."

Another reason to use "Replace Type Code with Subclasses" is the presence of type code–relevant behavior. After this refactoring you can use "Push Down Method" and "Push Down Field" to make specific data closer to specifically related behavior. This will free clients of the source class from managing variants on their side, leaving you free to add new behavior without the clients even knowing it: all you need to do is add a subclass.

Mechanics

- Self-encapsulate the type code, replacing the constructor with a factory method if needed.

- Create a subclass for each type code value. Override the type code accessor in the new subclass to return the relevant code. This value can even be hardcoded in the method return by now.

- Run tests after each type code is replaced with a subclass.

- Remove type code attributes in the parent class. Declare the type code accessor method and the whole parent class as abstract.

- Run tests.

Example

Let's consider an Order class and its test:

```
class Order:

{
  const GOLD = 0;
  const SILVER = 1;
  const BRONZE = 2;
```

```php
  protected $promotion;

  public function __construct($promotion)
  {
    $this->promotion = $promotion;
  }
}

class TestableOrder extends Order
{
  public function getPromotion()
  {
    return $this->promotion;
  }
}

class OrderTest extends PHPUnit_Framework_TestCase
{
  public function testPromotionType()
  {
    $order = new TestableOrder(Order::GOLD);
    $this->assertEquals(Order::GOLD, $order->getPromotion());
    $order = new TestableOrder(Order::SILVER);
    $this->assertEquals(Order::SILVER, $order->getPromotion());
    $order = new TestableOrder(Order::BRONZE);
    $this->assertEquals(Order::BRONZE, $order->getPromotion());
  }
}
```

Note how we extended the tested class to facilitate its testing with a public method to probe its internal state. Since we are passing the type code into the constructor, we create a factory method after using "Self-Encapsulate Field" type code:

```php
class Order
{
  const GOLD = 0;
  const SILVER = 1;
  const BRONZE = 2;

  protected $promotion;

  static public function create($promotion)
  {
    return new Order($promotion);
  }

  private function __construct($promotion)
  {
    $this->promotion = $promotion;
  }

  public function getPromotion()
  {
    return $this->promotion;
  }
}
```

We need to change tests accordingly, and we can get rid of the `TestableOrder` class since we introduced a type code accessor in the tested class, too:

```
class OrderTest extends PHPUnit_Framework_TestCase
{
  public function testPromotionType()
  {
    $order = Order::create(Order::GOLD);
    $this->assertEquals(Order::GOLD, $order->getPromotion());
    $order = Order::create(Order::SILVER);
    $this->assertEquals(Order::SILVER, $order->getPromotion());
    $order = Order::create(Order::BRONZE);
    $this->assertEquals(Order::BRONZE, $order->getPromotion());
  }
}
```

We can now start creating the subclasses for the first type:

```
class BronzeOrder extends Order
{
  public function getPromotion()
  {
    return Order::BRONZE;
  }
}
```

Now we edit the factory method:

```
class Order
{
  [...]
  static public function create($promotion)
  {
    if ($promotion == self::BRONZE)
    {
      return new BronzeOrder($promotion);
    }
    else
    {
      return new Order($promotion);
    }
  }
  [...]
}
```

And tests continue to tell us that everything is OK. We can then create other subclasses related to SILVER and BRONZE promotions until we get to the end:

```
abstract class Order
{
  const GOLD = 0;
  const SILVER = 1;
  const BRONZE = 2;
```

```php
  static public function create($promotion)
  {
    if ($promotion == self::BRONZE)
    {
      return new BronzeOrder($promotion);
    }
    elseif ($promotion == self::SILVER)
    {
      return new SilverOrder($promotion);
    }
    elseif ($promotion == self::GOLD)
    {
      return new GoldOrder($promotion);
    }
    else
    {
      throw new Exception('Invalid promotion');
    }
  }

  private function __construct($promotion)
  {
    $this->promotion = $promotion;
  }

  abstract public function getPromotion();
}

class BronzeOrder extends Order
{
  public function getPromotion()
  {
    return Order::BRONZE;
  }
}

class SilverOrder extends Order
{
  public function getPromotion()
  {
    return Order::SILVER;
  }
}

class GoldOrder extends Order
{
  public function getPromotion()
  {
    return Order::GOLD;
  }
}
```

At this point you are free to move behavior up and down the hierarchy to avoid duplication or enhance specialization.

Replace Type Code with State/Strategy

Problem: "You have a type code affecting the class behavior, but you cannot use subclassing."

Solution: "Replace the type code with a state object."

Motivation

This is similar to the technique "Replace Type Code with Subclasses" but can be used in more general cases—if the type code changes after having created the typed class instance or if another reason prevents subclassing. State and strategy patterns [GoF] are similar and any distinction among the two is not useful here.

Mechanics

- Self-encapsulate the type code.
- Create a new class and name it after the purpose of the type code.
- Add one subclass of the new class for each type code.
- Create a data type abstract query method in the new class.
- Override the abstract query method in each subclass to return correct type code.
- Run tests.
- Create a new attribute in the old class for the new state object.
- Make the type code query method in the old class delegate to the new class query method.
- Make the type code setting method in the old class assign an instance of the right subclass.
- Run tests.

Example

We start from the now usual `Order` class to compute a discount policy depending on the Order type

```
class Order
{
  const GOLD = 0;
  const SILVER = 1;
  const BRONZE = 2;

  private $price = 100;
  private $promotion;

  public function __construct($promotion)
  {
    $this->promotion = $promotion;
  }
}
```

```php
  public function getFinalPrice()
  {
    $price = $this->price;

    switch ($this->promotion)
    {
      case self::GOLD:
        $price *= 0.7;
        break;
      case self::SILVER:
        $price *= 0.8;
        break;
      case self::BRONZE:
        $price *= 0.9;
        break;
    }

    return $price;
  }
}
```

We also provide tests to verify the method's correctness:

```php
class OrderTest extends PHPUnit_Framework_TestCase
{
  public function testPromotion()
  {
    $order = new Order(Order::GOLD);
    $this->assertEquals(70, $order->getFinalPrice());
    $order = new Order(Order::SILVER);
    $this->assertEquals(80, $order->getFinalPrice());
    $order = new Order(Order::BRONZE);
    $this->assertEquals(90, $order->getFinalPrice());
  }
}
```

We proceed with self-encapsulating the promotion field.

```php
class Order
{
  [...]
  public function __construct($promotion)
  {
    $this->setPromotion($promotion);
  }

  public function getPromotion()
  {
    return $this->promotion;
  }

  public function setPromotion($promotion)
  {
    $this->promotion = $promotion;
  }
```

```php
  public function getFinalPrice()
  {
    $price = $this->price;

    switch ($this->getPromotion())
    {
      [...]
    }

    return $price;
  }
}
```

We have now to declare the state class now. We will name it Promotion

```php
abstract class Promotion
{
  abstract public function getCode();
}
```

Now we can now start creating subclasses.

```php
class GoldPromotion extends Promotion
{
  public function getCode()
  {
    return Order::GOLD;
  }
}

class SilverPromotion extends Promotion
{
  public function getCode()
  {
    return Order::SILVER;
  }
}

class BronzePromotion extends Promotion
{
  public function getCode()
  {
    return Order::BRONZE;
  }
}
```

We run tests and everything is fine. Now is the moment to link the Order class to the Promotion hierarchy.

```php
class Order
{
  [...]
  public function getPromotion()
  {
```

```
    return $this->promotion->getCode();
  }

  public function setPromotion($promotion)
  {
    switch ($promotion)
    {
      case self::GOLD:
        $this->promotion = new GoldPromotion();
        break;
      case self::SILVER:
        $this->promotion = new SilverPromotion();
        break;
      case self::BRONZE:
        $this->promotion = new BronzePromotion();
        break;
      default:
        throw new Exception('Invalid promotion code');
    }
  }
  [...]
}
```

Tests are still green! Now we can polish things a bit by putting all the code using the type codes in the new class.

```
class Order
{
  private $price = 100;
  private $promotion;

  public function __construct($promotion)
  {
    $this->setPromotion($promotion);
  }

  public function getPromotion()
  {
    return $this->promotion->getCode();
  }

  public function setPromotion($promotion)
  {
    $this->promotion = Promotion::create($promotion);
  }

  public function getFinalPrice()
  {
    $price = $this->price;

    switch ($this->getPromotion())
    {
      case Promotion::GOLD:
        $price *= 0.7;
        break;
      case Promotion::SILVER:
        $price *= 0.8;
```

```php
        break;
      case Promotion::BRONZE:
        $price *= 0.9;
        break;
    }

    return $price;
  }
}

abstract class Promotion
{
  const GOLD = 0;
  const SILVER = 1;
  const BRONZE = 2;

  static public function create($promotion)
  {
    switch ($promotion)
    {
      case self::GOLD:
        return new GoldPromotion();
      case self::SILVER:
        return new SilverPromotion();
      case self::BRONZE:
        return new BronzePromotion();
      default:
        throw new Exception('Invalid promotion code');
    }
  }

  abstract public function getCode();
}

class GoldPromotion extends Promotion
{
  public function getCode()
  {
    return Promotion::GOLD;
  }
}

class SilverPromotion extends Promotion
{
  public function getCode()
  {
    return Promotion::SILVER;
  }
}

class BronzePromotion extends Promotion
{
  public function getCode()
  {
    return Promotion::BRONZE;
  }
}
```

And we update tests to reflect this little change:

```
class OrderTest extends PHPUnit_Framework_TestCase
{
  public function testPromotion()
  {
    $order = new Order(Promotion::GOLD);
    $this->assertEquals(70, $order->getFinalPrice());
    $order = new Order(Promotion::SILVER);
    $this->assertEquals(80, $order->getFinalPrice());
    $order = new Order(Promotion::BRONZE);
    $this->assertEquals(90, $order->getFinalPrice());
  }
}
```

Replace Subclass with Fields

Problem: "You have subclasses that vary only in methods that return constant data."

Solution: "Change the methods to super class fields and eliminate the subclasses."

Motivation

Constant methods are those returning a hardcoded value. Though they can be very useful in subclasses returning different values for an accessor defined in the super class, it is sometimes true that a subclass made only of constant methods is not worth its own existence. You can then remove those subclasses, move fields up to the super class, and get a less complex architecture with no subclassing.

Mechanics

- Use the technique "Replace Constructor with Factory Method" on the subclasses.

- Replace any reference to any subclass with a reference to the super class.

- Declare attributes on the super class for each constant method.

- Declare a protected super class constructor to initialize the attributes.

- Add or modify subclass constructors to call the new super class constructor.

- Run tests.

- Move each constant method from each subclass to the super class to return the related attribute.

- Run tests after each move.

- Use the "Inline Method" technique to inline the constructor into the factory method of the super class.

- Run tests.

- Remove subclass.

161

- Run tests.
- Repeat constructor inlining, subclass removal, and test cycle until all subclasses are removed.

Example

We have an abstract `Promotion` class extended by some subclasses defining the promotion type:

```
abstract class Promotion
{
  abstract public function isGold();
  abstract public function isSilver();
  abstract public function getCode();
}

class GoldPromotion extends Promotion
{
  public function isGold()
  {
    return true;
  }

  public function isSilver()
  {
    return false;
  }

  public function getCode()
  {
    return 0;
  }
}

class SilverPromotion extends Promotion
{
  public function isGold()
  {
    return false;
  }

  public function isSilver()
  {
    return true;
  }

  public function getCode()
  {
    return 1;
  }
}
```

The following tests certify their correctness:

```php
class OrderTest extends PHPUnit_Framework_TestCase
{
  public function testPromotion()
  {
    $order = new GoldPromotion();
    $this->assertEquals(0, $order->getCode());
    $this->assertTrue($order->isGold());
    $this->assertFalse($order->isSilver());
    $order = new SilverPromotion();
    $this->assertEquals(1, $order->getCode());
    $this->assertFalse($order->isGold());
    $this->assertTrue($order->isSilver());
  }
}
```

Now we can move on, applying the first step described in the mechanics. We perform "Replace Constructor with Factory Method."

```php
abstract class Promotion
{
  [...]
  static public function createGoldPromotion()
  {
    return new GoldPromotion();
  }

  static public function createSilverPromotion()
  {
    return new SilverPromotion();
  }
}
```

Then edit tests accordingly:

```php
class OrderTest extends PHPUnit_Framework_TestCase
{
  public function testPromotion()
  {
    $order = Promotion::createGoldPromotion();
    $this->assertEquals(0, $order->getCode());
    $this->assertTrue($order->isGold());
    $this->assertFalse($order->isSilver());
    $order = Promotion::createSilverPromotion();
    $this->assertEquals(1, $order->getCode());
    $this->assertFalse($order->isGold());
    $this->assertTrue($order->isSilver());
  }
```

We can add fields to manage each different kind of promotion:

```php
abstract class Promotion
{
  private $is_gold = false;
  private $is_silver = false;
```

```
private $code;
[...]
}
```

Now we define a protected constructor in the `Promotion` parent class and we use it in subclass constructors:

```
abstract class Promotion
{
  [...]
  protected function __construct($code)
  {
    if (0 === $code)
    {
      $this->is_gold = true;
    }
    elseif (1 === $code)
    {
      $this->is_silver = true;
    }
    else
    {
      throw new Exception('Invalid promotion code.');
    }

    $this->code = $code;
  }
}
```

We also do the following:

```
class GoldPromotion extends Promotion
{
  public function __construct()
  {
    parent::__construct(0);
  }
  [...]
}
```

```
class SilverPromotion extends Promotion
{
  public function __construct()
  {
    parent::__construct(1);
  }
  [...]
}
```

At this point we can run tests to verify our code's health. Thus we can move constant methods from subclasses up to the parent class, obtaining the following:

```
abstract class Promotion
{
  private $is_gold = false;
  private $is_silver = false;
```

```
  private $code;

  public function isGold()
  {
    return $this->is_gold;
  }

  public function isSilver()
  {
    return $this->is_silver;
  }

  public function getCode()
  {
    return $this->code;
  }
  [...]
}
```

And do the following:

```
class GoldPromotion extends Promotion
{
  public function __construct()
  {
    parent::__construct(0);
  }
}

class SilverPromotion extends Promotion
{
  public function __construct()
  {
    parent::__construct(1);
  }
}
```

We must remember to run tests after moving each of the three methods to check everything is right while we refactor our code, keeping ourselves in the *green zone*.

We just have to perform "Inline Method" on the subclass constructors, moving the subclasses' creation directly into the parent class's factory methods.

```
class Promotion
{
  [...]
  static public function createGoldPromotion()
  {
    return new Promotion(0);
  }

  static public function createSilverPromotion()
  {
    return new Promotion(1);
  }
}
```

Now we can get rid of the subclasses.

Summary

Objects are defined by data with some behavior attached. Though the most important side of their design lies in the interface they expose, still, the data they carry plays a crucial role. Objects' inner structure can influence the interface they expose and the right choice can make a developer's life a lot easier. In this chapter we saw a few techniques to better deal with data held inside our objects. In the next chapter we'll be back focusing on our methods, discovering ways to simplify our conditional expressions.

■ ■ ■

CHAPTER 10

Reducing to Essential Conditional Executions

When designing our applications, often we limit ourselves to creating the most important classes and then we create complex conditional logic in their methods to change their behavior, based on their configuration. This approach is typical of those who used procedural programming for a long time and are accustomed to a cascading code execution, rather than designing objects that communicate with each other.

In procedural programming styles, the only way to change the behavior of code flow is with conditional logic. In object-oriented programming, in many cases, the conditional logic can be implemented in different ways more consistent with the object's behavior.

The logic often tries to change the behavior of a certain object. If this is the intent, we must use polymorphism. But if the condition has sense and gives greater prominence to the details of the condition rather than the conditions themselves, decouple the details of the condition from the condition itself. In other cases, our conditions are used only to check limit cases. We must isolate these cases by adding guard clauses. Sometimes we also have nested conditional logic that uses only one exit point. In this case we can simplify by introducing multiple exit points.

In this chapter we'll see a collection of some refactoring methods created by Martin Fowler [FOW01]. For each method we'll see the motivation and situation for its use, the mechanism that will explain how we can apply the method to our existing code, and some examples showing how the method works in a real-world case.

Decompose Conditional

Problem: "You have a complicated conditional (*if/else*) statement."

Solution: "Extract methods from the condition, then extract the *if* part and then the *else* part."

Motivation

Having complex logical conditional inside our methods is one of the most typical things that happen when our code increases and our design isn't good enough. Such conditional logic can make a method very long and difficult to read. A readable code is easier to maintain. Conditional logics often explain what they do, but it is not easy to understand why they do it, information that is, in most cases, much more useful.

To simplify these pieces of code we need to clarify the intentions of conditional logic. We must be capable of understanding easily because we are entering a conditional branch. To do this we need to highlight the condition of conditional logic, extrapolating this piece of code in an external method, and then extrapolate to other private methods outside of the pieces of code for each individual branch.

Mechanics

- Write a unit test to design how to extract conditional chunks of code and branch chunks of code.

- Extract conditional chunks of code into a private method.

- Extract branch chunks of code into other external private methods.

- Run a unit test and check that all assertions pass.

Example

We want to decompose conditional for the method getAmount() of the following class.

```
class Sale
{
  public $expired_at;
  public $amount;

  public function getAmount()
  {
    if(!is_null($this->expired_at) && $this->expired_at < time())
    {
      $interest = 10;
      $this->amount = $this->amount + ($this->amount / 100 * $interest);
    }
    else
    {
      $discount = 10;
      $this->amount = $this->amount - ($this->amount / 100 * $discount);
    }
    return $this->amount;
  }
}
```

First of all, we write a unit test if we didn't before. We write it to confirm that the behavior doesn't change after refactoring. So, our test will be green at once.

```
class SaleTest extends PHPUnit_Framework_TestCase
{
  public function testAmount()
  {
    $sale = new Sale();
    $sale->amount = 10;
    $sale->expired_at = strtotime('-10 days');
    $this->assertEquals(10 + (10/100*10), $sale->getAmount());

    $sale = new Sale();
```

```
      $sale->amount = 10;
      $sale->expired_at = strtotime('+10 days');
      $this->assertEquals(10 - (10/100*10), $sale->getAmount());
  }
}
```

Run the test—it should be green. Now we can start refactoring. The first step of refactoring is to extract conditional code in a private method. We name the method isExpired() because our conditional chunk of code checks if the sale is expired. We create the private method isExpired() and, with the technique of extract method, we move chunks of code into the new method.

```
class Sale
{
  public $expired_at;
  public $amount;

  public function getAmount()
  {
    if($this->isExpired())
    {
      $interest = 10;
      $this->amount = $this->amount + ($this->amount / 100 * $interest);
    }
    else
    {
      $discount = 10;
      $this->amount = $this->amount - ($this->amount / 100 * $discount);
    }
    return $this->amount;
  }

  private function isExpired()
  {
    return !is_null($this->expired_at) && $this->expired_at < time();
  }
}
```

We run the unit test again and it should still be green.

```
PHPUnit 3.4.1 by Sebastian Bergmann.

.

Time: 0 seconds

OK (1 test, 2 assertions)
```

The next step is to move each branch of the condition in a private method. We do the same as we did before for each branch. So we create the private method getAmountWithInterest() for the first branch and the method getAmountWithDiscount() for the second branch.

```
class Sale
{
  public $expired_at;
  public $amount;
```

```
public function getAmount()
{
  if($this->isExpired())
  {
    return $this->getAmountWithInterest();
  }
  else
  {
    return $this->getAmountWithDiscount();
  }
}

private function isExpired()
{
  return !is_null($this->expired_at) && $this->expired_at < time();
}

private function getAmountWithInterest()
{
  $interest = 10;
  return $this->amount + ($this->amount / 100 * $interest);
}

private function getAmountWithDiscount()
{
  $discount = 10;
  return $this->amount - ($this->amount / 100 * $discount);
}
}
```

We run the unit test for the last time and it should still be green. Our refactoring works fine, and we have decomposed our conditional, simplifying the legibility of conditional code.

Consolidate Conditional Expression

Problem: "You have a sequence of conditional tests with the same result."

Solution: "Combine them into a single conditional expression and extract it."

Motivation

Sometimes we see a different set of conditional expressions that return all the same value. These expressions in most cases can be combined through logical operators AND/OR. There are two main advantages in unifying these conditions. The first is to express a single condition in a set of conditional interdependent logics. The second is to combine conditional expressions in a single condition using the "extract method" refactoring technique. These advantages improve the readability of the condition itself.

Sometimes the conditional expressions cannot be linked to each other, since they have strong identities. In this case it is not advisable to consolidate the expressions. It's better to leave them separated, despite returning the same result.

Mechanism

- Check that none of the conditional expressions has side effects. If there are side effects, you won't be able to do this refactoring.

- Write a unit test to confirm that behavior doesn't change after refactoring.

- Replace the sequence of conditionals with a single conditional expression statement using logical operators.

- Extract conditionals into a private method if useful.

- Run the test.

Example to Consolidate with ORs

In the example we saw earlier, we have a sequence of conditions that return the same result.

```
class Sale
{
  public $never_expired;
  public $expired_at;
  public $amount;

  public function expiredAmount()
  {
    if ($this->never_expired) return 0;
    if (is_null($this->expired_at)) return 0;
    if ($this->expired_at > time()) return 0;

    return $this->amount/100*10;
  }
}
```

In this case, any condition hides side effects and we can start with consolidation. First of all, we write a unit test to ensure that the behavior remains the same after the refactoring.

```
class SaleTest extends PHPUnit_Framework_TestCase
{
  public function testExpiredAmount()
  {
    $sale = new Sale();
    $sale->amount = 10;
    $this->assertEquals(0, $sale->expiredAmount());

    $sale->never_expired = true;
    $this->assertEquals(0, $sale->expiredAmount());

    $sale->never_expired = false;
    $sale->expired_at = strtotime('+10 days');
    $this->assertEquals(0, $sale->expiredAmount());

    $sale->expired_at = strtotime('-10 days');
    $this->assertEquals(1, $sale->expiredAmount());
  }
}
```

We run a test and verify that it is green. If everything is ok, we can start our refactoring. The first step of consolidation is to combine the sequence into a single condition through the conditional logical operators. In our case we can combine the conditions by the logical operator OR.

```php
class Sale
{
  public $never_expired;
  public $expired_at;
  public $amount;

  public function expiredAmount()
  {
    if ($this->never_expired || is_null($this->expired_at) || $this->expired_at > time())
      return 0;

  return $this->amount/100*10;
  }
}
```

We have connected conditions linked together in a single logical expression, creating a single point of return instead of three different ones.

To improve readability we can perform the last step of refactoring, extracting the conditional expression into a new private method:

```php
class Sale
{
  public $never_expired;
  public $expired_at;
  public $amount;

  public function expiredAmount()
  {
    if ($this->isNotExpired())
      return 0;

    return $this->amount/100*10;
  }

  private function isNotExpired()
  {
    return $this->never_expired || is_null($this->expired_at) || $this->expired_at > time();
  }
}
```

Run the unit tests again—everything should still work properly.

Example to Consolidate with AND

As we have seen, not-nested sequences can be linked by OR logic; nested sequences can be combined through the logical operator AND.

```php
if (!is_null($this->expired_at))
  if ($this->expired_at < time())
    return 10;
```

```
    else
        return 0;
else
    return 0;
```

This conditional block can be combined as follows:

```
if (!is_null($this->expired_at) AND $this->expired_at < time())
    return 10;
else
    return 0;
```

Where we have nested and not-nested conditional logic, we can try to use both AND and OR operators to consolidate the logic.

Consolidate Duplicate Conditional Fragments

Problem: "The same fragment of code is in all branches of a conditional expression."

Solution: "Move it outside of the expression."

Motivation

When we have repeated code lines within two conditional branches, we should extract them out and put them in the bottom of the conditional block.

Mechanism

- Write a unit test to confirm that the behavior of the method is guaranteed.

- Identify the common code that is executed in branch conditional logic.

- If the common code is at the beginning of the branches, extract the block of code at the beginning of the conditional block.

- If the common code is at the end of the branches, extract the block of code at the end of the conditional block.

- If the common code is between them, let us first move the code above. We run the test, and if everything is ok, we can extract the block of code before the conditional block. If the tests fail, try moving down. If the tests pass, move the common block after block conditionally. If the tests fail, we can still extract the common block in a new method.

- If we have multiple statements, we have to extract the block into a new method.

Example

In the following class we have a conditional block, and in each branch there are two equal lines duplicated.

```
class Sale
{
  public $expired_at;
  public $amount;
  ...
  public function getRealAmount()
  {
    if ($this->isExpired())
    {
      $amount = $this->getAmount() + 10;
      $this->setAmount($amount);
      return $this->getAmount();
    }
    else
    {
      $amount = $this->getAmount() - 5;
          $this->setAmount($amount);
          return $this->getAmount();
    }
  }
  ...
}
```

We write a unit test to confirm that the behavior of the Sale class remains the same after the refactoring.

```
class SaleTest extends PHPUnit_Framework_TestCase
{
  public function testSaleExpiredAmount()
  {
    $sale = new Sale();
    $sale->setExpiredAt(strtotime('yesterday'));
    $this->assertEquals(10, $sale->getRealAmount());

    $sale->setAmount(12);
    $this->assertEquals(22, $sale->getRealAmount());
  }

  public function testSaleNotExpiredAmount()
  {
    $sale = new Sale();
    $sale->setExpiredAt(strtotime('tomorrow'));
    $this->assertEquals(-5, $sale->getRealAmount());

    $sale->setAmount(10);
    $this->assertEquals(5, $sale->getRealAmount());
  }
}
```

First of all we need to identify the chunk of code in branches we want to extract. The method setAmount() is executed in both branch code and in the end of conditional code. So we can move this chunk of code after the conditional block.

```php
class Sale
{
  public $expired_at;
  public $amount;
  ...
  public function getRealAmount()
  {
    if ($this->isExpired())
    {
      $amount = $this->getAmount() + 10;
    }
    else
    {
      $amount = $this->getAmount() - 5;
    }
    $this->setAmount($amount);
    return $this->getAmount();
  }
  ...
}
```

Run the test—it should still be green.

Remove Control Flag

Problem: "You have a variable that is acting as a control flag for a series of boolean expressions."

Solution: "Use a break or return instead."

Motivation

When we write a control structure loop as while or for, frequently, we use conditions with control flag variables to understand when to exit from it.

The use of control flags comes from the rules of structured programming languages, allowing a single access point and one exit point. Fortunately, PHP allows you a single access point, but the ability to define multiple exit points. For the same reason, PHP provides control structures such as continue and breaks that allow you to exit a loop without using flag control.

It's truly incredible the value that you can give back to your code by removing control flags, which make our code very messy and difficult to read.

Mechanism

The easiest way to remove the control flags in PHP is to use control structures such as continue and breaks that allow you to stop the execution of a cycle when you need to.

- Write a unit test to confirm that the behavior of the method is guaranteed.
- Find the value of the control flag that makes you out of the loop.

- Replace the assignment of control flags with the control structure break or continue.

- Remove the condition that checks the control flag and all its references.

- Run a unit test and check that everything is ok.

There is also another way, perhaps even more elegant, to remove the control flag:

- Write a unit test to confirm that the behavior of the method is guaranteed.

- Extract the logic in a new private method.

- Find the value of the control flag that makes you out of the loop.

- Replace the assignment of the control flag with a return.

- Remove the condition that checks the control flag and all its references.

- Run a unit test after successfully replacing all the parts.

Example with Control Flag Replaced with Break

In the following example there is a `CreditCardRepository` class that contains all transactions made with a credit card in the current month. If a transaction exceeds the maximum acceptable limit, then the card is blocked for a month.

```
class CreditCardRepository
{
  public $transactions = array();
  public $max_amount = 10000;
  public $card_blocked = false;

  public function checkAmount()
  {
    $found = false;
    foreach($this->transactions as $transaction)
    {
      if(!$found)
      {
        if ($transaction > $this->max_amount)
        {
          $this->blockCreditCardForOneMonth(time());
          $found = true;
        }
      }
    }
  }

  public function blockCreditCardForOneMonth($time)
  {
    $this->card_blocked = $time;
  }
}
```

First of all, we write a unit test to confirm that the class behavior doesn't change after removing the control flag.

```php
class CreditCardRepositoryTest extends PHPUnit_Framework_TestCase
{
  public function testCheckAmount()
  {
    $card_repository = new CreditCardRepository();
    $this->assertFalse((boolean)$card_repository->card_blocked);
    $card_repository->transactions = array('100', '11000');
    $card_repository->checkAmount();
    $this->assertTrue((boolean)$card_repository->card_blocked);

    $card_repository = new CreditCardRepository();
    $card_repository->transactions = array('100', '200');
    $card_repository->checkAmount();
    $this->assertFalse($card_repository->card_blocked);
  }
}
```

In the unit test there are two assertions; the first checks that the card is blocked if there is one transaction that exceeds the maximum limit. The second test checks that the card is not blocked if the transactions are all below the maximum limit. We run the unit test and make sure the line is green. Yeah! It's time to refactor.

The first step is to identify the control flag. In our case it is the variable $found through which we verify that a transaction limit has been reached. Once we find the control flag, we can replace its assignment with the control structure break and remove the control flag conditions and its references.

```php
class CreditCardRepository
{
  ...
  public function checkAmount()
  {
    foreach($this->transactions as $transaction)
    {
      if ($transaction > $this->max_amount)
      {
        $this->blockCreditCardForOneMonth(time());
        break;
      }
    }
  }
  ...
}
```

Let's run tests to verify that everything works as before. With this refactoring, we also improved the performance of our routine. When it is interrupted, it just finds the first max transaction, rather than loop over all transactions.

Example Replacing Control Flag with a Return Exit Point

Consider the same example shown previously, with the difference that this time the variable $found is assigned the maximum value of the transaction, and then passed to a method that is executed outside the loop.

```
class CreditCardRepository
{
  ...
  public function checkAmount()
  {
    $found = false;
    foreach($this->transactions as $transaction)
    {
      if(!$found)
      {
        if ($transaction > $this->max_amount)
        {
          $this->blockCreditCardForOneMonth(time());
          $found = $transaction;
        }
      }
    }
    $this->setMaxTransaction($transction);
  }
  ...
}
```

First, write a unit test if you didn't before. In this case we want to use an exit point to stop our cycle instead of the control structure break. First we extract the logic into a new private method and return the value found.

```
class CreditCardRepository
{
  ...
  public function checkAmount()
  {
    $transaction = $this->maxTransaction();
    $this->setMaxTransaction($transaction);
  }

  private function maxTransaction()
  {
    $found = false;
    foreach($this->transactions as $transaction)
    {
      if(!$found)
      {
        if ($transaction > $this->max_amount)
        {
          $this->blockCreditCardForOneMonth(time());
          $found = $transaction;
        }
      }
    }
    return $found;
  }
  ...
}
```

Then we can replace the assignment of the control flags directly with a return, delete the final return, the conditional control flag, and all its references.

```
class CreditCardRepository
{
  ...
  private function maxTransaction()
  {
    foreach($this->transactions as $transaction)
    {
      if ($transaction > $this->max_amount)
      {
        $this->blockCreditCardForOneMonth(time());
        return $transaction;
      }
    }
  }
  ...
}
```

Let's run the unit tests and make sure the line is still green.

Replace Nested Conditional with Guard Clauses

Problem: "A method has conditional behavior that does not make clear the normal path of execution."

Solution: "Use guard clauses for all the special cases."

Motivation

Conditional forms occur, in most cases, in two forms. The first is one in which both branches of *if* and *else* check normal behavior. The second is where only one branch checks the normal case while the other checks some extreme cases that do not belong to the normal flow case studies. This happens especially with nested conditional control structures.

These two types of conditions are very different. In the first case it is necessary to express the condition through normal *if* and *else*, because both branches have the same weight and value. In the second case, extreme cases must be closed off from the normal condition. It must simply verify that the limit condition is true and return its result. These types of controls are called guard clauses [BACK].

The purpose of this refactoring is to highlight the borderline cases and isolate them from the normal flow applications. It must be clear that we have fallen into a borderline case and we must immediately return value and exit the method.

The use of nested conditional logic to express extreme cases is typical of those programmers who think that the exit point of a method or function can be only one. Fortunately it isn't true, and we can create many exit points, as many as there are guard clauses.

Mechanism

- Write a unit test to confirm that the behavior of the method is guaranteed.

- For each condition insert a guard clause that throws an exception or returns.

- For every guard clause, run the unit tests. If the clauses evaluated return all the same value, consolidate with logical expressions.

Example

In the following method we have two conditional branches representing two extreme cases. The first checks if today is the first day of the month, and the second checks if it is the last day of the month, assigning different discounts if the check passes. The last is the normal case where the standard discount is returned.

```php
public function getOfferDiscount()
{
  // Limit conditions
  if ($this->isFirstDayOfMonth())
  {
    $offer_discount = $this->getFirstDayDiscount();
  }
  else
  {
    if ($this->isLastDayOfMonth())
    {
      $offer_discount = $this->getLastDayDiscount();
    }
    else
    {
      $offer_discount = $this->getDiscount();
    }
  }
  return $offer_discount;
}
```

The nested conditional block, in this method, checks both extreme conditions and normal conditions, making it seem all of the same value. But the condition with greater value is the one that returns the standard discounts. Our task is to insert guard clauses to isolate the borderline cases and return the right value and visibility to normal conditions.

Like other techniques of refactoring, this technique may sound simple, but let's not forget to create a unit test to confirm that the behavior of the method does not change after refactoring. Run the unit test, and if the line is green you can start with the refactoring.

To simplify this conditional logic we can add guard clauses for the extreme conditions. Starting from the first condition, at the beginning of the branch, remove the variable $offer_discount and create an exit point that returns the value of the getFirstDayDiscount() method.

```php
public function getOfferDiscount()
{
  // Limit conditions
  if ($this->isFirstDayOfMonth())
  {
    return $this->getFirstDayDiscount();
  }
  else
  {
    if ($this->isLastDayOfMonth())
    {
      $offer_discount = $this->getLastDayDiscount();
    }
    else
    {
```

```
      $offer_discount = $this->getDiscount();
    }
  }
  return $offer_discount;
}
```

We can do the same type of operation for the other two conditions and remove the final return.

```php
public function getOfferDiscount()
{
  // Limit conditions
  if ($this->isFirstDayOfMonth())
  {
    return $this->getFirstDayDiscount();
  }
  else
  {
    if ($this->isLastDayOfMonth())
    {
      return $this->getLastDayDiscount();
    }
    else
    {
      return $this->getDiscount();
    }
  }
}
```

Now we can move the normal case outside the conditional block and remove the *else* branch that becomes useless, because it is empty.

```php
public function getOfferDiscount()
{
  // Limit conditions
  if ($this->isFirstDayOfMonth())
  {
    return $this->getFirstDayDiscount();
  }
  else
  {
    if ($this->isLastDayOfMonth())
    {
      return $this->getLastDayDiscount();
    }
  }
  return $this->getDiscount();
}
```

Now we can move down the conditional block, the second extreme case, and remove the *else*, because it is empty.

```php
public function getOfferDiscount()
{
  // Limit conditions
```

```
    if ($this->isFirstDayOfMonth())
    {
      return $this->getFirstDayDiscount();
    }

    if ($this->isLastDayOfMonth())
    {
      return $this->getLastDayDiscount();
    }

    return $this->getDiscount();
}
```

Removing the braces from the first clause of the guard, we can make it even easier to read.

```
public function getOfferDiscount()
{
  // Limit conditions
  if ($this->isFirstDayOfMonth()) return $this->getFirstDayDiscount();
  if ($this->isLastDayOfMonth()) return $this->getLastDayDiscount();
  return $this->getDiscount();
}
```

After each small step we run tests to make sure everything is working the way it worked before.

Replace Conditional with Polymorphism

Problem: "You have a conditional that chooses different behavior depending on the type of an object."

Solution: "Move each leg of the conditional to an overriding method in a subclass. Make the original method abstract."

Motivation

Polymorphism is one of the most charming features of object-oriented programming because it avoids the use of logical conditional on object type when we have an object that changes its behavior according to its type. When we have switch or nested *if-else* statements that control an object type to change its behavior, in reality we are not using the object-oriented programming paradigm properly.

An object must always have the same behavior, and it should not change depending on its configuration or parameter value. If that happens, we need to replace this code with a sub-class or through a state/strategy pattern.

The disadvantage of switch and *if-else* statements is that if we use a lot of them in the application, when we add a new type, we should change them all. Instead, through polymorphism we can simply add a new subclass and implement the methods required. All of that will remain hidden from customers who use this class. They will simply invoke the method and not know about the subclasses. This will make the system easier to extend and maintain, having small objects with a strong identity.

Mechanism

Before replacing conditional logic with polymorphism, we must have an inheritance structure implemented. Where we haven't, we can use the "Replace type code with subclasses" or "Replace type code with state/strategy pattern" refactoring methods. If the object has not yet been extended and its type does not change after it is created, we can use the subclasses. Instead, if the object has already been extended and/or its type can be changed after it is created, we have to use the state/strategy pattern.

Once you create the right structure, you can begin to change the conditional logic.

- Write a unit test to confirm that the behavior of the method is guaranteed.

- If the conditional logic is part of a very long method, just extract this logic into a new protected method.

- If the method belongs to the subclass, move it on a super class.

- Choose one of the subclasses and write a method that overwrites the parent method with conditional logic. Copy the branch of the conditional logic that refers to the behavior of this subclass and remove the branch from its super class method. Adjust it where necessary, changing the visibility of the method and/or parameters.

- Run unit tests.

- Repeat the same actions for each branch of conditional logic, until all the branch conditions are empty.

- At this point, empty the method of the parent class and make it abstract.

Example

We use an example common to most web services that use "freemium" policies. In these services we usually have three types of users: the administrator user, the premium user, and the base user. Their credentials for access to various services are different depending on their type. In our application we have a unique User class that assigns the credentials depending on user type and does it with an *if-else* statement. We want to remove it.

```
class User
{
  ...
  public function initCredentials()
  {
    if ($this->type == 'admin')
    {
      $this->addCredential('admin');
    }
    elseif($this->type == 'premium')
    {
      $this->addCredential('premium');
    }
    elseif($this->type == 'base')
    {
      $this->addCredential('base');
    }
    else
    {
```

```
        throw new Exception('Error: type is not valid');
    }
  }
  ...
  private function addCredential($credential)
  {
    $this->credentials[] = $credential;
  }
  ...
}
```

The User class has not yet been extended, and the user type does not change after creating the object. So we can use subclasses to make our refactoring. Lacking the structure of inheritance, we must first create it using the "Replace type code with subclasses" method.

At the end of this first refactoring we have the super class User and three subclasses for each type: Admin, Premium, and Basic.

We first write a unit test that confirms the functioning of our method with the new subclasses.

```
class UserTest extends PHPUnit_Framework_TestCase
{
  public function testAdminInitCredentials()
  {
    $admin = new Admin();
    $admin->initCredentials();
    $credentials = $admin->getCredentials();
    $this->assertEquals('base', $credentials[0]);
    $this->assertEquals('credential', $credentials[1]);
    $this->assertEquals('admin', $credentials[2]);
  }

  public function testPremiumInitCredentials()
  {
    $admin = new Premium();
    $admin->initCredentials();
    $credentials = $admin->getCredentials();
    $this->assertEquals('base', $credentials[0]);
    $this->assertEquals('credential', $credentials[1]);
    $this->assertEquals('premium', $credentials[2]);
  }

  public function testBaseInitCredentials()
  {
    $admin = new Base();
    $admin->initCredentials();
    $credentials = $admin->getCredentials();
    $this->assertEquals('base', $credentials[0]);
    $this->assertEquals('credential', $credentials[1]);
  }
}
```

Run the tests and make sure that everything is ok. The first step would be to move the method in the super class if it is present in the subclass. In our case the method is already in the super class, so we shouldn't move it.

We start from the Admin class and continue with the next refactoring operations. Create the method setCredential(), which overrides the same method of the super class, and add onto the method body the leg of conditional logic related to admin type behavior.

```
class Admin extends User
{
  ...
  public function setCredential()
  {
    $this->addCredential('admin');
  }
  ...
}
```

Remove from the super class method the *if* block related to admin type. We also need to change the visibility of the method addCredential() in the super class, from private to protected, otherwise the subclass cannot use it.

```
class User
{
  ...
  public function setCredential()
  {
    if($this->type == 'premium')
    {
      $this->credentials = array_merge($this->getBaseCredential(), 'premium');
    }
    elseif($this->type == 'base')
    {
      $this->credentials = $this->getBaseCredential();
    }
    throw new Exception('Error on getting credential: type is not valid');
  }
  ...
  private function addCredential($credential)
  {
    $this->credentials[] = $credential;
  }
  ...
}
```

Run unit tests and make sure that everything still works properly. At this point we repeat the same activity, first for the Premium class and then for the Base class.

```
class Premium extends User
{
  ...
  public function setCredential()
  {
    $this->addCredential('premium');
  }
  ...
}


class Base extends User
{
  ...
```

```
public function setCredential()
{
  $this->credentials = $this->getBaseCredential();
}
...
}
```

After deleting its conditional blocks one at a time, we make the super class and its methods abstract.

```
abstract class User
{
  protected $credentials;
  ...
  abstract public function setCredential();
  ...
}
```

Once the variable $type in our User class will not be used anymore in the conditional logic of our application (since it is replaced by polymorphism), we could remove the variable $type in subclasses.

Finally, we run the test again and make sure everything is working correctly.

Summary

In this chapter we learned how to simplify the conditional logic of our code, decomposing it, consolidating it, or removing its control flags. We learned that sometimes we introduce conditional because we code in a procedural way rather than with the object paradigm. To remove these procedural defects, we learned how to replace conditional logic with polymorphism. In the next chapter, we'll discuss how to simplify method calls.

CHAPTER 11

Simplifying Method Calls

The core of object-oriented programming is the way it gets us thinking in terms of behavior and collaboration instead of algorithms and data. Interfaces are the gateway for this mindset. A good interface communicates intentions and becomes a joining point between different parts of our architecture.

Most of the refactoring techniques shown here address the issue of making an interface clearer to understand, by renaming methods, changing method signatures, and moving and encapsulating parameters. We'll also see some ways to better detect and manage exceptional conditions to avoid tainting our interfaces.

Rename Method

Problem: "A method is not named to be self-explanatory."

Solution: "Rename the method."

Motivation

Widely-acknowledged good practices and even entire methodologies like "Domain Driven Design" promote the use of clearly-named class methods to improve both the readability and design of code. You shouldn't forget that if we were writing code for CPUs only, we wouldn't even consider using PHP. We are writing mostly human-oriented code. Indeed, the cost for a CPU to compile a longer method name is many times worth the cost of a bad or misunderstood design. While too many developers still rely on comments to make their intentions clear, we should pay attention to method signatures by good naming, good parameter selection, and good parameter ordering: everything adds up to quality.

Mechanics

- Check to see if the method is shared with a super/subclass. If so, take care of each of those related methods.

- Create a new method with the new name and copy the body of the old method into the new one.

- Make the old method use the new method.

- Run tests.

- Replace all references to the old method with references to the new method. Run tests after each change.

- Remove the old method. Since sometimes classes implement an interface to match some architectural constraint, if the old method is part of the interface and cannot be removed, you can just mark it as deprecated to keep your class compliance.

- Run tests.

Example

We have an Order class featuring a method to retrieve a discounted price. Here is the class along with its unit test:

```php
class Order
{
  public function __construct($price)
  {
    $this->price = $price;
  }

  public function getPriceRedByDis($discount)
  {
    return $this->price * (100 - $discount) / 100;
  }
}

class OrderTest extends PHPUnit_Framework_TestCase
{
  public function setUp()
  {
    $this->order = new Order(1500);
  }

  public function testGetDiscountedPrice()
  {
    $this->assertEquals(1050, $this->order->getPriceRedByDis(30));
  }
}
```

We don't like the getPriceRedByDis() method's name and we'd like to change it to something clearer: getDiscountedPrice() would fit.

We start by creating the new method and referencing it in the old one:

```php
public function getDiscountedPrice($discount)
{
  return $this->price * (100 - $discount) / 100;
}

public function getPriceRedByDis($discount)
{
  return $this->getDiscountedPrice($discount);
}
```

When we have to change all the references to the old method, making them refer to the new method, we must also change the test:

```
public function testGetDiscountedPrice()
{
    $this->assertEquals(1050, $this->order->getDiscountedPrice(30));
}
```

At last our Order class looks like the following:

```
class Order
{
    public function __construct($price)
    {
        $this->price = $price;
    }

    public function getDiscountedPrice($discount)
    {
        return $this->price * (100 - $discount) / 100;
    }
}
```

Add Parameter

Problem: "A method needs more data."

Solution: "Add a parameter to pass those data on."

Motivation

This refactoring technique is very easy to understand and very often used. Code will change, and once in a while you will need a method to do something new with data still not available for it. While this refactoring technique is very common, beware of unconsidered addition of parameters since we consider a long parameter list a bad smell. Other refactoring techniques in this chapter show other ways to overcome a growing parameter list.

Mechanics

- Check to see if the method is shared with a super/subclass. If so, take care of each of those related methods.

- Create a new method with the new parameter or parameters and copy the body of the old method into the new one.

- Make the old method use the new method.

- Run tests.

- Replace all references to the old method with references to the new method. Run tests after each change.

- Remove the old method. If it's part of the interface just mark it as deprecated.
- Run tests.

Example

Despite its deep effects, this is a very simple refactoring. Briefly, let's look at the `Order` class and its unit test shown just before and just after the refactoring.

```
class Order
{
  private $discount = 30;

  public function __construct($price)
  {
    $this->price = $price;
  }

  public function getDiscountedPrice()
  {
    return $this->price * (100 - $this->discount) / 100;
  }
}

class OrderTest extends PHPUnit_Framework_TestCase
{
  public function setUp()
  {
    $this->order = new Order(1500);
  }

  public function testGetDefaultDiscountedPrice()
  {
    $this->assertEquals(1050, $this->order->getDiscountedPrice());
  }
}
```

We want to refactor this class to manage a new `$discount` parameter. Following the refactoring steps we finally get the test as follows:

```
class OrderTest extends PHPUnit_Framework_TestCase
{
  public function setUp()
  {
    $this->order = new Order(1500);
  }

  public function testGetDefaultDiscountedPrice()
  {
    $this->assertEquals(1050, $this->order->getDiscountedPrice());
    // after refactoring
    $this->assertEquals(600, $this->order->getDiscountedPrice(60));
  }
}
```

Test is satisfied by the Order class modified in the following manner.

```php
class Order
{
  private $discount = 30;

  public function __construct($price)
  {
    $this->price = $price;
  }

  public function getDiscountedPrice($discount = null)
  {
    $actual_discount = is_null($discount) ? $this->discount : (int)$discount;

    return $this->price * (100 - $actual_discount) / 100;
  }
}
```

Remove Parameter

Problem: "A parameter is no longer used within a method's body."

Solution: "Remove it."

Motivation

While an extra, unused parameter seems harmless for our software, we have more than one reason to get rid of it. First, it's just another way for our eye to get distracted and disturbed. Code readability also comes through brevity. Remember that the less code we write, the clearer it will be. Second, for anyone using your class, one more parameter means one more thing to care about: "What's the right value to pass as that parameter?", "When should I pass that parameter on?", or "Wait... *why should I* pass that parameter on?" Third, fewer parameters make any further refactoring often easier and always quicker. Fewer things must be moved back and forth and around. Last, but absolutely not least, by reducing the parameter count you are simplifying the method interface, eventually removing unneeded dependencies.

The only case you should pay more attention to is when coping with polymorphic methods. These interfaces are shared across a hierarchy and any change to the methods signature must be considered with respect to its side effects. Though this is something to be taken into consideration, "Remove Parameter" is such a cheap refactoring technique that we should never miss the chance to perform it.

Mechanics

- Check to see if the method is shared with a super/subclass. If so, take care of each of those related methods. If one or more of the related methods use the parameter, just stop.

- Create a new method with the new parameter or parameters and copy the body of the old method into the new one.

- Make the old method use the new method.

- Run tests.

- Replace all references to the old method with references to the new method. Run tests after each change.

- Remove the old method. If it's part of the interface, just mark it as deprecated.

- Run tests.

Separate Query from Modifier

Problem: "A method returns a value and changes the internal state of an object too."

Solution: "Split the method in two methods, one for the query, the other setting the new state."

Motivation

A method just returning a value with no effect on the internal state of an object is called a *function* [EVA] and is very easy to manage. Eric Evans [EVA] says "a function can be called multiple times and return the same value each time. A function can call on other functions without worrying about the depth of nesting. Functions are much easier to test than operations that have side effects. For these reasons, functions lower risk." Therefore we should place as much logic as possible into side effect methods, segregating the unavoidable and even needed side effects into very simple methods not returning data.

While this separation always helps, it shouldn't become your next dogma: if you meet a method that returns a value while also changing the object state, then that's the time for you to try—at least—to separate the query from the modifier.

Mechanics

- Declare a new query method returning the same value as the original method. Beware of any temp assignment.

- Make the original method call the new one to return the result.

- Run tests.

- Replace all calls of the original method with a call to the query and add a call to the original method at the line before.

- Run tests.

- Remove all return expressions from the original method.

- Run tests.

Example

The following PHPunit test verifies that an instance of the Order class exposes a method called deliver() that sets its state to *delivered* while returning the expected delivery date.

```
class OrderTest extends PHPUnit_Framework_TestCase
{
  public function setUp()
  {
```

```
    $this->order = new Order(strtotime('yesterday'));
  }

  public function testDelivery()
  {
    $this->assertFalse($this->order->isDelivered());
    $this->assertEquals(date('Y-m-d', strtotime('tomorrow')), date('Y-m-d', $this->↵
order->deliver()));
    $this->assertTrue($this->order->isDelivered());
  }
}
```

The class code to satisfy this test is the following:

```
class Order
{
  const DELIVERY_TIME = '2 days';

  private $placed_at;
  private $delivered = false;

  public function __construct($placed_at)
  {
    $this->placed_at = $placed_at;
  }

  public function deliver()
  {
    $this->delivered = true;
    return strtotime('+'.self::DELIVERY_TIME, $this->placed_at);
  }

  public function isDelivered()
  {
    return $this->delivered;
  }
}
```

We perform the refactoring step by step, beginning with the new query method:

```
public function getDeliveryTime()
{
  return strtotime('+'.self::DELIVERY_TIME, $this->placed_at);
}
```

We use it in the original method:

```
public function deliver()
{
  $this->delivered = true;
  return $this->getDeliveryTime();
}
```

Thereafter we replace each call to the original method with a double call—don't forget the test is a caller too—and remove the return expression:

```php
class OrderTest extends PHPUnit_Framework_TestCase
{
  public function setUp()
  {
    $this->order = new Order(strtotime('yesterday'));
  }

  public function testDelivery()
  {
    $this->assertFalse($this->order->isDelivered());
    $this->order->deliver();
    $this->assertEquals(date('Y-m-d', strtotime('tomorrow')), date('Y-m-d', $this->↩
order->getDeliveryTime()));
    $this->assertTrue($this->order->isDelivered());
  }
}
class Order
{
  const DELIVERY_TIME = '2 days';

  private $placed_at;
  private $delivered = false;

  public function __construct($placed_at)
  {
    $this->placed_at = $placed_at;
  }

  public function deliver()
  {
    $this->delivered = true;
  }

  public function getDeliveryTime()
  {
    return strtotime('+'.self::DELIVERY_TIME, $this->placed_at);
  }

  public function isDelivered()
  {
    return $this->delivered;
  }
}
```

Parameterize Method

Problem: "More methods implement the same logic with different values."

Solution: "Declare one method accepting those changing values as parameters."

Motivation

Code duplication is one of the easiest bad smells to understand and agree upon. Removing duplicated code facilitates the maintenance of existing code while offering more chances to extend the functionalities of our software just by adding parameters. In this refactoring technique, you abstract similar methods into a common one, getting the desired behavior by isolating mutable values into parameters.

Mechanics

- Declare a parameterized method behaving like the methods we want to remove. If you find you can parameterize just a fragment of a method, use the "Extract Method" technique before the "Parameterize Method" technique.

- Replace one call to an old method with a call to the new one.

- Run tests.

- Repeat, replacing and testing for each remaining old method.

Example

Suppose in our `Order` class we have a couple of methods to compute two different price discount policies: one applying a 10% discount, the other a 20% discount.

```php
class Order
{
  public function __construct($price)
  {
    $this->price = $price;
  }

  public function getTenPercentDiscountedPrice()
  {
    return $this->price * 0.9;
  }

  public function getTwentyPercentDiscountedPrice()
  {
    return $this->price * 0.8;
  }
}
```

Class Order is tested by the following unit test.

```php
class OrderTest extends PHPUnit_Framework_TestCase
{
  public function setUp()
  {
    $this->order = new Order(1500);
  }

  public function testGetDiscountedPrice()
  {
    $this->assertEquals(1350, $this->order->getTenPercentDiscountedPrice());
    $this->assertEquals(1200, $this->order->getTwentyPercentDiscountedPrice());
  }
}
```

After the refactoring mechanics, we create a new method:

```php
public function getDiscountedPrice($discount_factor)
{
  return $this->price * $discount_factor;
}
```

We replace all calls to our two old methods, updating tests as well:

```php
class OrderTest extends PHPUnit_Framework_TestCase
{
  public function setUp()
  {
    $this->order = new Order(1500);
  }

  public function testGetDiscountedPrice()
  {
    $this->assertEquals(1350, $this->order->getDiscountedPrice(0.9));
    $this->assertEquals(1200, $this->order->getDiscountedPrice(0.8));
  }
}
```

We change code in the following manner to obtain the final Order class.

```php
class Order
{
  public function __construct($price)
  {
    $this->price = $price;
  }

  public function getDiscountedPrice($discount_factor)
  {
    return $this->price * $discount_factor;
  }
}
```

Replace Parameter with Explicit Method

Problem: "A method behaves differently depending on an enumerated parameter."

Solution: "Extract a method for each enumerated value."

Motivation

Sometimes you find a situation where the caller of the method has to tell the method itself how to behave by setting a parameter, or where the method behaves differently according to the value of the parameter. Both situations smell bad. We don't want a caller to cope with the responsibility of returning the proper result for a given situation, neither do we want a nasty conditional block in our method to manage different cases. Our goal is to provide a self-explaining interface along with a design that is easy to maintain and extend.

Mechanics

- Declare an explicit method for each enumerated value of the parameter.
- Make each leg of the conditional call the appropriate method.
- Run tests after changing each leg.
- Replace each caller of the original method with a call to the right method.
- Run tests after changing each caller.
- When all callers are changed, remove the original method.
- Run tests.

Example

Our `Order` class implements two different discounting logics depending on the value passed as the discount. If it's an integer, it lowers the price by that amount; if it's a floating-point number we apply that discount factor.

```php
class Order
{
  public function __construct($price)
  {
    $this->price = $price;
  }

  public function getDiscountedPrice($discount)
  {
    if (is_int($discount))
    {
      return $this->price - $discount;
    }
    elseif (is_float($discount))
    {
      return $this->price * $discount;
    }

    throw new Exception('Invalid discount type');
  }
}
```

It works, as stated by the next test:

```php
class OrderTest extends PHPUnit_Framework_TestCase
{
  public function setUp()
  {
    $this->order = new Order(1500);
  }

  public function testGetDiscountedPrice()
  {
```

```
    $this->assertEquals(1350, $this->order->getDiscountedPrice(0.9));

    $this->assertEquals(1400, $this->order->getDiscountedPrice(100));
  }
}
```

It works correctly, but we find this logic horrible indeed. Users of this class cannot be confident in passing values to the method since they fear that the behavior will change unexpectedly depending on the value passed on. We want two different methods to manage each of the two discount strategies.

Let's perform the refactoring step by step. First, we add two new methods:

```
public function getFixedDiscountedPrice($discount)
{
  return $this->price - $discount;
}

public function getPercentDiscountedPrice($discount)
{
  return $this->price * $discount;
}
```

Then we use those methods in the original one:

```
public function getDiscountedPrice($discount)
{
  if (is_int($discount))
  {
    return $this->getFixedDiscountedPrice($discount);
  }
  elseif (is_float($discount))
  {
    return $this->getPercentDiscountedPrice($discount);
  }

  throw new Exception('Invalid discount type');
}
```

We can run tests at any time, and we still get *green tests*. Before we can remove the original method, though, we have to change the callers, tests included.

```
class OrderTest extends PHPUnit_Framework_TestCase
{
  public function setUp()
  {
    $this->order = new Order(1500);
  }

  public function testGetDiscountedPrice()
  {
    $this->assertEquals(1350, $this->order->getPercentDiscountedPrice(0.9));

    $this->assertEquals(1400, $this->order->getFixedDiscountedPrice(100));
  }
}
```

Now we can remove the method.

```
class Order
{
  public function __construct($price)
  {
    $this->price = $price;
  }

  public function getFixedDiscountedPrice($discount)
  {
    return $this->price - $discount;
  }

  public function getPercentDiscountedPrice($discount)
  {
    return $this->price * $discount;
  }
}
```

Preserve Whole Object

Problem: "A method needs many parameters and those values are coming from an object."

Solution: "Pass the whole object on as a single parameter."

Motivation

A long parameter list is a bad smell, and having to compute the single values needed by the caller each time it's invoked can be a problem, at least in terms of performance. Instead, passing the whole object containing those values as single parameters simplifies the method's signature and lets it get access to real-time data, by means of the passed object getter and query methods.

On the other hand, passing an object as a parameter means adding a new dependency between the calling class and the called one. Furthermore, a method depending too much on another class's values suggests that method should belong to the called class. The decision depends on the context, and you should always consider "Move Method" before performing this refactoring technique.

Mechanics

- Create a new parameter to host the new whole object parameter. Assign it a default value if needed to ease the next steps.

- Run tests.

- Replace one parameter with a call to the appropriate method on the whole object parameter.

- Run tests and repeat for each parameter whose value can be got from the whole object.

- If the calling method features some code to obtain the old parameter values and it doesn't need those values anymore, remove that code.

- Add whole object parameter type if you want or need a stricter type check.
- Run tests.

Example

Our Order class features a checkout() method, setting final discounted price and delivery date depending on two parameters, both belonging to the Customer.

```
class Order
{
  public function __construct($price)
  {
    $this->price = $price;
  }

  public function checkOut($discount, $policy)
  {
    $this->delivery_time = strtotime('+'.$policy);
    $this->final_price = $this->price * $discount;
  }

  public function getFinalPrice()
  {
    return $this->final_price;
  }

  public function getDeliveryTime()
  {
    return $this->delivery_time;
  }
}
```

In our test we provide a stub class to represent the Customer role:

```
class MockCustomer implements Customer
{
  private $discount;
  private $delivery_policy;

  public function __construct($discount, $delivery_policy)
  {
    $this->delivery_policy = $delivery_policy;
    $this->discount = $discount;
  }

  public function getDeliveryPolicy()
  {
    return $this->delivery_policy;
  }

  public function getDiscount()
  {
```

```
    return $this->discount;
  }
}

class OrderTest extends PHPUnit_Framework_TestCase
{
  public function setUp()
  {
    $this->order = new Order(1500);
  }

  public function testDeliver()
  {
    $customer = new MockCustomer(0.8, '2 days');

    $this->order->checkOut($customer);

    $this->assertEquals(1200, $this->order->getFinalPrice());
    $this->assertEquals(date('Y-m-d', strtotime('+2 days')), date('Y-m-d', $this->
order->getDeliveryTime()));
  }
}
```

To satisfy this test we just have to follow the refactoring steps. At first we add the new $customer parameter to checkout().

```
public function checkOut($discount, $policy, $customer = null)
{
  $this->delivery_time = strtotime('+'.$policy);
  $this->final_price = $this->price * $discount;
}
```

Note we set $customer to null by default, so that it's easier to manage the transitions towards the final version of the method. After that we make the method use values coming from the whole object:

```
$this->delivery_time = strtotime('+'.$customer->getDeliveryPolicy());
$this->final_price = $this->price * $customer->getDiscount();
```

This change of code let us to remove useless parameters and add type hinting.

```
public function checkOut(Customer $customer)
{
  $this->delivery_time = strtotime('+'.$customer->getDeliveryPolicy());
  $this->final_price = $this->price * $customer->getDiscount();
}
```

Replace Parameter with Method

Problem: "A receiver method gets a parameter whose value comes from another object the receiver can get access to."

Solution: "Remove the parameter and make the receiver call the proper method."

Motivation

If an object is calling a method on itself to get the value to use in another method of its own, or if the object already holds a reference to the object owning the needed value, we should exploit this condition to shorten the parameter list. Any time an object can retrieve a value not using parameters in a method's signature, we should consider the chance to reduce the parameter list, since they are hard to understand.

Mechanics

- Use the "Extract Method" technique if needed.
- Replace references to the parameter with references to the method.
- Run tests after each replacement.
- Use the "Remove Parameter" technique on the replaced parameter.
- Run tests.

Example

The next test shows the use of an Order class to get a discounted price, starting from a total price derived from the same object.

```
class OrderTest extends PHPUnit_Framework_TestCase
{
  public function setUp()
  {
    $this->order = new Order(1500, 2);
  }

  public function testGetDiscountedPrice()
  {
    $this->assertEquals(2400, $this->order->getDiscountedPrice($this->order->↵
getOverallPrice(), 0.8));
  }
}
```

The class making this test *green* looks like the following:

```
class Order
{
  public function __construct($base_price, $quantity)
  {
    $this->base_price = $base_price;
    $this->quantity = $quantity;
  }

  public function getOverallPrice()
  {
    return $this->base_price * $this->quantity;
  }
```

```
public function getDiscountedPrice($overall_price, $discount)
{
  return $overall_price * $discount;
}
}
```

Executing the few steps described in this refactoring's mechanics, we get the following Order class and unit test.

```
class Order
{

  public function __construct($base_price, $quantity)
  {
    $this->base_price = $base_price;
    $this->quantity = $quantity;
  }

  public function getOverallPrice()
  {
    return $this->base_price * $this->quantity;
  }

  public function getDiscountedPrice($discount)
  {
    return $this->getOverallPrice() * $discount;
  }
}

class OrderTest extends PHPUnit_Framework_TestCase
{
  public function setUp()
  {
    $this->order = new Order(1500, 2);
  }
  public function testGetDiscountedPrice()
  {
    $this->assertEquals(2400, $this->order->getDiscountedPrice(0.8));
  }
}
```

Introduce Parameter Object

Problem: "You have a group of parameters that would make more sense collected together."

Solution: "Collect them in a new object."

Motivation

This easy refactoring technique would be worth the time spent on it even if it returned only the benefit of reducing the size of the parameter list. We already know how stiff a long parameter list is, and we have tried to shorten it every time we could, especially in this chapter.

By the way, you can get a greater benefit by applying this refactoring technique. Once the parameters have their own shared class, you can start adding new behavior in new methods or moving existing behavior from client classes to this new one, further reducing code duplication.

Mechanics

- Declare a new class to represent the group of parameters to be replaced.
- Use the "Preserve Whole Object" technique.
- Run tests.
- Inspect your code to detect methods (or fragments) to be moved into the new class with the "Move Method" technique after using the "Extract Method" technique, if needed.

Remove Setting Method

Problem: "An attribute should be set at creation time once for all."

Solution: "Remove setters for that attribute."

Motivation

If you don't want a value to change, then don't offer a way to change it. You should remove any unneeded setter, communicating your design and then your intention in a clearer way.

Mechanics

- Check the setter is called only in the constructor.
- Make the constructor have access to the attribute.
- Run tests.
- Remove the setter.
- Run tests.

Example

The GoldOrder class still offers a setter for the discount, while the discount factor should be defined only by the *Gold* policy, as reflected by the DISCOUNT constant.

```
class GoldOrder
{
  const DISCOUNT = 0.9;

  private $discount;

  public function __construct($price)
  {
```

```
    $this->price = $price;
    $this->setDiscount(self::DISCOUNT);
  }

  public function setDiscount($discount)
  {
    $this->discount = $discount;
  }

  public function getDiscountedPrice()
  {
    return $this->price * $this->discount;
  }
}
```

A simple test will provide us with feedback about the correctness of the refactoring.

```
class GoldOrderTest extends PHPUnit_Framework_TestCase
{
  public function setUp()
  {
    $this->order = new GoldOrder(1500);
  }

  public function testGetDiscountedPrice()
  {
    $this->assertEquals(1350, $this->order->getDiscountedPrice());
  }
}
```

Executing the refactoring is easy and brings us here:

```
class GoldOrder
{
  const DISCOUNT = 0.9;

  private $discount;

  public function __construct($price)
  {
    $this->price = $price;
    $this->discount = self::DISCOUNT;
  }

  public function getDiscountedPrice()
  {
    return $this->price * $this->discount;
  }
}
```

Hide Method

Problem: "No client class uses a method."

Solution: "Make the method private."

Motivation

We can hide methods for reasons similar to the ones for removing parameters from a method's signature. All in all, we are just simplifying our interface, making it easier to understand for ourselves and other developers. We should try to spot unused methods as often as we can. A quite common circumstance occurs when adding behavior to a class and making the transition from a simple data holder to a mature class—its setters become useless. However, if a method becomes useless to the owning class as well, we should remove even it.

Mechanics

- Spot a method not used anymore by other classes.

- Make the method protected. Make it private if you can.

- Run tests.

Replace Constructor with Factory Method

Problem: "You want more flexibility in creating instances of a class."

Solution: "Replace the constructor with a factory method."

Motivation

The factory method [GOF] is a well-known object-oriented design pattern to implement the concept of factories, according to which we delegate to some object the creation of other objects. In other words, factories are an abstraction of constructors. This pattern then deals with the problem of creating objects without specifying the exact class of object that will be created. Since the constructor is abstracted in a class method, its subclasses can then override it to specify the right class to be created.

Factory methods are commonly used in frameworks where the library code needs to use objects of classes that may be subclassed by applications using the framework. Also, parallel class hierarchies often require objects from one hierarchy to be able to create appropriate objects from the other.

Other benefits in using a factory method lie in having a better interface for the constructor—since constructor methods can be named only `__constructor()`—and a clearer encapsulation of the construction process, also leading to easier ways to test our classes.

Constructors can return only an instance of the class they belong to. This is too limited when we don't know the exact subclass of a hierarchy that we want to create an instance of. With a factory method we overcome this stiffness and make our code a lot smarter.

Mechanics

- Create a factory method. Make it call the current constructor.

- Replace all calls to the constructor with a call to the factory method.

- Run tests after each replacement.

- Make the constructor private.

- Run tests.

Example

A really meaningful example would require a chapter of its own. Refer to *Gang of Four Design Pattern* [GOF] for a detailed explanation of the pattern called *factory method*. In our case we will see just a simple example to make the mechanics clear. We have a Person class extended by Male and Female classes.

```
class Person
{
  public function __construct() {}
}
class Male extends Person {}
class Female extends Person {}
```

Creation of this class is tested by a very simple test:

```
class PersonTest extends PHPUnit_Framework_TestCase
{
  public function testInstances()
  {
    $person = new Male();
    $this->assertTrue($person instanceof Male);
    $person = new Female();
    $this->assertTrue($person instanceof Female);
  }
}
```

According to the first step described in the mechanics we create a new static method in the Person class.

```
public static function create($subclass)
{
  return new $subclass();
}
```

Then we finalize the refactoring to obtain PersonTest unit test and the final Person class.

```
class PersonTest extends PHPUnit_Framework_TestCase
{
  public function testInstances()
  {
    $person = Person::create('Male');
    $this->assertTrue($person instanceof Male);
    $person = Person::create('Female');
```

```
    $this->assertTrue($person instanceof Female);
  }


class Person
{
  public static function create($subclass)
  {
    return new $subclass();
  }

  private function __construct() {}
}
```

Replace Error Code with Exception

Problem: "A method returns a special code to indicate an error."

Solution: "Throw an exception instead."

Motivation

Exceptions are a powerful way to spot and manage errors while not tainting our good design. They let you write how things should go if nothing bad happens, delegating the decision about what to do if something goes wrong to the right agent. More traditional PHP developers rely on error codes returned by methods, standing loyal to a tradition coming from C, Perl, and other good old-fashioned procedural languages. Though valid for decades, we think this approach should now be deprecated in PHP since exceptions allow for a much clearer design.

Mechanics

- Find all the method callers and make them expect a possible exception by means of a try/catch block. Tests must be updated too.

- Change the method body to raise an appropriate exception when needed.

- Run tests.

Example

The BankAccount class lets us safely withdraw any amount of money, returning an error code in case the $amount withdrawn exceeds our availability.

```
class BankAccount
{
  public $balance = 1500;

  public function safeWithdraw($amount)
  {
    if ($amount > $this->balance)
    {
```

```
      return -1;
    }
    else
    {
      $this->balance -= $amount;
      return 0;
    }
  }
}
```

We test this behavior like this:

```
class BankAccountTest extends PHPUnit_Framework_TestCase
{
  public function setUp()
  {
    $this->account = new BankAccount();
  }

  public function testSafeWithdraw()
  {
    $this->assertEquals(0, $this->account->safeWithdraw(30));
    $this->account->safeWithdraw(30);
    $this->assertEquals(1470, $this->account->balance);

    $this->assertEquals(-1, $this->account->safeWithdraw(1480));
    $this->assertEquals(1470, $this->account->balance);
  }
}
```

PHPUnit features an elegant way to test for exceptions, so we can first update our test:

```
class BankAccountTest extends PHPUnit_Framework_TestCase
{
...
  /**
   * @expectedException BalanceException
   */
  public function testSafeWithdraw()
  {
    $this->account->safeWithdraw(30);
    $this->assertEquals(1470, $this->account->balance);

    $this->account->safeWithdraw(1480);
    $this->assertEquals(1470, $this->account->balance);
  }
}
```

Now, we can perform the refactoring in BankAccount class.

```
class BankAccount
{
  public $balance = 1500;
```

```
public function safeWithdraw($amount)
{
  if ($amount > $this->balance)
  {
    throw new BalanceException();
  }

  $this->balance -= $amount;
}
}
```

At the end we provide our new exception type, class BalanceException extends Exception {}.

Replace Exception with Test

Problem: "An exception is thrown on a condition that could have been checked first."

Solution: "Change the caller to perform the test first."

Motivation

Though we think exceptions are a powerful device, they can be overused. Not all bound conditions are to be considered exceptional. For example, an empty record set returned from a query is a peculiar condition, but it should be managed with a simple test, not requiring an exception to be raised.

Mechanics

- Update tests and copy the code from the catch block into the right conditional fragment.

- Rethrow any raised exception caught in the catch block to notify you whether the catch block itself is ever executed.

- Run tests.

- Repeat and test for any other catch block to be removed.

- Remove the try block when all catch blocks are gone.

- Run tests.

Summary

Making method calls easier to understand is a key point in object-oriented programming. By means of a simple "Method Rename" or by adding a new error management device like an exception, we should always put our effort into getting a clear collaboration between objects so that purpose and focus are well exposed. This way any further change in the future becomes clear in its location and its effects easier to predict. Don't ever forget that object-oriented programming is all about interfaces.

■ ■ ■

CHAPTER 12

Simplifying Generalization Relationships

With the generalization methods we want to introduce order and clarity in class hierarchies. There are methods that deal with moving class features in hierarchy to the subclass or to the super class (pull up/down attributes, pull up/down method), there is a method that takes care of standardizing the constructor and extracts it on the super class (pull up constructor body), and another very interesting method that helps us to implement the template method pattern of "Gang of Four"[GOF], which is useful when we have methods that perform the same steps but the steps are different.

We will see how to extract subclasses or super classes, useful when the single class tends to encapsulate different behaviors in different instances, or to help us understand how to collapse a hierarchy when useless.

Using inheritance in object-oriented programming is a good habit, but sometimes it can create confusion—for example, when some super class methods or parameters do not represent their subclasses, and it would be better to implement a delegation,. In this chapter we will also see how we can replace inheritance with delegation or replace the delegation with inheritance.

The collection of refactoring techniques that we'll present in this chapter was created by Martin Fowler [FOW01]. For each method, we'll see the motivation and situation for using it, the mechanism that will explain how we can apply the method to our existing code, and some examples of how each method works in a real-world case.

Pull Up Field

Problem: "Two subclasses have the same field."

Solution: "Move the field to the super class."

Motivation

When we find two classes that extend the same super class having the same attributes, we can move these duplicated attributes in the super class.

It may happen that the same attributes have different names. In this case, check that the attributes are equal, and that they are used in the same way. If we are sure, we can rename the attribute in one of two classes, move it to the super class and remove them from their subclasses.

Mechanism

- Write unit tests to confirm that the behavior doesn't change after refactoring.

- Find similar attributes.

- Check that they are used in the same way.

- If attributes do not have the same name, rename one of the two with the same name of the other.

- Run tests and make sure everything still works properly.

- Create a new attribute in the super class with protected visibility so that the subclasses can access it.

- Delete the attributes in the subclasses.

- Run tests and make sure everything still works properly.

Example

After some refactoring steps, we have two classes—User and Admin—that extend the BaseUser class. These two classes were initially independent, and therefore both have the same attribute $username.

```php
class User extends BaseUser
{
  public $username;

  public function getUsernameWithLabel()
  {
    return 'User: '.$this->username;
  }
}

class Admin extends BaseUser
{
  public $username;

  public function getUsernameWithLabel()
  {
    return 'Admin: '.$this->username;
  }
}
```

Before moving the common attribute in the super class, we write a unit test that preserves the proper class behavior.

```php
class UserTest extends PHPUnit_Framework_TestCase
{
  public function testGetUsername()
  {
    $admin = new Admin();
    $admin->username = 'cphp';
    $this->assertEquals('Admin: cphp', $admin->getUsernameWithLabel());

    $user = new User();
```

```
    $user->username = 'cphp';
    $this->assertEquals('User: cphp', $user->getUsernameWithLabel());
  }
}
```

Run the test and verify that everything works.

```
PHPUnit 3.4.1 by Sebastian Bergmann.

.

Time: 1 second

OK (1 test, 2 assertions)
```

At this point, following the mechanism, we identify similar class attributes. In our case we have the $username attribute that is duplicated in both classes. After checking that it's used in the same way both in the User class and in the Admin class, we can create a new attribute with the same name in a super class and remove it from the subclasses.

```
abstract class BaseUser
{
  public $username;
}

class User extends BaseUser
{
  public function getUsernameWithLabel()
  {
    return 'User: '.$this->username;
  }
}

class Admin extends BaseUser
{
  public function getUsernameWithLabel()
  {
    return 'Admin: '.$this->username;
  }
}
```

Run the unit test again and verify that the behavior of the classes has not changed.

Pull Up Method

Problem: "You have methods with identical results on subclasses."

Solution: "Move them to the super class."

Motivation

As we have said several times, duplicate code is one of the most dangerous bad smells, because where there is duplicate code, bugs can proliferate. Every time we duplicate even a single line of code, we should ask what would happen if we apply a change in one of the two lines, forgetting the other.

213

Through the copy and paste action often we can find the exact same methods duplicated in subclasses that extend the same super class. In this case we can move the duplicated method in the super class and delete it from all subclasses.

In other cases we have methods with the same body but with different interfaces. In these cases we must standardize the interface, move the method in the super class, and remove the original methods from the subclasses.

Another case is when we have a method of a subclass, which overrides a super class method, and the body remains unchanged, producing the same behavior.

If we move the method body into the super class, but we have other methods and attributes that aren't in the super class, we can implement some strategies If we're using attributes present only in a subclass, we can move these attributes to a super class. If we're using methods present only in a subclass we can move these methods to a super class if all subclasses use it, or create an abstract method on a super class.

If we have similar methods that are not exactly equal, we can apply the "Form Template" technique, which we'll see after in this chapter.

Mechanism

- Identify methods that appear to be duplicated.

- Check that the behavior of the methods is the same. If methods do the same thing but in different ways, you can align the two bodies through the technique of "Replacement Algorithm."

- If the methods have different interfaces, align them with a more significant interface.

- Create a new method in the super class with the same interface, copy in the new method body one of two origin methods, fix it where needed, and run tests. If the method uses some methods present only in the subclass, declare an abstract method in the super class. If the method uses an attribute of the subclass, move the attribute in the super class, or encapsulate it and declare getter and setter methods in the abstract super class.

- Delete the method in one of the subclasses, and run the tests.

- For each subclass remove the method and run tests until the method remains only in the super class.

Example

Consider an abstract super class `BaseUser` with two subclasses, `Admin` and `User`.

```
abstract class BaseUser
{
  protected $credentials;

  public function hasCredential($credential)
  {
    return in_array($credential, $this->credentials);
  }
}
```

```php
class Admin extends BaseUser
{
  public function initCredentials($credentials)
  {
    $this->credentials = array_merge($credentials, $this->getBaseCredentials());
  }

  public function getBaseCredentials()
  {
    return array('admin', 'base');
  }
}

class User extends BaseUser
{
  public function initCredentials($credentials)
  {
    $this->credentials = array_merge($credentials, $this->getBaseCredentials());
  }

  public function getBaseCredentials()
  {
    return array('user', 'base');
  }
}
```

The initCredential() method is the same in both classes, but the getBaseCredential() method used inside the initCredential() method is different. First of all, we write a unit test to prevent class behavior.

```php
class UserTest extends PHPUnit_Framework_TestCase
{
  public function testGetCredential()
  {
    $admin = new Admin();
    $admin->initCredentials(array('editor'));
    $this->assertTrue($admin->hasCredential('base'));
    $this->assertTrue($admin->hasCredential('admin'));
    $this->assertTrue($admin->hasCredential('editor'));
    $this->assertTrue(!$admin->hasCredential('user'));

    $user = new User();
    $user->initCredentials(array('editor'));
    $this->assertTrue($user->hasCredential('base'));
    $this->assertTrue($user->hasCredential('user'));
    $this->assertTrue($user->hasCredential('editor'));
    $this->assertTrue(!$user->hasCredential('admin'));
  }
}
```

Run the test and verify that everything works. Now, before moving the method, we must define the getBaseCredentials() method as abstract in the super class.

```php
abstract class BaseUser
{
  ...
```

215

```
  abstract protected function getBaseCredentials();
  ...
}
```

Then we can move the initCredential() method in the super class and remove it from each subclass. Every time we remove a method we run a unit test.

```
abstract class BaseUser
{
  protected $credentials;

  abstract protected function getBaseCredentials();

  public function hasCredential($credential)
  {
    return in_array($credential, $this->credentials);
  }

  public function initCredentials($credentials)
  {
    $this->credentials = array_merge($credentials, $this->getBaseCredentials());
  }
}

class Admin extends BaseUser
{
  protected function getBaseCredentials()
  {
    return array('admin', 'base');
  }
}

class User extends BaseUser
{
  protected function getBaseCredentials()
  {
    return array('user', 'base');
  }
}
```

Pull Up Constructor Body

Problem: "You have constructors on subclasses with mostly identical bodies."

Solution: "Create a super class constructor; call this from the subclass methods."

Motivation

The constructor of a class is usually the delegate method to initialize the values of the object instantiated. When we find subclasses that implement the same constructor, we can move it into the super class. In PHP, when we create an instance of a subclass, if the constructor is not implemented, it uses the constructor of the parent class.

If the constructors of the subclasses share only a part of their body, we can extract only this part and put it into a super class constructor, calling the parent constructor inside the subclass constructor. In PHP it is possible to override the parent constructor, changing its interface.

Mechanism

- Write a unit test of the class to confirm that the behavior doesn't change after refactoring.
- Identify the body or the partial body of constructors to extract.
- Define the constructor in the super class.

Now, you can have two cases. In the first, you have to extract all of the constructor's body:

- Extract the body of the subclass constructor into the constructor of the super class.
- Remove the constructors from the subclasses.
- Run a unit test.

In the second case, we have to extract only a part of the subclass's constructor body:

- Move the body part of the constructor in the super class.
- Replace the body part with a call to the constructor of the super class.
- Run a test.

Where we have other equal code to call after the execution of the constructor of the subclass, we can extract a new method and move it in the super class.

Example

We have two classes—News and Events—that extend the Article class. After some refactoring steps we have already moved fields and methods in the super class. But now we have a part of the body of the subclasses' constructor duplicate.

```php
class Article
{
  protected $title;
  protected $author;

  public function getTitle()
  {
    return $this->title;
  }
}

class Event extends Article
{
  protected $start_date;
```

```php
  protected $end_date;

  public function __construct($title, $author, $start_date, $end_date)
  {
    $this->title = $title;
    $this->author = $author;
    $this->start_date = $start_date;
    $this->end_date = $end_date;
  }

  public function getStartDate()
  {
    return $this->start_date;
  }

  public function getEndDate()
  {
    return $this->end_date;
  }
}

class News extends Article
{
  protected $date;

  public function __construct($title, $author, $date)
  {
    $this->title = $title;
    $this->author = $author;
    $this->date = $date;
  }

  public function getDate()
  {
    return $this->date;
  }
}
```

Before starting the refactoring, we write two unit tests, one for the Event class and one for the News class, if we have not already done so. In the unit test we check the behavior of the constructor. We first implement the Event class unit test.

```php
class EventTest extends PHPUnit_Framework_TestCase
{
  public function testEvent()
  {
    $event = new Event('New event', 'Francesco Trucchia', strtotime('5/10/2010 8:00 am'), ↵
strtotime('5/11/2010 6:00 pm'));
    $this->assertTrue($event instanceof Article);
    $this->assertEquals('New event', $event->getTitle());
    $this->assertEquals(strtotime('5/10/2010 8:00 am'), $event->getStartDate());
    $this->assertEquals(strtotime('5/11/2010 6:00 pm'), $event->getEndDate());
  }
}
```

Then we implement a unit test for the News class.

```
class NewsTest extends PHPUnit_Framework_TestCase
{
  public function testNews()
  {
    $news = new News('New news', 'Francesco Trucchia', strtotime('5/10/2010 8:00 am'));
    $this->assertTrue($news instanceof Article);
    $this->assertEquals('New news', $news->getTitle());
    $this->assertEquals(strtotime('5/10/2010 8:00 am'), $news->getDate());
  }
}
```

Run the tests and make sure that everything works right. If the tests are running properly, we can begin the steps of refactoring. The first step is to identify the duplicated block of code in the constructor to move to the super class. Looking at the class constructors News and Events, we realize that the first two lines are the same. We implement the constructor method in the super class and extract the two lines of code.

```
class Article
{
  ...
  public function construct($title, $author)
  {
    $this->title = $title;
    $this->author = $author;
  }
  ...
}
```

Then replace the two lines just copied with the call to the constructor of the super class.

```
class News extends Article
{
  ...
  public function __construct($title, $author, $date)
  {
    parent::__construct($title, $author);
    $this->date = $date;
  }
  ...
}

class Event extends Article
{
  ...
  public function __construct($title, $author, $start_date, $end_date)
  {
    parent::__construct($title, $author);
    $this->start_date = $start_date;
    $this->end_date = $end_date;
  }
  ...
}
```

We run tests and make sure that everything runs correctly.

Push Down Method

Problem: "Behavior on a super class is relevant only for some of its subclasses."

Solution: "Move it to those subclasses."

Motivation

The "Push Down" method is the opposite of the "Move Up" method. We can use this refactoring technique when a certain method in the super class is meaningful only for a certain subclass. In this case you must move the method from the super class to a subclass.

Mechanism

- Write a unit test of the class to confirm that the behavior doesn't change after refactoring.

- Identify the method to move down.

- Implement the method in each subclass. If the attributes to method access are private, we must change their visibility, becoming protected, or implement the accessory methods if we cannot change the visibility.

- Remove the method from the super class.

- Run a unit test.

- Remove the origin method from the subclasses.

- Remove the method from subclasses that it doesn't represent.

- Run the unit test again.

Example

Consider an abstract super class `BaseUser` with two subclasses, `Premium` and `User`.

```
abstract class BaseUser
{
  ...
  public function getPaymentDate()
  {
    return $this->payment_date + $this->duration_time;
  }

  public function haveToPay()
  {
    return $this->getPaymentDate() < strtotime('today');
  }
  ...
}
```

```php
class Premium extends BaseUser
{
  ...
}

class User extends BaseUser
{
  ...
}
```

Methods getPaymentDate() and haveToPay() are used only with Premium instances and never with User. So we want to push down these two methods, from the BaseUser class to the Premium class. First, write a test to confirm that the behavior doesn't change. We also add a check that methods getPaymentDate() and haveToPay() can't be called by the User instance.

```php
--- PremiumTest.php ---
<?php

class PremiumTest extends PHPUnit_Framework_TestCase
{
  public function setUp()
  {
    $this->user = new Premium();
  }

  public function testHaveToPay()
  {
    $this->user->duration_time = 60*60*24*30;
    $this->user->payment_date = strtotime('5/1/2009');

    $this->assertEquals('31-05-2009', date('d-m-Y', $this->user->getPaymentDate()));
    $this->assertTrue($this->user->haveToPay());

    $this->user->payment_date = strtotime('+2 days');
    $this->assertFalse($this->user->haveToPay());
  }
}

--- UserTest.php ---

class UserTest extends PHPUnit_Framework_TestCase
{
  public function setUp()
  {
    $this->user = new User();
  }

  public function testHaveToPay()
  {
    $this->assertTrue($this->user instanceof BaseUser);
    $this->assertFalse(method_exists($this->user, 'getPaymentDate'));
    $this->assertFalse(method_exists($this->user, 'haveToPay'));
  }
}
```

If we run tests, PremiumTest is ok, and UserTest fails because getPaymentDate() and haveToPay() are still methods of the User class. The next step of refactoring is to implement the getPaymentDate() and haveToPay() methods in each subclassing and remove them from the super class.

```
abstract class BaseUser
{
  ...
}

class Premium extends BaseUser
{
  ...
  public function getPaymentDate()
  {
    return $this->payment_date + $this->duration_time;
  }

  public function haveToPay()
  {
    return $this->getPaymentDate() < strtotime('today');
  }
  ...
}

class User extends BaseUser
{
  ...
  public function getPaymentDate()
  {
    return $this->payment_date + $this->duration_time;
  }

  public function haveToPay()
  {
    return $this->getPaymentDate() < strtotime('today');
  }
  ...
}
```

At the end, we need to remove the two methods from the User class, because they don't represent the User object.

```
class User extends BaseUser
{
  ...
}
```

We run tests and everything works fine.

```
PHPUnit 3.4.1 by Sebastian Bergmann.

.

Time: 0 seconds

OK (1 test, 3 assertions)
```

Push Down Field

Problem: "A field is used only by some subclasses."

Solution: "Move the field to those subclasses."

Motivation

"Push Down Field" is the opposite of "Move Up Field." We can use this refactoring technique when a certain attribute in the super class is significant only in one of the subclasses.

Mechanism

- Write a unit test of the class to confirm that the behavior doesn't change after refactoring.

- Declare the attribute in all subclasses.

- Remove the attribute in the super class.

- Run the unit test.

- Remove the attribute in classes where it is not necessary.

- Run the unit test again.

Example

After some refactoring steps we have two classes—Developer and Manager—that extend the abstract class Employee.

```
abstract class Employee
{
  protected $project_manager;
  protected $assigned_projects;
}

class Developer extends Employee
{
  public function setProjectManager($project_manager)
  {
    $this->project_manager = $project_manager;
  }
}

class Manager extends Employee
{
  public function setAssignedProjects($assigned_projects)
  {
    $this->assigned_projects = $assigned_projects;
  }

  public function getAssignedProjects()
  {
```

```
    return $this->assigned_projects;
  }
}
```

The Employee class has two properties, $project_manager and $assigned_projects. These two parameters don't represent both classes and they need to be moved to subclasses. $project_manager has to be moved to the Developer class and $assigned_projects to the Manager class.

We write a test to check that the two classes don't have the wrong parameter; if needed, we have to check their behavior to confirm that it doesn't change after refactoring.

```
--- ManagerTest.php ---

include(dirname(__FILE__).'/Employee.php');

class ManagerTest extends PHPUnit_Framework_TestCase
{
  public function setUp()
  {
    $this->manager = new Manager();
  }

  public function testProjectManagerPropertyDoesntExists()
  {
    $reflection_manager = new ReflectionObject($this->manager);
    $this->assertFalse($reflection_manager->hasProperty('project_manager'));
  }
}

--- DeveloperTest.php ---

class DeveloperTest extends PHPUnit_Framework_TestCase
{
  public function setUp()
  {
    $this->developer = new Developer();
  }

  public function testAssignedProjectsPropertyDoesntExists()
  {
    $reflection_developer = new ReflectionObject($this->developer);
    $this->assertFalse($reflection_developer->hasProperty('assigned_projects'));
  }
}
```

Tests fail because the classes still have the wrong properties. To push down fields we need first to copy all the properties we want to move from the super class to the subclasses, and remove them from the super class.

```
abstract class Employee { }

class Developer extends Employee
{
  protected $project_manager;
  protected $assigned_projects;
```

```
  public function setProjectManager($project_manager)
  {
    $this->project_manager = $project_manager;
  }
}

class Manager extends Employee
{
  protected $project_manager;
  protected $assigned_projects;

  public function setAssignedProjects($assigned_projects)
  {
    $this->assigned_projects = $assigned_projects;
  }

  public function getAssignedProjects()
  {
    return $this->assigned_projects;
  }
}
```

At the end we can remove the fields that don't represent the class where they are—for example, we have to remove $project_manager from the Manager class, and $assigned_projects from the Developer class.

```
class Developer extends Employee
{
  protected $project_manager;

  public function setProjectManager($project_manager)
  {
    $this->project_manager = $project_manager;
  }
}

class Manager extends Employee
{
  protected $assigned_projects;

  public function setAssignedProjects($assigned_projects)
  {
    $this->assigned_projects = $assigned_projects;
  }

  public function getAssignedProjects()
  {
    return $this->assigned_projects;
  }
}
```

We run tests and confirm that everything works fine.

```
$ phpunit DeveloperTest.php
PHPUnit 3.4.1 by Sebastian Bergmann.

.

Time: 0 seconds

OK (1 test, 1 assertion)

---

$ phpunit ManagerTest.php
PHPUnit 3.4.1 by Sebastian Bergmann.

.

Time: 0 seconds

OK (1 test, 1 assertion
```

Extract Subclass

Problem: "A class has features that are used only in some instances."

Solution: "Create a subclass for that subset of features."

Motivation

There are some classes where it's useful to extract a subclass when we realize that a set of its features is used only in certain instances of the class. We have already seen that in other refactoring techniques, it is recommended to extract classes, such as when we have a type attribute because we can remove the attribute adding subclasses or remove it through the state/strategy pattern.

When we don't have the type attribute, we can extract the class or perform this refactoring by extracting a subclass. The leading choice in both cases is to choose between inheritance and delegation. If the object typology needs to change after being instantiated, we must delegate. Otherwise we can use the inheritance.

Mechanism

- Write a unit test to confirm that the behavior doesn't change after refactoring.

- Define a new subclass of the initial class.

- Find all instances of the class source in your code and replace it with instances of the subclass where necessary. If you find that the constructor of the subclass may be different from that of the super class, we can implement it in the subclass with the new interface and then call the parent constructor into the child subclass constructor. If we see that the super class is not more instantiated, but only its subclass are instantiated, let's make it abstract.

- Run the test and verify that it is still correct.

- Move the methods required by the super class to the subclass.

- Run the test again and verify that it is still correct.

- Move the class attributes from the super class to the subclass.

- Find each attribute of the super class that expresses the same information now expressed by heredity, and remove it, encapsulating the attributes and replacing the getter body with the constants class.

- Run tests and verify that it is still correct.

Example

We have the Subscription class, which is used both for annual subscriptions and monthly subscriptions. Through the $is_yearly attribute we can understand whether the subscription is yearly or monthly. The method getPrice() implements different behaviors based on this attribute.

```
class Subscription
{
  private $price;
  private $is_yearly;
  private $discount;

  public function __construct($price, $is_yearly = false, $discount = 0)
  {
    $this->price = $price;
    $this->is_yearly = $is_yearly;
    $this->discount = $discount;
  }

  public function getPrice()
  {
    if ($this->is_yearly)
    {
      $price = $this->price * 12;
      return $price - ($price / 100 * $this->discount);
    }

    return $this->price;
  }

  public function getDiscount()
  {
    return $this->discount;
  }

  public function isYearly()
  {
    return $this->is_yearly;
  }
}
```

We want to extract a YearSubscription subclass from the Subscription class, in order to isolate different behaviors in different classes. Let's start writing a unit test for the Subscription class.

```
class SubscriptionTest extends PHPUnit_Framework_TestCase
{
  public function testSubscription()
  {
    $subscription = new Subscription(100);
    $this->assertEquals(100, $subscription->getPrice());
    $this->assertEquals(false, $subscription->isYearly());
  }

  public function testYearlysubscription()
  {
    $yearly_subscription = new Subscription(100, true, 20);
    $this->assertEquals((100*12)-((100*12)/100*20), $yearly_subscription->getPrice());
    $this->assertEquals(true, $yearly_subscription->isYearly());
  }
}
```

We use a unit test to move through the refactoring steps. First we want the annual subscription to be an instance of a new class called YearSubscription, so we modify the testYearlysubscription() method of the unit test, changing the class to instance.

```
class SubscriptionTest extends PHPUnit_Framework_TestCase
{
  ...
  public function testYearlysubscription()
  {
    $yearly_subscription = new YearSubscription(100, true, 20);
    $this->assertEquals((100*12)-((100*12)/100*20), $yearly_subscription->getPrice());
    $this->assertEquals(true, $yearly_subscription->isYearly());
  }
  ...
}
```

We implement the class YearSubscription that extends the class Subscription.

```
class YearSubscription extends Subscription { }
```

Now we can change the class interface of Subscription, because the $discount attribute belongs only to the YearSubscription class. To do that, we override the constructor in the YearSubscription class.

```
class YearSubscription extends Subscription
{
  public function __construct($price, $is_yearly = false, $discount = 0)
  {
    parent::__construct($price, $is_yearly, $discount);
  }
}
```

Then we modify the interface of the Subscription class and move the assignment of the $discount attribute in the constructor of the subclass. We also change the visibility of this attribute from private to protected in the super class, so we can access it in the YearSubscription subclass.

```php
class Subscription
{
  private $price;
  private $is_yearly;
  protected $discount;

  public function __construct($price, $is_yearly = false)
  {
    $this->price = $price;
    $this->is_yearly = $is_yearly;
  }
  ...
}
```

In the constructor body of the YearSubscription class, we must change the call to the parent constructor, just modified, and set the $discount attribute directly.

```php
class YearSubscription extends Subscription
{
  public function __construct($price, $discount = 0)
  {
    parent::__construct($price, true);
    $this->discount = $discount;
  }
}
```

Now we can move the methods that are only of the subclass. The method getDiscount() of the Subscription class is used only with the class YearSubscription, so push it down.

```php
class YearSubscription extends Subscription
{
  public function __construct($price, $discount = 0)
  {
    parent::__construct($price, true);
    $this->discount = $discount;
  }

  public function getDiscount()
  {
    return $this->discount;
  }
}
```

We also push down the attribute $discount of the super class that is used only with the subclass.

```php
class YearSubscription extends Subscription
{
  protected $discount;

  public function __construct($price, $discount = 0)
  {
    parent::__construct($price, true);
    $this->discount = $discount;
  }
```

```
public function getDiscount()
{
  return $this->discount;
}
}
```

We also remove the $is_yearly attribute that represents the same information given by inheritance. To do this we must change the method isYearly() in the super class to return a constant value. The same thing should be done also in the subclass.

```
class Subscription
{
  ...
  public function isYearly()
  {
    return false;
  }
}

class YearSubscription
{
  ...
  public function isYearly()
  {
    return true;
  }
}
```

To remove the $is_yearly attribute, we must first remove the conditional logic of the method getPrice() with the polymorphism. In practice, we modify the method in the super class and then we do an override in the subclass. We must also change the visibility of the attribute price, otherwise the subclass cannot access it.

```
class Subscription
{
  protected $price;
  ...
  public function getPrice()
  {
    return $this->price;
  }
}

class YearSubscription
{
  ...
  public function getPrice()
  {
    $price = $this->price * 12;
    return $price - ($price / 100 * $this->discount);
  }
}
```

Now we can remove all references to the $is_yearly attribute in the Subscription class.

```
class Subscription
{
  protected $price;

  public function __construct($price)
  {
    $this->price = $price;
  }

  public function getPrice()
  {
    return $this->price;
  }

  public function isYearly()
  {
    return false;
  }
}
```

Remember to run the tests at every step of refactoring to verify that the correct behavior is maintained.

Extract Super Class

Problem: "You have two classes with similar features."

Solution: "Create a super class and move the common features to the super class."

Motivation

When we have two classes doing the same things in the same way, or similar things in different ways, we can extract a super class and standardize some of their behavior to avoid duplicated code.

Once we have extracted the super class, we can use all the refactoring techniques seen in this chapter to remove duplicated code. We can push attributes and methods up or down, we can rename the methods that do the same thing but are named differently and move them to the super class, we can pull up the constructor, and so on.

We can also use inheritance to remove duplication. When we cannot use inheritance, we can use delegation. It isn't always easy to know at first what is better to use. Don't worry—we use a KISS approach (http://en.wikipedia.org/wiki/K.I.S.S.), and if we are wrong, we can always refactor, replacing inheritance with delegation and vice versa.

Mechanism

- Identify classes that do the same thing or something similar.

- Write a unit test for each class to confirm that the behavior doesn't change after refactoring.

- Extract a super class and make sure that the origin classes extend it.

- Move attributes and common methods one at a time. It is best to start from the attributes, changing the visibility where needed. Then continue with the methods. Where methods have different interfaces, rename them and then move them. Where only part of the method is the same, extract the method first, and then move it to the super class. Where the bodies of the methods are different but do the same thing, try replacing the algorithm, and then move the method in the super class.

- Run the unit test to confirm every change.

- Check for instances of classes. If no client needs to instantiate the super class, make it abstract.

Example

We have two classes—Order and Estimate—that have the same behavior.

```
class Order
{
  private $id;
  private $number;
  private $details = array();

  public function setId($id)
  {
    $this->id = $id;
  }

  public function setNumber($number)
  {
    $this->number = $number;
  }

  public function addDetail($detail)
  {
    $this->details[] = $detail;
  }

  public function getTotal()
  {
    $total = 0;
    foreach($this->details as $detail)
    {
      $total += $detail->getTotal();
    }
    return $total;
  }
}

class Estimate
{
  private $id;
  private $number;
  private $details = array();
```

```php
public function setId($id)
{
 $this->id = $id;
}

public function setNumber($number)
{
 $this->number = $number;
}

public function addDetail($detail)
{
 $this->details[] = $detail;
}

public function getTotal()
{
   $total = 0;
   foreach($this->details as $detail)
   {
     $total += $detail->getTotal();
   }
   return $total;
}
}
```

We want to extract the super class Document in order to remove the duplication of code, because both classes have the same attributes and the same methods. First of all, we write a unit test for each class.

```php
class DocumentIntegrationTest extends PHPUnit_Framework_TestCase
{
  private function detail($price, $amount, $description)
  {
    $detail = new Detail();
    $detail->setPrice($price);
    $detail->setAmount($amount);
    $detail->setDescription($description);
    return $detail;
  }

  public function testOrder()
  {
    $order = new Order();
    $order->setId(10);
    $order->setNumber(100);
    $order->addDetail($this->detail(100, 10, 'Detail 1'));

    $this->assertEquals(1000, $order->getTotal());
  }

  public function testEtimate()
  {
    $estimate = new Estimate();
    $estimate->setId(10);
    $estimate->setNumber(100);
```

```
    $estimate->addDetail($this->detail(100, 10, 'Detail 1'));

    $this->assertEquals(1000, $estimate->getTotal());
  }
}
?>
</pre>
```

Create a super class `Document` and make sure that the classes `Order` and `Estimate` extend it. Add a test that checks the inheritance to the unit test.

```
class Document {}

class Order extends Document { ... }

class Estimate extends Document { ... }

class DocumentIntegrationTest extends PHPUnit_Framework_TestCase
{
  public function testOrder()
  {
    ...
    $this->assertTrue($order instanceof Document);
    $this->assertEquals(1000, $order->getTotal());
  }

  public function testEtimate()
  {
    ...
    $this->assertTrue($estimate instanceof Document);
    $this->assertEquals(1000, $estimate->getTotal());
  }
}
```

We run the unit test and verify it is correct. If everything is ok, we can begin to pull up the attributes of the duplicated classes in the super class `Document`, changing their visibility where needed. In our case we pull up the `$id`, `$number`, and `$details` attributes, changing their visibility from private to protected. Once moved in the super class, we can remove them from the subclasses.

```
class Document
{
  protected $id;
  protected $number;
  protected $details = array();
}
```

Then pull up the methods from the subclasses to the super class, one at a time, and run the unit tests at each time. After moving the method, remove it from the other subclasses.

```
class Document
{
  protected $id;
  protected $number;
  protected $details = array();
```

```php
public function setId($id)
{
 $this->id = $id;
}

public function setNumber($number)
{
 $this->number = $number;
}

public function addDetail($detail)
{
 $this->details[] = $detail;
}

public function getTotal()
{
  $total = 0;
  foreach($this->details as $detail)
  {
    $total += $detail->getTotal();
  }
  return $total;
}
}

class Estimate extends Document { }

class Order extends Document { }
```

Collapse Hierarchy

Problem: "A super class and subclass are not very different."

Solution: "Merge them together."

Motivation

When we realize that a single class hierarchy doesn't give value to any of the classes in the hierarchy, we can do a merge of the hierarchy and create a single class. If we are often moving methods or attributes up and down the hierarchy, it probably means that we can't give the right meaning to any of the classes in the hierarchy. So we must merge them.

Mechanism

- Identify the hierarchy that you want to merge and decide whether to keep the super class or subclass.

- Write a unit test for the class we want to keep to confirm that the behavior doesn't change after refactoring.

- Move the class methods and attributes up or down as needed.

235

- Run the unit test and check that everything is ok.

- Adjust calls to the class that you want to remove, including calls to its methods or attributes.

- Run the unit test again and check that everything is ok.

- Remove the class.

- Run the unit test for the last time.

Example

We have a Salesman class that extends an abstract class, Employee. The class Salesman is the only one that extends the Employee class, so we want to remove the Employee class, pushing down all methods and properties merging the hierarchy.

```
abstract class Employee
{
  protected $firstname;
  protected $lastname;
}

class Salesman extends Employee
{
  public function setFirstname($firstname)
  {
    $this->firstname = $firstname;
  }

  public function setLastname($lastname)
  {
    $this->lastname = $lastname;
  }

  public function getFirstname()
  {
    return $this->firstname;
  }

  public function getLastname()
  {
    return $this->lastname;
  }
}
```

We write a test for the Salesman class, to confirm its behavior doesn't change after merging.

```
class CollapseHierarchyTest extends PHPUnit_Framework_TestCase
{
  public function testCollapse()
  {
    $salesman = new Salesman();
    $salesman->setFirstname('Francesco');
    $salesman->setLastname('Trucchia');
    $this->assertEquals('Francesco', $salesman->getFirstname());
```

```
    $this->assertEquals('Trucchia', $salesman->getLastname());
  }
}
```

The `Employee` class has only two properties, and we move them to `Salesman` with the "Push Down Field" technique.

```
abstract class Employee
{

}

class Salesman extends Employee
{
  protected $firstname;
  protected $lastname;

  public function setFirstname($firstname)
  {
    $this->firstname = $firstname;
  }

  public function setLastname($lastname)
  {
    $this->lastname = $lastname;
  }

  public function getFirstname()
  {
    return $this->firstname;
  }

  public function getLastname()
  {
    return $this->lastname;
  }
}
```

Then, we remove the hierarchy from `Salesman` and run the unit test.

```
class Salesman
{
  protected $firstname;
  protected $lastname;

  public function setFirstname($firstname)
  {
    $this->firstname = $firstname;
  }

  public function setLastname($lastname)
  {
    $this->lastname = $lastname;
  }
```

```
public function getFirstname()
{
  return $this->firstname;
}

public function getLastname()
{
  return $this->lastname;
}
}
```

If the test is ok, we remove the Employee class also and run all unit tests again.

Form Template Method

Problem: "You have two methods in subclasses that perform similar steps in the same order, yet the steps are different."

Solution: "Get the steps into methods with the same signature, so that the original methods become the same. Then you can pull them up."

Motivation

There are cases in which removing code duplication between the methods of our hierarchies may seem impossible, since these methods differ very little on features, but enough to not be able to pull methods and/or move them to the super class.

One of these cases is when we have two methods that perform operations in the same order, but the operations are different, sometimes so quite. The Gang of Four, to solve this problem, introduced the "Template Pattern"[GOF]. In essence, the pattern is to implement a method in the super class that calls each step in sequence through methods that may be on the super class or subclass. At this point, the methods of the steps, through polymorphism, can be quite different. The important thing is that they have the same interface.

Mechanism

- Write a unit test for the class to confirm that the behavior doesn't change after refactoring.

- Split the method in steps, so that steps of the method are identical or completely different.

- Move the identical methods in the super class.

- Rename the different methods if needed so that the name is the same.

- Run the unit test every time you rename a method.

- Move one of the origin methods in the super class and define step methods as abstract in the super class.

- Run the unit test.

- Remove duplicate methods by subclasses.

- Run the unit test for the last time.

Example

The Article class provides two methods for printing the article in HTML or TEXTILE format
(http://en.wikipedia.org/wiki/Textile_%28markup_language%29).

```
class Article
{
  ...
  public function texttileView()
  {
    $output = 'h1. '.$this->getTitle().PHP_EOL.PHP_EOL;
    $output .= $this->getIntro().PHP_EOL.PHP_EOL;
    $output .= $this->getBody().PHP_EOL.PHP_EOL;
    $output .= '_Written by '.$this->getAuthor().' on '.date('m/d/Y', $this->getDate()).'_';
    return $output;
  }

  public function htmlView()
  {
    $output = '<h2>'.$this->getTitle().'</h2>'.PHP_EOL;
    $output .= '<p>'.$this->getIntro().'</p>'.PHP_EOL;
    $output .= '<p>'.$this->getBody().'</p>'.PHP_EOL;
    $output .= '<em>Written by '.$this->getAuthor().' on '.date('m/d/Y', ↩
$this->getDate()).'</em>';
    return $output;
  }
}
```

These two methods are very similar because they implement the same steps, but each step is very different from each other. Therefore we want to remove the duplication of some code introducing the "Template Pattern" [GOF]. Before starting our refactoring, we extract a new class from the article class, which will be delegated only to print the template.

Extract the ArticleView class from the Article class that implements only the textileView() and htmlView() methods.

```
class ArticleView
{
  public function textileView($article)
  {
    $output = 'h1. '.$article->getTitle().PHP_EOL.PHP_EOL;
    $output .= $article->getIntro().PHP_EOL.PHP_EOL;
    $output .= $article->getBody().PHP_EOL.PHP_EOL;
    $output .= '_Written by '.$article->getAuthor().' on '.date('m/d/Y', $article->getDate()).'_';
    return $output;
  }

  public function htmlView($article)
  {
    $output = '<h2>'.$article->getTitle().'</h2>'.PHP_EOL;
    $output .= '<p>'.$article->getIntro().'</p>'.PHP_EOL;
    $output .= '<p>'.$article->getBody().'</p>'.PHP_EOL;
    $output .= '<em>Written by '.$article->getAuthor().' on '.date('m/d/Y', ↩
$article->getDate()).'</em>';
    return $output;
  }
}
```

```php
class Article
{
  ...
  public function textileView()
  {
    $view = new ArticleView();
    return $view->textileView($this);
  }

  public function htmlView()
  {
    $view = new ArticleView();
    return $view->htmlView($this);
  }
  ...
}
```

From the `ArticleView` class, we can extract two subclasses, `ArticleTextile` and `ArticleHtml`. One implements the method `textileView()`, and the other implements the method `htmlView()`. As the method name would be redundant with the class name, rename both methods in `view()`. Once the class is extracted, we also fix the calls to the class on clients.

```php
class ArticleView
{

}

class ArticleTextile extends ArticleView
{
  public function view($article)
  {
    $output = 'h1. '.$article->getTitle().PHP_EOL.PHP_EOL;
    $output .= $article->getIntro().PHP_EOL.PHP_EOL;
    $output .= $article->getBody().PHP_EOL.PHP_EOL;
    $output .= '_Written by '.$article->getAuthor().' on '.date('m/d/Y', $article->getDate()).'_';
    return $output;
  }
}

class ArticleHtml extends ArticleView
{
  public function view($article)
  {
    $output = '<h2>'.$article->getTitle().'</h2>'.PHP_EOL;
    $output .= '<p>'.$article->getIntro().'</p>'.PHP_EOL;
    $output .= '<p>'.$article->getBody().'</p>'.PHP_EOL;
    $output .= '<em>Written by '.$article->getAuthor().' on '.date('m/d/Y', ↵
$article->getDate()).'</em>';
    return $output;
  }
}

class Article
{
  ...
```

```
  public function textileView()
  {
    $view = new ArticleTextile();
    return $view->view($this);
  }

  public function htmlView()
  {
    $view = new ArticleHtml();
    return $view->view($this);
  }
  ...
}
?>
</pre>
```

We run the tests and make sure that everything is correct. At this point we can start implementing the "Form Template" technique for the view() method of the ArticleTextile and ArticleHtml classes. Split the method into steps so that all the steps are separated. We start from the class ArticleTextile.

```
class ArticleTextile extends ArticleView
{
  protected function title($article)
  {
    return 'h1. '.$article->getTitle().PHP_EOL.PHP_EOL;
  }

  protected function intro($article)
  {
    return $article->getIntro().PHP_EOL.PHP_EOL;
  }

  protected function body($article)
  {
    return $article->getBody().PHP_EOL.PHP_EOL;
  }

  protected function footer($article)
  {
    return '_Written by '.$article->getAuthor().' on '.date('m/d/Y', $article->getDate()).'_';
  }

  public function view($article)
  {
    return $this->title($article)
         .$this->intro($article)
         .$this->body($article)
         .$this->footer($article);
  }
}
```

We do the same thing for the `ArticleHtml` class.

```
class ArticleHtml extends ArticleView
{
  protected function title($article)
  {
    return '<h2>'.$article->getTitle().'</h2>'.PHP_EOL;
  }

  protected function intro($article)
  {
    return '<p>'.$article->getIntro().'</p>'.PHP_EOL;
  }

  protected function body($article)
  {
    return '<p>'.$article->getBody().'</p>'.PHP_EOL;
  }

  protected function footer($article)
  {
    return '<em>Written by '.$article->getAuthor().' on '.date('m/d/Y', ↵
$article->getDate()).'</em>';
  }

  public function view($article)
  {
    return $this->title($article)
         .$this->intro($article)
         .$this->body($article)
         .$this->footer($article);
  }
}
```

Finally we can move the `view()` method in the super class `ArticleView`, and remove it from the subclasses.

```
class ArticleView
{
  public function view($article)
  {
    return $this->title($article)
         .$this->intro($article)
         .$this->body($article)
         .$this->footer($article);
  }
}

class ArticleTextile extends ArticleView
{
  protected function title($article)
  {
    return 'h1. '.$article->getTitle().PHP_EOL.PHP_EOL;
  }
```

```php
  protected function intro($article)
  {
    return $article->getIntro().PHP_EOL.PHP_EOL;
  }

  protected function body($article)
  {
    return $article->getBody().PHP_EOL.PHP_EOL;
  }

  protected function footer($article)
  {
    return '_Written by '.$article->getAuthor().' on '.date('m/d/Y', $article->getDate()).'_';
  }
}
class ArticleHtml extends ArticleView
{
  protected function title($article)
  {
    return '<h2>'.$article->getTitle().'</h2>'.PHP_EOL;
  }

  protected function intro($article)
  {
    return '<p>'.$article->getIntro().'</p>'.PHP_EOL;
  }

  protected function body($article)
  {
    return '<p>'.$article->getBody().'</p>'.PHP_EOL;
  }

  protected function footer($article)
  {
    return '<em>Written by '.$article->getAuthor().' on '.date('m/d/Y', ↩
$article->getDate()).'</em>';
  }
}
```

We run the unit test for the last time and make sure that everything works fine.

Replace Inheritance with Delegation

Problem: "A subclass uses only part of a super class's interface or does not want to inherit data."

Solution: "Create a field for the super class, adjust methods to delegate to the super class, and remove the subclass."

Motivation

Inheritance is a very important feature of object-oriented programming. We must use it in the right way, otherwise it could create confusion. When we have classes that use few methods of the super class, classes that are not represented in the data and methods of their super class, or represented only partially, we must ask whether the choice of inheritance is the right choice.

Sometimes, it can be right anyway, but others may be better off using delegation rather than inheritance. Through delegation we explain in a better way what we need of the delegated class, how it represents our class, and what we can ignore. There is a payable fee, which is rewriting many methods of the delegated class, but, on the other hand, the advantage is that it increases the code's clarity.

Mechanism

- Write a unit test for the subclass.

- Add a new attribute on the subclass referred to the super class. Assign an instance of object itself to this attribute.

- Change each subclass method that uses super class fields, with the delegated fields.

- Remove the hierarchy from the subclass and assign to the super class attribute an instance of a new super class object.

- Add a delegating method for each super class method used by the subclass.

- Run the unit test.

Example

The class Car extends the class Engine, but it uses only one attribute of this class, the attribute $CV. So the Engine class is only partially described from the Car class. In fact, the engine should be an attribute of the Car class and not its super class, since there is a more general set of the car. We can confirm that in this case it would be better to use delegation rather than inheritance.

```
class Engine
{
  protected $fuel_type;
  protected $kW;
  protected $CV;

  public function getFuel()
  {
    return $this->fuel;
  }

  public function getKW()
  {
    return $this->kW;
  }

  public function getCV()
  {
    return $this->CV;
  }

  public function setFuel($fuel)
  {
```

```php
      $this->fuel = $fuel;
  }

  public function setKW($kw)
  {
      $this->kW = $kw;
  }

  public function setCV($cv)
  {
      $this->CV = $cv;
  }
}

class Car extends Engine
{
  protected $brand;
  protected $model;

  public function __toString()
  {
      return $this->brand.' '.$this->model.' ('.$this->getCV().'CV)';
  }

  public function setModel($model)
  {
      $this->model = $model;
  }

  public function getModel()
  {
      return $this->model;
  }

  public function setBrand($brand)
  {
      $this->brand = $brand;
  }

  public function getBrand()
  {
      return $this->brand;
  }

}
```

Following the mechanism, we must first write a unit test for the `Car` subclass.

```php
class CarTest extends PHPUnit_Framework_TestCase
{
  public function testEngine()
  {
      $car = new Car();
      $car->setBrand('Audi');
      $car->setModel('A3');
      $car->setCV('250');

      $this->assertEquals('Audi', $car->getBrand());
```

```
    $this->assertEquals('A3', $car->getModel());
    $this->assertEquals('250', $car->getCV());

    $this->assertEquals('Audi A3 (250CV)', (string)$car);
  }
}
```

We run the test and verify that it doesn't fail. To replace inheritance, we must, first of all, create an attribute $engine in the Car class that is an instance of itself.

```
class Car extends Engine
{
  ...
  protected $engine;

  public function __construct()
  {
    $this->engine = $this;
  }
  ...
}
```

Replace, in the methods of the Car class, the calls to methods or attributes of the super class with the delegated attribute. In our case, the only method that makes use of attributes of the super class is the __toString() method.

```
class Car extends Engine
{
  ...
  public function __toString()
  {
    return $this->brand.' '.$this->model.' ('.$this->engine->getCV().'CV)';
  }
  ...
}
```

Remove inheritance from the Car class and assign to the $engine attribute a new instance of object engine.

```
class Car
{
  ...
  protected $engine;

  public function __construct()
  {
    $this->engine = new Engine();
  }
  ...
}
```

Finally, add the proxy method `setCV()` in the `Car` class to set the attribute `$CV` of the `Engine` class.

```
class Car
{
  ...
  public function setCV($cv)
  {
    $this->engine->setCV($cv);
  }
  ...
}
```

Run the unit test and verify that everything is correct.

Replace Delegation with Inheritance

Problem: "You're using delegation and are often writing many simple delegations for the entire interface."

Solution: "Make the delegating class a subclass of the delegate."

Motivation

This technique is the opposite of the technique "Replace Inheritance with Delegation." When a class uses all the methods of a delegate class, and when we add a new method in the delegate class, we must always add it in the delegating class. We can "Replace Delegation with Inheritance."

If the delegating class doesn't use all the methods of the delegate class, we cannot use this refactoring technique, because with inheritance all methods of the super class become interfaces for subclasses. If we cannot replace the delegation, we can use other methods. For example, we can directly make access clients to the delegated class, so we don't have to rewrite all delegate methods, or we can extract a super class from the delegate class to isolate the common interface and then inherit from it.

If the delegate class is shared with other objects and may change after you have instantiated it, we cannot replace it with inheritance, because then we couldn't share it.

Mechanism

- Make the delegating class a subclass of the delegate class.
- Set the delegate attribute as an instance of the object itself.
- Remove the delegate methods.
- Run the unit test.
- Replace all other delegations with attributes or methods of the object itself.
- Remove the delegate attribute.

Example

We have an `Employee` class, without attributes, which delegates all its behaviors to the `Person` class.

```php
class Person
{
  protected $name;

  public function setName($name)
  {
    $this->name = $name;
  }

  public function getName()
  {
    return $this->name;
  }

  public function getLastName()
  {
    list(,$lastname) = explode(' ', $this->getName());
    return $lastname;
  }
}

class Employee
{
  protected $person;

  public function __construct()
  {
    $this->person = new Person();
  }

  public function __toString()
  {
    return 'Emp: '.$this->person->getLastName();
  }

  public function getName()
  {
    return $this->person->getName();
  }

  public function setName($name)
  {
    $this->person->setName($name);
  }
}
```

Write a unit test to confirm that the behaviors remain unchanged at the end of refactoring.

```php
class EmployeeTest extends PHPUnit_Framework_TestCase
{
  public function testEngine()
  {
    $employee = new Employee();
```

```
    $employee->setName('Francesco Trucchia');

    $this->assertEquals('Emp: Trucchia', (string)$employee);
    $this->assertEquals('Trucchia', $employee->getLastName());
    $this->assertEquals('Francesco Trucchia', $employee->getName());
  }
}
```

Define inheritance from the `Person` class in the `Employee` class.

```
class Employee extends Person {...}
```

We run the tests and make sure everything is still correct. Afterwards, we assign an instance of the object itself to the delegate attribute and remove accessory methods.

```
class Employee extends Person
{
  protected $person;

  public function __construct()
  {
    $this->person = $this;
  }

  public function __toString()
  {
    return 'Emp: '.$this->person->getLastName();
  }
}
```

At this point, we can directly call the methods of the `Person` class and remove the delegate attribute.

```
class Employee extends Person
{
  public function __toString()
  {
    return 'Emp: '.$this->getLastName();
  }
}
```

Run the tests and verify that the behaviors don't change.

Summary

In this chapter we learned how to simplify and modify our class hierarchies. We learned how to move methods and properties up and down in hierarchical classes, how to collapse unnecessary hierarchies, and how to extract super classes or subclasses in the presence of over-responsible classes. Learning how to manage generalization facilitates a very simple and easily maintainable code.

CHAPTER 13

■ ■ ■

Legacy Code

Back in 2004 Robert C. Martin mercilessly wrote that "software systems almost always degrade into a mess. What starts as a clean crystalline design in the minds of the programmers rots, over time, like a piece of bad meat." [LEGACY] We would bet that anyone reading this book has faced this situation during her life as a developer. Our best intentions are to build a perfect code base, but time constraints and the tendency to entropy claim their fee. We have always tried to blame this on the customers and their senseless will to keep changing requirements, but the reality is that we don't have to change customers as much as we have to change ourselves.

Reality being what it is and not what we would like it to be, if customers need to change their requirements we better upgrade our code and manage software projects in a way more closely matching this fact. Developers who best meet that challenge while preserving the underlying quality of their code will be able to better position themselves in the market, slowly overwhelming developers still sticking to the old way of blaming software projects and their stakeholders for changing.

The key to embracing changes and indeed to seeing them as an opportunity to improve the system is to avoid writing stiff code that doesn't tolerate changing requirements. This is the real goal of every software project. This book shows you many techniques to improve the quality of your design step by step by changing the code, with no effect on external functionality. By the way, solutions never come too early, so everyone has come to some nasty unmanageable code in his life. Furthermore, even the most committed developer will need time to master the refactoring techniques, and thus he will keep writing some *ugly* code in the meantime.

That ugly code has many names. In this book we will call it *legacy code*. Legacy code is what you get when for some reason you haven't been able to fight entropy. Legacy code is something you cannot get rid of in a single refactoring step or by some other sort of magic. For this reason, we decided to dedicate this last part of our book to some higher-level ways to distill a better structure from your old or new legacy code. We hope it will help those PHP developers out there who are still working on old applications but are willing to join the wonders of well-structured and safe programming. In this chapter we will introduce a simple application built with a procedural style, and in the following chapters we will show you how to refactor it towards a better architecture.

Ugly Code

This section will be based on a sample application Francesco Trucchia created for one of his workshops on refactoring techniques. It's nothing more than a system to manage a contact list: you can list, add, edit, and delete names, phone numbers, and mobile phone numbers, as shown in Figures 13-1 through 13-3.

Contacts Book

New contact

Last Name	First Name	Phone	Mobile	
Romei	Jacopo	0543123543	34012345	[X]
Trucchia	Francesco	+44 2 1234567	234 12345	[X]

All © Francesco Trucchia & Jacopo Romei - Pro PHP Refactoring

Figure 13-1. *The list view of our application*

Contacts Book

First Name*

Last Name*

Phone*

Mobile

Save Cancel

(Mandatory fields)*

All © Francesco Trucchia & Jacopo Romei - Pro PHP Refactoring

Figure 13-2. *The contact creation form of our application*

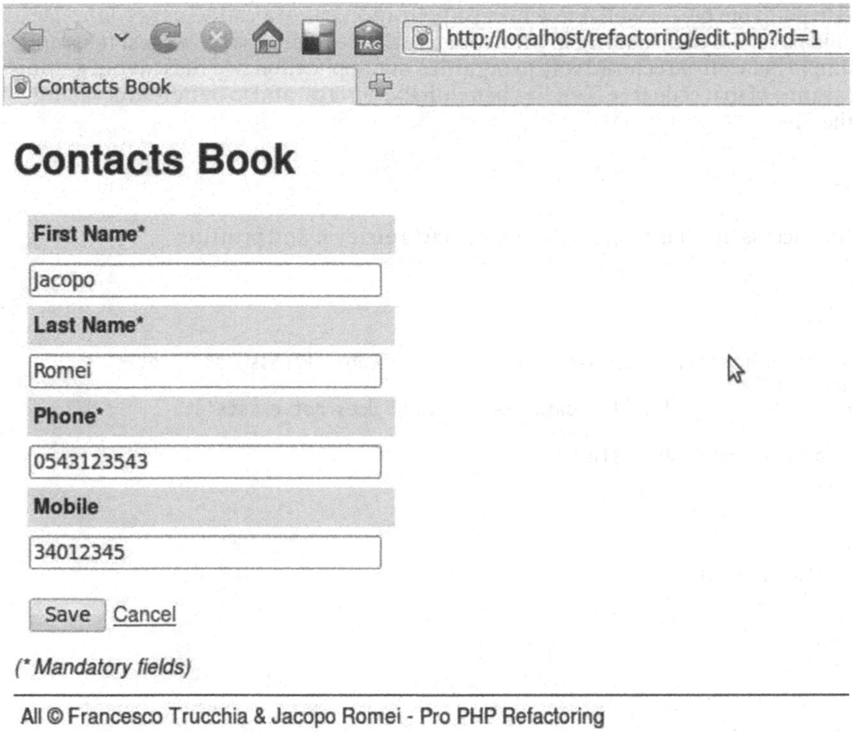
http://localhost/refactoring/edit.php?id=1
Contacts Book
Contacts Book
First Name*
Jacopo
Last Name*
Romei
Phone*
0543123543
Mobile
34012345
Save
Cancel
(* Mandatory fields)
All © Francesco Trucchia & Jacopo Romei - Pro PHP Refactoring

Figure 13-3. *The form to edit a contact is the same as that in the contact creation screen, but filled with editable data.*

We kept its code intentionally *ugly*. Some of you reading the code in the next chapters might be amazed by what we are calling ugly and argue that the principles it seems written on are the same applied by many open-source and well-known PHP applications out there. We agree—that's true. Right now we prefer not to explain why we think that's ugly code—we will return to that later in this chapter. Now it's time to check our code.

The application is built mainly upon a set of nine files, each focusing on a single task and including code belonging to every logical layer, from database access to HTML code rendering through SQL and plain PHP logic. Those files are the following:

config.php
edit.php
footer.php
_form.php
functions.php
header.php
index.php
new.php
remove.php

We could be tempted to point out here a well-known web application pattern called *page controller*, according to which we could have one path leading to a file for each single logical page request to handle. Though this would be a simple but well-structured way to organize our application, we must avoid getting misled by the outer appearance of that code tree. Evil lies beneath the surface, and to better understand this, let's have a look at the files.

index.php

This is the main application access file. It is responsible for contact retrieval and printing.

```php
<?php
include_once('config.php');

$db = @mysql_connect($database['host'], $database['username'], $database['password']) or↵
die('Can\'t connect to database');
@mysql_select_db($database['name']) or die('The database selected does not exists');

$query = 'SELECT * FROM contacts ORDER BY lastname';
$rs = mysql_query($query);

if (!$rs)
{
  die_with_error(mysql_error(), $query);
}

$num = mysql_num_rows($rs);

?>

<?php include_once('header.php') ?>

<div class="actions">
  <a href="new.php">New contact</a>
 </div>

<?php if ($num) : ?>
  <table border="1" cellspacing="0" cellpadding="5">
  <tr>
    <th>Last Name</th>
    <th>First Name</th>
    <th>Phone</th>
    <th>Mobile</th>
    <th> </th>
  </tr>
  <?php while($row = mysql_fetch_assoc($rs)) : ?>
    <tr>
      <td><a href="edit.php?id=<?php echo $row['id']?>" title="Edit"><?php echo ↵
$row['lastname']?></a></td>
      <td><?php echo $row['firstname']?></a></td>
      <td><a href="callto://<?php echo $row['phone']?>"><?php echo $row['phone']?></a></td>
      <td><a href="callto://<?php echo $row['mobile']?>"><?php echo $row['mobile']?></a></td>
      <td>[<a href="remove.php?id=<?php echo $row['id']?>" title="Delete" onclick="if ↵
(confirm('Are you sure?')) {return true;} return false;">X</a>]</td>
    </tr>
  <?php endwhile;?>
```

```
  </table>

 <?php else : ?>
  Database is empty
<?php endif ?>

<?php include_once('footer.php') ?>

<?php
  mysql_free_result($rs);
  mysql_close($db);
?>
```

We start by including config.php, a system configuration file. Then we connect to a MySQL database and execute the query to retrieve all contacts ordered by lastname. After having included the header.php template file, we print some additional HTML code and perform a conditional branching based on the amount of records returned by the query. In the case of a non-empty record set, we draw a table iterating over the recordset. Thereafter we include another template file called footer.php, and then we close the MySQL connection.

Even at a first glance you may well see how data-oriented code is interleaved with business logic code and template view code. In spite of being a small file it features an amazingly tangled portion of code, where database queries are next to HTML code. We know that separating code into layers is one of the most widely acknowledged ways to keep code readable and maintainable. In this case we are completely missing this goal.

config.php

This is the main application configuration file. It is responsible for setting database access parameters. It also takes care of including a mandatory application specific library.

```php
<?php

$database['host'] = 'localhost';
$database['username'] = 'root';
$database['password'] = null;
$database['name'] = 'contacts';

require_once('functions.php');

?>
```

functions.php

This is the main application library file. It is responsible for the definition of a couple of functions used throughout the application.

```php
<?php

/**
 * Validate form
 *
 * @param array $mandatory_fields
 * @param array $fields
 * @return array
```

```
    */
function validate($mandatory_fields, $fields)
{
  $errors = array();

  foreach ($mandatory_fields as $field)
  {
    if($fields[$field] == '')
    {
      $errors[] = 'The ' . $field . ' field is mandatory';
    }
  }

  return $errors;
}

function die_with_error($error_msg, $query)
{
  $message  = 'Invalid query: ' . $error_msg. "\n";
  $message .= 'Whole query: ' . $query;
  die($message);
}

?>
```

We define a validate() function that will be used by files requiring the validation of values coming from a form. Then we define an SQL error management function called die_with_error().

header.php

This is the main template file. It is responsible for the HTML code to be printed before our main page content.

```
<html>
  <head>
    <title>Contacts Book</title>

    <style>
    body{
      font-family: Helvetica;
      font-size: 14px;
    }

    label{
      display: block;
      background-color: #ddd;
      margin: 5px 0px;
      padding: 4px;
      font-weight: bold;
      width: 250px;
    }

    form{
      margin-left: 10px;
    }

    input[type="text"]{
```

```
  width: 250px;
}

.actions{
  margin-bottom: 10px;
}

#footer{
  padding: 5px;
  border-top: 1px solid #000;
  margin-top: 10px;
}
</style>
</head>

<body>

<div id="header">
  <h1>Contacts Book</h1>
</div>

<div id="content">
```

No PHP code or output buffering here: this HTML code gets sent to the client as soon as the `header.php` file is included.

footer.php

This is the footer template file. It is responsible for printing the HTML after our main page content.

```
  </div>

  <div id="footer">
  All &copy; Francesco Trucchia & Jacopo Romei - Pro PHP Refactoring
  </div>
</body>
</html>
```

The HTML code printed here must closely match the HTML code featured in `header.php`. Any mismatch could make the overall HTML code not well formed, thus leading to rendering errors in the browser and, at least, to invalid HTML code.

new.php

This is the new contact page. It is responsible for the creation of a new contact.

```
<?php
include_once('config.php');

if($_SERVER['REQUEST_METHOD'] == 'POST')
{
  $errors = validate(array('firstname', 'lastname', 'phone'), $_POST);

  if(count($errors) == 0)
  {
```

```
    $db = @mysql_connect($database['host'], $database['username'], $database['password']) or ↵
die('Can\'t connect do database');
    @mysql_select_db($database['name']) or die('The database selected does not exists');

    $query = sprintf("INSERT INTO contacts (firstname, lastname, phone, mobile) VALUES ('%s', ↵
'%s', '%s', '%s')",
                     mysql_real_escape_string($_POST['firstname']),
                     mysql_real_escape_string($_POST['lastname']),
                     mysql_real_escape_string($_POST['phone']),
                     mysql_real_escape_string($_POST['mobile'])
                    );

    $rs = mysql_query($query);

    if (!$rs)
    {
      die_with_error(mysql_error(), $query);
    }

    mysql_close($db);

    header('Location: index.php');

  }
}
?>

<?php include_once('header.php') ?>

<?php include_once('_form.php') ?>

<?php include_once('footer.php') ?>
```

We start by including the configuration file and, after checking the request HTTP method and form parameter validity, we perform a MySQL connection and an INSERT query. After a successful query, since we haven't output any HTML code yet, we can redirect the client to index.php, the contact list where we will see the contact we just created. At the end of the file we manage the case of a GET request by including three template files to render a new contact form.

edit.php

This is the edit contact page. It is responsible for the editing of an existing contact.

```
<?php

include_once('config.php');

if(!$_GET['id'])
{
 die('Some error occured!!');
}

$db = @mysql_connect($database['host'], $database['username'], $database['password']) or ↵
die('Can\'t connect do database');
@mysql_select_db($database['name']) or die('The database selected does not exists');
```

```php
if($_SERVER['REQUEST_METHOD'] == 'POST')
{
  $errors = validate(array('id', 'firstname', 'lastname', 'phone'), $_POST);

  if(count($errors) == 0)
  {
    $query = sprintf("UPDATE contacts set firstname = '%s',
                                              lastname = '%s',
                                              phone = '%s',
                                              mobile = '%s' WHERE id = %s",
                      mysql_real_escape_string($_POST['firstname']),
                      mysql_real_escape_string($_POST['lastname']),
                      mysql_real_escape_string($_POST['phone']),
                      mysql_real_escape_string($_POST['mobile']),
                      mysql_real_escape_string($_POST['id'])
                    );

    $rs = mysql_query($query);

    if (!$rs)
    {
      die_with_error(mysql_error(), $query);
    }

    header('Location: index.php');
  }
}
else
{
  $query = sprintf('SELECT * FROM contacts WHERE id = %s', mysql_real_escape_string($_GET['id']));

  $rs = mysql_query($query);

  if (!$rs)
  {
    die_with_error(mysql_error(), $query);
  }

  $row = mysql_fetch_assoc($rs);

  $_POST['id'] = $row['id'];
  $_POST['firstname'] = $row['firstname'];
  $_POST['lastname'] = $row['lastname'];
  $_POST['phone'] = $row['phone'];
  $_POST['mobile'] = $row['mobile'];
}

mysql_close($db);

?>

<?php include_once('header.php') ?>

<?php include_once('_form.php') ?>

<?php include_once('footer.php') ?>
```

We are now used to this: we start by including the configuration file. We connect to the MySQL database and then we perform actions similar to those we found in new.php: in the case of a POST request we perform the data validation, the query to update the right record, and the client redirection to index.php; in the case of a GET request or invalid POST parameters we render an HTML form loaded with default values coming from the requested record.

_form.php

This is the main contact form file. It is responsible for printing the form to create or edit a contact.

```php
<form method="post">

<?php if (isset($errors) and count($errors)) : ?>
  <ul class="errors">
  <?php foreach ($errors as $error) : ?>
    <li><?php echo $error ?></li>
  <?php endforeach;?>
  </ul>
<?php endif ?>

<input type="hidden" name="id" value="<?php echo $_POST['id']?>" />

<label for="firstname">First Name*</label>
<input type="text" id="firstname" name="firstname" value="<?php echo $_POST['firstname'] ?>" />

<label for="lastname">Last Name*</label>
<input type="text" id="lastname" name="lastname" value="<?php echo $_POST['lastname'] ?>" />

<label for="phone">Phone*</label>
<input type="text" id="phone" name="phone" value="<?php echo $_POST['phone'] ?>" />

<label for="mobile">Mobile</label>
<input type="text" id="mobile" name="mobile" value="<?php echo $_POST['mobile'] ?>" />

<br/><br/>
<input type="submit" value="Save" />
<a href="index.php" >Cancel</a>
</form>
<em>(* Mandatory fields)</em>
```

remove.php

This is the remove contact file. It is responsible for contact removal.

```php
<?php
include_once('config.php');

if(!$_GET['id'])
{
 die('Some error occured!!');
}

$db = @mysql_connect($database['host'], $database['username'], $database['password']) or ↵
die('Can\'t connect do database');
@mysql_select_db($database['name']) or die('The database selected does not exists');
```

```
$query = sprintf('DELETE FROM contacts where ID = %s',
                 mysql_real_escape_string($_GET['id']));

if(!mysql_query($query))
{
  die_with_error(mysql_error(), $query);
}

mysql_close($db);

header('Location: index.php');

?>
```

Also here, for the last time, we include the configuration file named config.php. We check whether the ID of the record we want to delete is defined, we connect to our MySQL database, and we perform the record deletion query before redirecting the client to index.php or dying because of a MySQL error.

Maintenance

This application is very hard to maintain. There is no separation of layers and no abstraction at all. Because the code is affected by a strong entanglement between business logic code, workflow, data-oriented code, and template rendering, it makes any change request a nightmare for the developer. We are not talking about new features but just about maintenance of this code. Let's see a few examples.

Example: SQL injection

After launching our Contacts Book application, we realize we are vulnerable to SQL injection attacks. Just by requesting this URL, we could delete all the data in our database:

http://<hostname>/remove.php?id=3%20or%20id%20is%20not%20null (or just http://<hostname>/remove.php?id=3 or id is not null on modern browsers).

In the remove.php file we execute the following code:

```
$query = sprintf('DELETE FROM contacts where ID = %s', mysql_real_escape_string($_GET['id']));
```

This lets us inject some foreign SQL by means of the $_GET['id'] variable. Then, requesting the preceding URL, our code would execute the following query:

```
DELETE FROM contacts where ID = 3 or id is not null;
```

This has easy-to-understand and ruinous consequences. To make things worse, it looks like we are exposing many other similar security holes. In edit.php we could perform the same attack by exploiting the $_POST['id'] variable.

Please don't think it's just a simple security hole that no serious PHP developer would introduce. It may be, but the point here is that with this application structure we cannot manage this maintenance issue in a single, clear, and well-defined spot. When called to fix such a simple security bug, we have to arrange a solution scattered throughout the code tree. This example application is obviously small and likely not worth this worry, but how would you manage the same issue if it featured hundreds of pages?

Example: Database Portability

One year after the first public launch of our Contacts Book application the managers made a request: the application must be ported to some proprietary database technology due to both new partnerships and sponsorships. Good for the business, but how good for the developers? In our application the code managing our database connections and queries is closely tangled with the rest of the PHP code and completely MySQL specific.

Please note we are not simply advocating the use of an abstraction layer here, as you may think. The real problem is having no single focal point to manage DB-oriented code. We could even agree on using native DB libraries offered by PHP, but the way our application is structured now forces us to cope with lots of code duplication and lots of chaos: what if our application were a real one with hundreds of files needing a connection to the DB? Wouldn't it be insane to go through all of them replacing the `mysql_connect()` call with the new one?

Many other examples could show you how hard the maintenance of an application like this would be. What if we need to change some HTTP header depending on the output of code executed after the `header.php` file is included, preventing us from sending further HTTP headers? What if we need an error log, considering we manage errors only by means of conditional logic, and thus only errors we thought of well in advance and not those emerging from the complexity of our application?

Keeping maintenance simple is the key to keeping software cheap. Keeping software cheap makes us successful and desirable developers, providing our customers with winning solutions, and no compromise on quality.

New Features

Things can get awkward when it comes to new features, too. A good design paves the way for new features to be put in place quickly and cheaply. Here we will provide just a couple of brief examples, but other similar situations are easy to imagine.

Dynamic Layouts

Our application grew up strong and full of data. Thousands of contacts populate our database and the list shown in `index.php` is very long now. The customer, together with her usability experts, decide to ask the development team for a few user-centered features: a box in every page containing the form to create a new contact without loading a whole new page by means of an AJAX asynchronous request, and another box showing the ten most recently added contacts.

From a customer point of view it should be no big deal, and you have to admit all the logic required is there already: we have a form, contact creation business logic, and a list template and a query to retrieve lists of contacts. Well, actually the listing query should be tweaked somehow to make it ordered by record creation time and limited to ten records, but we know it's absolutely something you cannot tell the customer it's hard to do. The truth is different, though.

We have a big problem here: a simple problem gets complicated because of our own code. Portions of our existing code are not suitable to be used out of their own context. We cannot just include the `new.php` file in a div tag in the `header.php` file to get a working new contact form in every page, since the `new.php` execution brings another HTML layout in with itself. If we were to include just the `_form.php` template we would miss the right action attribute and some server-side action would have to be performed to return a clean AJAX-oriented output.

Concerning the list of the ten most recently added contacts, we have similar issues to cope with. As we noted already, we have a query to retrieve lists of contacts in `index.php`:

```
$query = 'SELECT * FROM contacts ORDER BY lastname';
```

The first problem here is about query reuse. Though we could just append the needed LIMIT clause, being the query written in native SQL there is no way to edit the ORDER BY clause if we don't want to use some awkward string replacement routine. The worst has yet to come: that query is buried deep into the `index.php` file, once again tainted by the whole HTML page layout. So we have no ready-to-use query to base our new feature upon, leading to higher development costs.

Internationalization

At first we planned for a local user community and we didn't need an internationalization framework. Then our customer discovered her own web site had grown outside of national boundaries, and now she wants it to be capable of speaking its user's language. She plans a meeting with the development team and happily announces a translation team will be providing the developers with a folder of well-structured files with translations of every string featured on the web site for each planned new language, according to the format that the developers judge best to use. We get caught red-handed here. All in all the customer did her homework: she didn't ask the developers to do something other than developing, she kept her options open by making the translation team deliver the best material to be used by the developers, and she didn't even ask for the developers to extract all the strings used in the user interface.

The reason the upgrade of the system to feature translations seems so expensive lies on the design side. The missing separation of layers makes it very hard to spot all the user interface strings used across the application, and even the most patient developer who spotted all of them would have a hard time injecting the translation behavior with no loss in readability and no risk of side effects. With a real layered structure, tasks like this get a lot easier and coding new features gets lots cheaper.

Break the Cycle

Changing existing code always costs something. Introducing unintended changes along with desired ones costs a lot more. Most development teams facing the need for a change in code will react in a conservative way, in a struggle to minimize change. All in all, if it works, why change it? Consequently, new features are just plainly *added* as new lines right into the methods or functions that apparently need them, involving fewer changes and less uncertainty.

As time passes, we get ever-worse code, and we are progressively less confident in the changes you are requested to perform to maintain or upgrade the code base. The less confident we are, the less we are incentivized to improve our design, since it requires the code to be changed. This endless loop diverges to the point where a rewrite from scratch is needed, and we lose all the value injected for months or even years in the software we are about to throw away. It's an unsustainable damage for most companies.

OK, we know that avoiding change is bad, but how can we avoid the fear of change? Working with more attention, though considered a must for every professional, may be not enough. It would be like asking a free climber to be more cautious as a security policy instead of making climbing harnesses mandatory. To remove fear, we need a safety net. A safety net is something that leaves you free to move but gently saves you in case something goes wrong. What kind of safety net is available to us?

We already learned about a safety net tool while reading this book: automated tests. We can cover our legacy code with tests, and when we have a good set of tests wrapping our system, we can make changes and quickly find bad effects caused by our changes. We still preserve our care, due to the customer as professionals, but with the quick and complete feedback we get by means of tests, we are able to make changes faster and more carefully. When we are equipped with such a safety net, the fear of change starts to fade away, motivating us to transform legacy code into a maintainable code base able to host new features very cheaply.

As long as we define legacy code as the code that becomes unmaintainable with time, we can now come to the conclusion that with adequate test coverage, legacy code doesn't deserve the "legacy" attribute anymore. Legacy code exists only where an adequate set of tests doesn't. Those kinds of tests are called *regression tests*.

Summary

In this chapter we introduced a legacy application and defined what we mean by legacy code. We learned how legacy code is created by the absence of proper test coverage, and how, from a certain perspective, an apparently well-structured software application can be considered low-quality. In the next chapter, we will show you how to face the big challenge of making a good application from a poor one. Keep reading!

CHAPTER 14

■ ■ ■

Regression Tests

The big challenge has begun. In the previous chapter we have been asked to add new features to an old PHP legacy application in a very complex company context. The application has not been maintained for a long time, since the person who developed it no longer works at the company. Management wants some new features and has absolutely no budget to rewrite it from scratch. The development team is paralyzed by this kind of situation. How could we tackle this critical situation?

Ugly But Valuable

Within many companies, there is old software that, despite its age, continues to return great value for the business processes. They are usually ignored by the entire IT department, the members of which are frightened by the thought of having to change. Users don't want new features anymore, because they know that won't have them. If this software could start to grow again, adapting to new business processes, it would be even more valuable for the company.

Throughout this book we have learned about many little refactoring techniques that allow us to maintain the value of software while we grow or maintain it, making it easier to accommodate future implementations. In this case, these small techniques cannot be applied because our code is not object-oriented, and it is not tested. So it has the worst smell that software can have.

For this kind of situation, we can't talk about "refactoring" but about "big refactoring." This term is intended to indicate major refactoring activities that take a lot of time at the beginning, but once done, they will allow us to have better software which to apply the classic refactoring to.

In the next chapters we will see how to apply some of the big refactoring techniques to transform our legacy web application, introduced in the previous chapter, into an object-oriented application that best fits the requirements of implementation and design.

Specifically we will introduce the following techniques of "big refactoring."

- Putting chaos in a cage
- Transforming procedural code into object-oriented code
- Introducing ORM instead of SQL
- Separating business logic from presentation

To demonstrate these techniques we will use the following steps:

- Write the regression tests for the application, so as not to lose value when refactoring.
- Transform procedural code into object code through the "Facade Pattern."

- Replace the SQL logic by introducing an Object Relational Mapper (ORM).

- Separate the whole application logic from presentation logic through the "MVC" and "Template View" patterns.

- Add new presentation logic to display the web application on mobile devices.

Keeping Value vs. Wasting Value

The concept of software value is complex to explain, because it can change between different companies or between different products. For example, a web portal can have great value, because the company needs it to communicate to the outside, and e-commerce is important because a certain company sells its products in markets that normally it could not reach. An intranet is important because it improves the internal company processes and knowledge, and a social software is important because it connects people and makes the company money through advertising or aggregated data selling.

The only thing all these examples have in common is that if a software has value, but cannot grow with the company or follow the market and customer requirements, that software loses value. Even the company itself loses value because it wastes money recreating the same value from scratch.

When you are afraid to modify software, and you don't have the courage to embrace the changes, first you have to understand why. Usually, the reasons are

- The code is old.

- The code is not tested.

- The code is very messy and was not designed clearly.

- The code is very large.

Usually these reasons are presented all together, which we must learn to deal with. A software that cannot be changed is a dead but walking software.

First we need to be able to change it without the risk of introducing bugs. The best tool we have at our disposal to measure the changes are automated tests. Our first goal is to put our software in a cage of regression functional tests. Through these tests we can avoid introducing bugs, since the tests will notify a failure before it is put into production.

Now we'll see a refactoring technique in the same format viewed in the previous chapters but with an extended example, where we'll learn how to test procedural code with regression functional tests.

Putting the Chaos in a Cage

Problem: "I have an untested procedural application."

Solution: "Cage the application with regression functional tests."

Motivation

When we are asked to change or add features to an untested application, the first thing we must do is confine them in regression tests.

Regression tests ensure that we can modify the application without losing the original value, since any change affecting the standard behavior will be notified directly by the tests. In this way we will be free to apply major refactoring in order to make an old application young again.

Where the application is procedural, we can use functional tests to test the macro functionality and unit tests to test the functions. If an application is already written with an object-oriented paradigm we can use unit tests.

Another advantage of writing the regression tests is to know the application domain inside. If there isn't technical documentation of the application, by writing tests, we will go inside the business logic mechanism and at the same time begin to create documentation for the application, because tests can be part of documentation.

With very large applications, we should write tests with an expert user of the software who can help us to identify all of the features, including hidden gems. The work will be a long process but it's necessary to not lose the value the software already has.

Mechanics

1. Separate the user application actions. For example, in web management common actions are related to actions on the same entity (CRUD). In the case of an intranet or internet portals, common actions are related to the navigation in a single information section (navigating a tree of content, research, etc.) and the actions possible there.

2. Prepare the fixtures to be used in testing, in order to have independent tests.

3. For each set of common actions, create a new suite of test cases.

4. For every action, add a new test case, with test navigation, assertion, and verification, especially taking care to test the critical actions that can fail.

5. Add the test case to the suite.

6. Run the test suite to make sure everything is correct.

7. Continue until you have tested all user actions.

Examples

For our examples, we will use the web application "Contacts Book," seen in the previous chapter. Following the mechanism, the first thing we must do is to separate the application into common user actions. The application is a web application that performs web actions on the contact entity. We can add, edit, read, and delete a contact record in a database.

First prepare the relevant data that will load when we start each test, so that the tests will be independent. To do this, we start doing a dump only of the data of the application and not of the structure. Once we do the dump, remove the useless records, and keep only a significant number of records per entity. Remember that, before the data is loaded, we always must empty the table, otherwise the data is added to the bottom.

```
--- fixtures/contacts.sql ---
TRUNCATE TABLE contacts;

LOCK TABLES contacts WRITE;
INSERT INTO contacts (firstname, lastname, phone, mobile) VALUES ('Jacopo', 'Romei', ↵
'0543123543', '34012345');
INSERT INTO contacts (firstname, lastname, phone, mobile) VALUES ('Francesco', 'Trucchia', ↵
'12345', '234 12345');
UNLOCK TABLES;
```

PHPUnit could support the ability to upload data in XML or CSV, but when using the extension for Selenium, we can't use this feature, because both are extensions and in PHPUnit we can use only one extension at a time. We will load the fixtures in SQL directly running a command shell.

We create the folder tests in the root of application, and put the fixtures and functional folder inside the tests folder. In the fixture folder we will put fixture files and in the functional folder we'll put all the functional tests. As mentioned previously, we make a dump of the database and save it in the fixtures folder with the name contacts.sql.

We create also a new folder called contact inside the functional folder, where we put all the test cases related by common actions we can make with the contact entity.

The result should be the following:

```
...
tests
|- fixtures
|  |- contacts.sql
|- functional
|  |- contacts
...
```

At this point, through the PHPUnit Selenium extension, we begin to write our functional tests for each action we can perform with the contact entity. The actions we can perform are:

- Add a new contact

- Edit a contact

- Display a list of contacts sorted by last name

- Remove contact

- Validate inserting or editing a contact

For each of these actions we will write a new test case, with its regression tests inside.

Add a New Record

This test is on adding a new contact record.

```php
<?php
require_once 'PHPUnit/Extensions/SeleniumTestCase.php';

class Contact_AddTest extends PHPUnit_Extensions_SeleniumTestCase
{
    function setUp()
    {
        shell_exec('mysql -u root contacts < '.dirname(__FILE__).'/../../fixtures/contacts.sql');

        $this->setBrowser("*firefox");
        $this->setBrowserUrl("http://localhost/");
    }

    function testAdd()
    {
        $this->open("/refactoring/index.php");
        $this->click("link=New contact");
```

```
        $this->waitForPageToLoad("30000");

        $this->assertEquals("Contacts Book", $this->getTitle());
        $this->assertEquals("Contacts Book", $this->getText("//div[@id='header']/h1"));

        $this->assertEquals("First Name*", $this->getText("//div[@id='content']/form/label[1]"));
        $this->assertEquals("Last Name*", $this->getText("//div[@id='content']/form/label[2]"));
        $this->assertEquals("Phone*", $this->getText("//div[@id='content']/form/label[3]"));
        $this->assertEquals("Mobile", $this->getText("//div[@id='content']/form/label[4]"));

        $this->assertTrue($this->isElementPresent("firstname"));
        $this->assertTrue($this->isElementPresent("lastname"));
        $this->assertTrue($this->isElementPresent("phone"));
        $this->assertTrue($this->isElementPresent("mobile"));
        $this->assertTrue($this->isElementPresent("link=Cancel"));

        $this->assertEquals("(* Mandatory fields)", $this->getText("//div[@id='content']/em"));
        $this->assertEquals("All © Francesco Trucchia & Jacopo Romei - Pro PHP Refactoring", ↵
$this->getText("footer"));

        $this->type("firstname", "Girolamo");
        $this->type("lastname", "Pompei");
        $this->type("phone", "098245678");
        $this->type("mobile", "3402343879");
        $this->click("//input[@value='Save']");
        $this->waitForPageToLoad("30000");

        $this->assertEquals("Pompei", $this->getTable("//div[@id='content']/table.1.0"));
        $this->assertEquals("Girolamo", $this->getTable("//div[@id='content']/table.1.1"));
        $this->assertEquals("098245678", $this->getTable("//div[@id='content']/table.1.2"));
        $this->assertEquals("3402343879", $this->getTable("//div[@id='content']/table.1.3"));
        $this->assertEquals("[X]", $this->getTable("//div[@id='content']/table.1.4"));

        $this->assertTrue($this->getXpathCount('//table/tbody/tr') == 4);

    }
}
?>
```

In the setUp() method we load the fixtures in the database, run the web browser, and set the BasePath of the application. In the testAdd() method we verify that a new record is properly inserted.

We run the tests and verify that everything is ok. We start the Selenium RC server if we have not started it before, as seen in Chapter 5.

```
$ phpunit tests/functional/contact/addTest.php
PHPUnit 3.4.1 by Sebastian Bergmann.

.

Time: 10 seconds

OK (1 test, 19 assertions)
```

Edit a Record

The second test is related to editing a contact record.

```php
<?php

require_once 'PHPUnit/Extensions/SeleniumTestCase.php';

class Contact_EditTest extends PHPUnit_Extensions_SeleniumTestCase
{
  function setUp()
  {
    shell_exec('mysql -u root contacts < '.dirname(__FILE__).'/../../fixtures/contacts.sql');

    $this->setBrowser("*firefox");
    $this->setBrowserUrl("http://localhost/");
  }

  function testEdit()
  {
    $this->open("/refactoring/index.php");

    $this->click("link=Trucchia");
    $this->waitForPageToLoad("30000");

    $this->assertEquals("Contacts Book", $this->getTitle());
    $this->assertEquals("Contacts Book", $this->getText("//div[@id='header']/h1"));

    $this->assertEquals("First Name*", $this->getText("//div[@id='content']/form/label[1]"));
    $this->assertEquals("Last Name*", $this->getText("//div[@id='content']/form/label[2]"));
    $this->assertEquals("Phone*", $this->getText("//div[@id='content']/form/label[3]"));
    $this->assertEquals("Mobile", $this->getText("//div[@id='content']/form/label[4]"));

    $this->assertTrue($this->isElementPresent("firstname"));
    $this->assertTrue($this->isElementPresent("lastname"));
    $this->assertTrue($this->isElementPresent("phone"));
    $this->assertTrue($this->isElementPresent("mobile"));
    $this->assertTrue($this->isElementPresent("link=Cancel"));

    $this->assertEquals("Francesco", $this->getValue("firstname"));
    $this->assertEquals("Trucchia", $this->getValue("lastname"));
    $this->assertEquals("12345", $this->getValue("phone"));
    $this->assertEquals("234 12345", $this->getValue("mobile"));

    $this->assertEquals("(* Mandatory fields)", $this->getText("//div[@id='content']/em"));
    $this->assertEquals("All © Francesco Trucchia & Jacopo Romei - Pro PHP Refactoring", ↵
$this->getText("footer"));

    $this->type("firstname", "Piergiacomo");
    $this->type("phone", "1234");
    $this->click("//input[@value='Save']");
    $this->waitForPageToLoad("30000");

    $this->assertEquals("Trucchia", $this->getTable("//div[@id='content']/table.2.0"));
    $this->assertEquals("Piergiacomo", $this->getTable("//div[@id='content']/table.2.1"));
```

```
        $this->assertEquals("1234", $this->getTable("//div[@id='content']/table.2.2"));
    }
}
?>
```

As in the previous test in the setUp() method, we load the fixtures in the database, start the browser, and set the base path. In the testEdit() method we verify that a record is edited in the correct way.

Run the tests and verify that everything is ok.

```
$ phpunit tests/functional/contact/EditTest.php
PHPUnit 3.4.1 by Sebastian Bergmann.

.

Time: 9 seconds

OK (1 test, 20 assertions)
```

Read a List of Records

The third test is on displaying a list of contact records.

```php
<?php

require_once 'PHPUnit/Extensions/SeleniumTestCase.php';

class Contact_ListTest extends PHPUnit_Extensions_SeleniumTestCase
{
    function setUp()
    {
        shell_exec('mysql -u root contacts < '.dirname(__FILE__).'/../../fixtures/contacts.sql');

        $this->setBrowser("*firefox");
        $this->setBrowserUrl("http://localhost/");
    }

    function testList()
    {
        $this->open("/refactoring/index.php");
        $this->assertEquals("Contacts Book", $this->getTitle());

        $this->assertEquals("Contacts Book", $this->getText("//div[@id='header']/h1"));
        $this->assertEquals("New contact", $this->getText("link=New contact"));

        $this->assertEquals("Last Name", $this->getTable("//div[@id='content']/table.0.0"));
        $this->assertEquals("First Name", $this->getTable("//div[@id='content']/table.0.1"));
        $this->assertEquals("Phone", $this->getTable("//div[@id='content']/table.0.2"));
        $this->assertEquals("Mobile", $this->getTable("//div[@id='content']/table.0.3"));


        $this->assertEquals("Romei", $this->getTable("//div[@id='content']/table.1.0"));
        $this->assertEquals("Romei", $this->getText("link=Romei"));

        $this->assertEquals("Jacopo", $this->getTable("//div[@id='content']/table.1.1"));
        $this->assertEquals("0543123543", $this->getTable("//div[@id='content']/table.1.2"));
```

271

```php
    $this->assertEquals("0543123543", $this->getText("link=0543123543"));
    $this->assertEquals("34012345", $this->getTable("//div[@id='content']/table.1.3"));
    $this->assertEquals("34012345", $this->getText("link=34012345"));
    $this->assertEquals("[X]", $this->getTable("//div[@id='content']/table.1.4"));
    $this->assertEquals("X", $this->getText("link=X"));

    $this->assertEquals("Trucchia", $this->getTable("//div[@id='content']/table.2.0"));
    $this->assertEquals("Trucchia", $this->getText("link=Trucchia"));
    $this->assertEquals("Francesco", $this->getTable("//div[@id='content']/table.2.1"));
    $this->assertEquals("12345", $this->getTable("//div[@id='content']/table.2.2"));
    $this->assertEquals("12345", $this->getText("link=12345"));
    $this->assertEquals("234 12345", $this->getTable("//div[@id='content']/table.2.3"));
    $this->assertEquals("234 12345", $this->getText("link=234 12345"));
    $this->assertEquals("[X]", $this->getTable("//div[@id='content']/table.2.4"));
  }
}
?>
```

As in the previous test in the setUp() method, we load the fixtures in the database, start the browser, and set the base path. In the testList() method, we verify that the contact list is displayed correctly.

Run the tests and verify that everything is ok.

```
$ phpunit tests/functional/contact/ListTest.php
PHPUnit 3.4.1 by Sebastian Bergmann.

.

Time: 9 seconds

OK (1 test, 24 assertions)
```

Remove a Record

This test is on removing a contact record.

```php
<?php

require_once 'PHPUnit/Extensions/SeleniumTestCase.php';

class Contact_RemoveTest extends PHPUnit_Extensions_SeleniumTestCase
{
  function setUp()
  {
    shell_exec('mysql -u root contacts < '.dirname(__FILE__).'/../../fixtures/contacts.sql');

    $this->setBrowser("*firefox");
    $this->setBrowserUrl("http://localhost/");
  }

  function testRemove()
  {
    $this->open("/refactoring/index.php");

    $this->assertEquals(3, $this->getXpathCount('//table/tbody/tr'));
    $this->assertEquals("Romei", $this->getTable("//div[@id='content']/table.1.0"));
```

```
        $this->assertEquals("Trucchia", $this->getTable("//div[@id='content']/table.2.0"));

        // Delete first record
        $this->click("//div[@id='content']/table/tbody/tr[2]/td[5]/a");
        $this->assertEquals('Are you sure?', $this->getConfirmation());
        $this->chooseOkOnNextConfirmation();

        $this->assertEquals(2, $this->getXpathCount('//table/tbody/tr'));
        $this->assertEquals("Trucchia", $this->getTable("//div[@id='content']/table.1.0"));
    }
}
?>
```

As in the previous test in the setUp() method, we load the fixtures in the database, start the browser, and set the base path. In the testRemove() method, we verify that a contact record is successfully deleted from our contact list.

Run the tests and verify that everything is ok.

```
$ phpunit tests/functional/contact/RemoveTest.php
PHPUnit 3.4.1 by Sebastian Bergmann.


.


Time: 8 seconds

OK (1 test, 3 assertions)
```

Validate a Record

This test is on validating a record when we insert a new one or modify an existing one.

```
<?php

require_once 'PHPUnit/Extensions/SeleniumTestCase.php';

class Contact_ValidateTest extends PHPUnit_Extensions_SeleniumTestCase
{
    function setUp()
    {
        shell_exec('mysql -u root contacts < '.dirname(__FILE__).'/../../fixtures/contacts.sql');

        $this->setBrowser("*firefox");
        $this->setBrowserUrl("http://localhost/");
    }

    function testValidation()
    {
        $this->open("/refactoring/index.php");
        $this->click("link=New contact");
        $this->waitForPageToLoad("30000");

        $this->click("//input[@value='Save']");
        $this->waitForPageToLoad("30000");
```

```
    $this->assertEquals("The firstname field is mandatory", ↩
$this->getText("//div[@id='content']/form/ul/li[1]"));
    $this->assertEquals("The lastname field is mandatory", ↩
$this->getText("//div[@id='content']/form/ul/li[2]"));
    $this->assertEquals("The phone field is mandatory", ↩
$this->getText("//div[@id='content']/form/ul/li[3]"));

    $this->assertTrue($this->getXpathCount("//div[@id='content']/form/ul/li") == 3);

    $this->type("firstname", "Francesco");
    $this->click("//input[@value='Save']");
    $this->waitForPageToLoad("30000");

    $this->assertEquals("The lastname field is mandatory", ↩
$this->getText("//div[@id='content']/form/ul/li[1]"));
    $this->assertEquals("The phone field is mandatory", ↩
$this->getText("//div[@id='content']/form/ul/li[2]"));

    $this->assertTrue($this->getXpathCount("//div[@id='content']/form/ul/li") == 2);
    $this->assertEquals("Francesco", $this->getValue("firstname"));

    $this->type("lastname", "Trucchia");
    $this->click("//input[@value='Save']");
    $this->waitForPageToLoad("30000");

    $this->assertEquals("The phone field is mandatory", ↩
$this->getText("//div[@id='content']/form/ul/li[1]"));

    $this->assertTrue($this->getXpathCount("//div[@id='content']/form/ul/li") == 1);

  }
}
?>
```

As in the previous test in the setUp() method, we load the fixtures in the database, start the browser, and set the base path. In the testValidate() method, we verify that the validation system works correctly when we add and modify a contact record.

Run the tests and verify that everything is ok.

```
$ phpunit tests/functional/contact/ValidateTest.php
PHPUnit 3.4.1 by Sebastian Bergmann.

.

Time: 9 seconds

OK (1 test, 10 assertions)
```

Test Refactoring

If we look at the code written so far for our tests, do we notice any familiar bad smells? Well, we would say yes, the setUp() method is the same in all tests, and duplicate code is a bad smell. Remember that the tests, both functional and unit, must be maintained like the rest of our code, so that we have simple tests that are written clearly. To improve the code of our tests written so far, we can apply two refactoring techniques, "Extract Super Class" and "Move Method."

Through the "Extract Super Class" technique we create a new class, which we will call Contacts_TestCase, which extends PHPUnit_Extensions_SeleniumTestCase, and we move within it the setUp() method. At this point all our tests should extend the class Contacts_TestCase.

```php
require_once 'PHPUnit/Extensions/SeleniumTestCase.php';

class ContactsTestCase extends PHPUnit_Extensions_SeleniumTestCase
{
  function setUp()
  {
    shell_exec('mysql -u root contacts < '.dirname(__FILE__).'/../fixtures/contacts.sql');

    $this->setBrowser("*firefox");
    $this->setBrowserUrl("http://localhost/");
  }
}

...

class Contact_AddTest extends ContactsTestCase {...}

...

class Contact_EditTest extends ContactsTestCase {...}

...

class Contact_ListTest extends ContactsTestCase {...}

...

class Contact_RemoveTest extends ContactsTestCase{...}

...

class Contact_ValidateTest extends ContactsTestCase {...}
```

In this way we will not have duplicated code, and it will be easier to maintain our functional tests. Run the tests again and check that everything is still correct.

```
$ phpunit tests/functional/contact/
PHPUnit 3.4.1 by Sebastian Bergmann.

.....

Time: 45 seconds

OK (5 tests, 76 assertions)
```

Unify Test Cases in a Suite

We added all the tests for the contact entity. Now we can group them into a suite test, so we can organize them in the best way. We create a suite.php file inside the functional folder with the following class:

```php
<?php
require_once('AddTest.php');
require_once('EditTest.php');
```

```php
require_once('ListTest.php');
require_once('RemoveTest.php');
require_once('ValidateTest.php');

class Contact_Suite extends PHPUnit_Framework_TestSuite
{
  public static function suite()
  {
    $suite = new PHPUnit_Framework_TestSuite('Contact');
    $suite->addTestSuite('Contact_AddTest');
    $suite->addTestSuite('Contact_EditTest');
    $suite->addTestSuite('Contact_ListTest');
    $suite->addTestSuite('Contact_RemoveTest');
    $suite->addTestSuite('Contact_ValidateTest');

    return $suite;
  }
}
?>
```

Now we can use this suite class to run tests.

Summary

In this chapter we have begun the process of "big refactoring" of an old PHP application in order to add new features without losing the value of the application itself. We learned how to cage our application in functional regression tests so that we can detect bad changes in our refactoring work when they happen.

In the next chapter we'll learn how to improve the quality of procedural code with techniques of refactoring according to patterns.

■ ■ ■

CHAPTER 15

Refactoring with Patterns

In this chapter we will see how some big refactoring techniques can improve the design of a procedural PHP application by refactoring with design patterns. All of the techniques attempt to solve common design problems with many common models, which helps us make the design of our application better and easier to maintain. Big refactoring techniques, in contrast to refactoring techniques, require a lot of time and care, because we are changing the software at the architectural level. We explain the mechanisms of big refactoring techniques using the legacy PHP application used in previous chapters.

If you are completely refactoring a procedural PHP application, follow the techniques in the same order suggested; otherwise you can also apply the techniques one by one as needed.

Design Patterns

The big refactoring techniques we use in this chapter use some object-oriented design patterns and architectural patterns often used for developing PHP applications to solve design problems. What are the design patterns, why do you need to use them, and when can you use them?

What Are Design Patterns?

> *Each pattern describes a problem which occurs over and over again in our environment, and then describes the core of the solution to that problem, in such a way that you can use this solution a million times over, without ever doing it the same way twice.*

—Christopher Alexander [AIS+77]

In PHP, as in many other object-oriented languages, you can apply design patterns, because they are not related to languages but to models of common solutions.

The patterns are divided into object-oriented patterns, which typically show relationships and interactions between classes and objects, and architectural patterns that, at the highest level, describe how the system components communicate with each other. One famous architectural pattern is Model View Control.

The difference between an algorithm and a design pattern is that the first solves computational problems, while the second is related to the design aspects of the software.

The most famous design patterns have been cataloged by the Gang of Four [GOF] and are divided into these groups:

- **Creational:** Solve problems relating to the creation of dynamic objects on the fly.

- **Structural:** Allow reuse of existing objects by providing users with a more suitable interface.

- **Behavior:** Resolve all common problems associated with the interaction between objects.

Each category has a collection of patterns suitable for solving a certain set of common design problems.

There are also other types of design patterns:

- **Architectural:** Solve problems related to communication between macro components in large systems.

- **Methodology:** Solve problems through the use of methodologies.

- **Competition:** Solve problems related to concurrent programming and transmission of objects in concurrent environments.

Why Do I Need to Use Design Patterns?

As engineers, our daily task is to find design solutions to known problems. In my experience as a PHP developer I've read a lot of code written by different developers that, while solving similar problems, presented very different design, making it difficult to understand the solution. If a problem is known, why doesn't everyone apply a similar solution from a model that is equally well known?

Using design patterns to solve common problems greatly simplifies the understanding of the software, because we do not have to reinvent the wheel every time. When you recognize the pattern in the code, you instantly understand that component design.

Communication within a team and solving design problems with design patterns become much clearer when you can explain the solution in minutes.

When Do I Need to Use Them?

Design patterns are used as much as possible when programming with objects. If you can identify the solution to a problem in a pattern, it should be used. There are no contraindications for using design patterns. As for refactoring, the important thing is to follow the right model—you can't create hybrid models that don't conform to the pattern. Sometimes we can't immediately recognize a problem in a certain pattern, but we can always solve it in the simplest way and then change the design to design patterns with refactoring.

Refactoring with Patterns

In some of the techniques we will see later, we will try to apply refactoring techniques to solve the design problems of a procedural application through design patterns. Specifically we will apply the Façade pattern to transform the procedural code into object code, the Template View pattern and the Decorator Design pattern to separate the business logic from the representational logic, and, finally, the MVC pattern to further improve the design of our application and decouple its components.

Transform Procedural Code into Object-Oriented Code

Problem: "A PHP application is written in procedural code."

Solution: "Using the Façade pattern, we transform the code from procedural to object-oriented."

Motivation

PHP is characterized by its procedural nature and simplicity of use, due to a very permissive language. PHP 4 has very basic object support, and most of the applications using that version are written in a procedural manner. The presence of procedural code is a bad smell if we plan to code with objects, because procedural software is very difficult to maintain. For these reasons, there are important applications for some companies that cannot longer grow because they are written with PHP 4 and are now difficult to change.

With this technique we will learn how to begin the transformation from procedural code to object-oriented code. Obviously it is first necessary to bring the software to PHP 5 before starting this process. The migration from PHP4 to PHP5 is not covered in this book, but I recommend reading the official manual section on the php.net portal[1], and the book *php|architect's Guide to PHP 5 Migration* [PRI08].

Design patterns help us in solving this long-standing problem, and the specific pattern that we will use to solve this design problem is the structural pattern Façade (shown in Figure 15-1).

> *Façade provides a unified interface to a set of interfaces in a subsystem. Façade defines a higher-level interface that makes the subsystem easier to use.*

> —Erich Gamma [GOF]

The typical architecture of procedural software written in PHP consists of a set of scripts, which can be accessed through a certain URL. Each script typically performs a series of common operations that can be driven by parameters passing via POST or GET. If we see each of these scripts as a complex interface to query, the Façade pattern can solve the problem of simplifying these interfaces.

---

[1] PHP migration, www.php.net/manual/en/migration5.php.

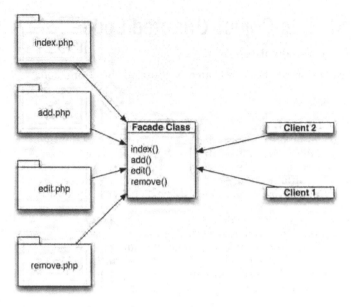

Figure 15-1. The Façade structural pattern

Mechanism

1. Identify which methods you need to create in the Façade class. The methods coincide with the PHP scripts you can call from an URL.

2. Create a new test case for the Façade class also called the Main class.

3. Prepare the fixtures and configure the test cases to load them.

For each class method Main identified, carry out the following steps:

1. Create functional tests verifying that the method has the correct behavior even if the request doesn't pass through a web server.

2. Extract the PHP code from the script and create a new method in the Main class with script code.

3. Adjust the code where necessary.

4. Run unit tests and verify that the behavior has not changed.

5. Replace in script procedural code with a new instance of Main class and call the method just created.

6. Run the functional tests previously prepared and verify that the behavior is unchanged.

Example

In the following example we will use the PHP legacy application "Contacts Book," already shown in previous chapters. The application has been caged in functional tests in Chapter 14, and these tests will ensure consistency of behavior in this process of big refactoring.

The first thing we need to do is identify what scripts we can call from an URL. Looking through the code we see that the scripts we can call are the following:

- index.php
- new.php
- edit.php
- remove.php

Then we will create four methods in the Main class that will replace procedural PHP code in our scripts. The methods are

- index()
- add()
- edit()
- remove()

Working with Fixtures

In Chapter 5 we saw that PHPUnit supports loading fixtures in the database from XML and CSV files. We use this feature to load data in our database. It's important that data is reloaded for each test to ensure independence between unit tests. With our favorite tools, export the database in .csv format, adjusted according to the PHPUnit specifications, and save it in the folder tests/fixtures/contacts.csv.

Now we can start writing a unit test for the Main class that we call ContactsBookMain, so we call the test case class ContactsBookMainTest.

```
--- tests/unit/ContactsBookMainTest.php ---

require_once 'PHPUnit/Extensions/Database/TestCase.php';
require_once 'PHPUnit/Extensions/Database/DataSet/CsvDataSet.php';
require_once dirname(__FILE__).'/../../lib/ContactsBookMain.php';

class ContactsBookMainTest extends PHPUnit_Extensions_Database_TestCase
{

  protected function getConnection()
  {
    $pdo = new PDO('mysql:host=localhost;dbname=contacts', 'root', '');
    return $this->createDefaultDBConnection($pdo, 'contacts');
  }

  protected function getDataSet()
  {
    $dataSet = new PHPUnit_Extensions_Database_DataSet_CsvDataSet();
    $dataSet->addTable('contacts', dirname(__FILE__).'/../fixtures/contacts.csv');

    return $dataSet;
  }
}
```

The class extends the class of the PHPUnit framework PHPUnit_Extensions_Database_TestCase, which implements the interface to load the fixtures database from CSV files.

Next we will see the implementation of each method of the Façade class ContactsBookMain that simplifies the method we will use to simplify calls within the script application.

Index Action

The first method we implement is the index method that coincides with the call to the index.php script. We write the unit test and we verify that the output of the method is a valid DOM document. We do this check because the output of a call to index.php is a valid DOM document. To test the output we use the PHP output control functions.

```
--- tests/unit/ContactsBookMainTest.php ---
...
class ContactsBookMainTest extends PHPUnit_Extensions_Database_TestCase
{
  ...
  public function testIndex()
  {
    ob_start();
    $contacts_book_main = new ContactsBookMain();
    $contacts_book_main->index();
    $output = ob_get_contents();
    ob_end_clean();
    ob_end_flush();

    error_reporting(E_ALL | E_STRICT);

    try
    {
      $dom = new DOMDocument();
      $dom->loadHTML($output);
    }
    catch (Exception $e)
    {
      $this->fail('Not valid dom document - '.$e->getMessage());
    }
  }
}
```

It is recommended, almost required, to write unit tests so that all PHP errors occur. Since the application sets errors such as E_ALL & ~ E_NOTICE, it could probably hide some surprises. To prevent this kind of surprise and to ensure that we identify all errors, we again set error reporting to E_ALL | E_STRICT after the call to the index() method.

Now we can run the unit test. First it fails because the class ContactsBookMain doesn't exist. We create it, and then the unit test fails because the index() method doesn't exist. We create it, too, extracting the code from the index.php script in the method. We adjust the code where needed. Pay attention to PHP open and close tags, and fix the path of the file included.

```
--- lib/ContactsBookMain.php ---
...
class ContactsBookMain
{
```

```php
public static function index()
{

include(dirname(__FILE__).'/../config.php');

$db = @mysql_connect($database['host'], $database['username'], $database['password'])
    or die('Can\'t connect do database');

    @mysql_select_db($database['name'])
    or die('The database selected does not exists');

$query = 'SELECT * FROM contacts ORDER BY lastname';
$rs = mysql_query($query);

if (!$rs)
{
  die_with_error(mysql_error(), $query);
}

$num = mysql_num_rows($rs);

?>

<?php include(dirname(__FILE__).'/../header.php') ?>

<div class="actions">
  <a href="new.php">New contact</a>
 </div>

<?php if ($num) : ?>
  <table border="1" cellspacing="0" cellpadding="5">
  <tr>
    <th>Last Name</th>
    <th>First Name</th>
    <th>Phone</th>
    <th>Mobile</th>
    <th> </th>
  </tr>
  <?php while($row = mysql_fetch_assoc($rs)) :?>
    <tr>
      <td><a href="edit.php?id=<?php echo $row['id']?>" title="Edit"><?php echo ↵
$row['lastname']?></a></td>
      <td><?php echo $row['firstname']?></a></td>
      <td><a href="callto://<?php echo $row['phone']?>"><?php echo $row['phone']?></a></td>
      <td><a href="callto://<?php echo $row['mobile']?>"><?php echo $row['mobile']?></a></td>
      <td>[<a href="remove.php?id=<?php echo $row['id']?>" title="Delete" onclick="if ↵
(confirm('Are you sure?')) {return true;} return false;">X</a>]</td>
    </tr>
  <?php endwhile;?>
  </table>

 <?php else: ?>
  Database is empty
<?php endif ?>

<?php include(dirname(__FILE__).'/../footer.php') ?>
```

```php
<?php
  mysql_free_result($rs);
  mysql_close($db);
  }
}
```

We run the test and there is another failure.

```
$ phpunit tests/unit/ContactsBookMainTest.php
PHPUnit 3.4.1 by Sebastian Bergmann.

F

Time: 0 seconds

There was 1 failure:

1) ContactsBookMainTest::testIndex
Not valid dom document - DOMDocument::loadHTML(): Unexpected end tag : a in Entity, line: 65

/Users/cphp/Dropbox/Progetti/Libri/Apress/ProPHPRefactoring/chapters/bundled_code/↵
bigrefactoring/tests/unit/ContactsBookMainTest.php:43

FAILURES!
Tests: 1, Assertions: 0, Failures: 1.
```

Oops—this is a bug. The HTML created by our application is not a valid DOM document. While doing refactoring we can find bugs. We fix the bug, deleting the unexpected tag, and run the test again.

```php
--- lib/ContactsBookMain.php ---
...
public static function index()
{
  ...
    <td><?php echo $row['firstname']?></td>
  ...
}
```

After running the test we find another unexpected error with the "&" character not admitted in the footer. We change "&" with the HTML entity "&" and run the test again.

```php
--- footer.php ---
...
All &copy; Francesco Trucchia &amp; Jacopo Romei - Pro PHP Refactoring
...
```

Now the tests are OK.

```
$ phpunit tests/unit/ContactsBookMainTest.php
PHPUnit 3.4.1 by Sebastian Bergmann.

.

Time: 0 seconds

OK (1 test, 0 assertions)
```

Now we integrate the unit test to verify that the HTML output is correct. We use the functional test that we created for Selenium as a starting point. Not using the extension for Selenium, we don't have the same methods to query the DOM. However, using the XPath object is useful to make queries in the DOM document, and we can easily do the same checks.

```
--- tests/unit/ContactsBookMainTest.php ---
...
class ContactsBookMainTest extends PHPUnit_Extensions_Database_TestCase
{
  ...
  public function testIndex()
  {
    ...
    $xpath = new DOMXPath($dom);

    $this->assertEquals('Contacts Book', $this->getText($xpath, '//head/title'));
    $this->assertEquals('Contacts Book', $this->getText($xpath, '//div[@id="header"]/h1'));
    $this->assertEquals('New contact', $this->getText($xpath, '//div[@class="actions"]/a'));

    $this->assertEquals('Last Name', $this->getText($xpath, '//table/tr/th[1]'));
    $this->assertEquals('First Name', $this->getText($xpath, '//table/tr/th[2]'));
    $this->assertEquals('Phone', $this->getText($xpath, '//table/tr/th[3]'));
    $this->assertEquals('Mobile', $this->getText($xpath, '//table/tr/th[4]'));

    $this->assertEquals('Romei', $this->getText($xpath, '//table/tr[2]/td[1]'));
    $this->assertEquals('Romei', $this->getText($xpath, '//table/tr[2]/td[1]/a'));
    $this->assertEquals('Jacopo', $this->getText($xpath, '//table/tr[2]/td[2]'));
    $this->assertEquals('0543123543', $this->getText($xpath, '//table/tr[2]/td[3]'));
    $this->assertEquals('0543123543', $this->getText($xpath, '//table/tr[2]/td[3]/a'));
    $this->assertEquals('34012345', $this->getText($xpath, '//table/tr[2]/td[4]'));
    $this->assertEquals('34012345', $this->getText($xpath, '//table/tr[2]/td[4]/a'));
    $this->assertEquals('[X]', $this->getText($xpath, '//table/tr[2]/td[5]'));
    $this->assertEquals('X', $this->getText($xpath, '//table/tr[2]/td[5]/a'));

    $this->assertEquals('Trucchia', $this->getText($xpath, '//table/tr[3]/td[1]'));
    $this->assertEquals('Trucchia', $this->getText($xpath, '//table/tr[3]/td[1]/a'));
    $this->assertEquals('Francesco', $this->getText($xpath, '//table/tr[3]/td[2]'));
    $this->assertEquals('12345', $this->getText($xpath, '//table/tr[3]/td[3]'));
    $this->assertEquals('12345', $this->getText($xpath, '//table/tr[3]/td[3]/a'));
    $this->assertEquals('234 12345', $this->getText($xpath, '//table/tr[3]/td[4]'));
    $this->assertEquals('234 12345', $this->getText($xpath, '//table/tr[3]/td[4]/a'));
    $this->assertEquals('[X]', $this->getText($xpath, '//table/tr[3]/td[5]'));
    $this->assertEquals('X', $this->getText($xpath, '//table/tr[3]/td[5]/a'));
  }

  private function getText(DOMXPath $xpath, $query)
  {
    if ($xpath->query($query)->length == 0)
    {
      throw new Exception('Text not found in query ' . $query);
    }

    return $xpath->query($query)->item(0)->nodeValue;
  }
}
```

We run the test again and verify that all assertions are correct. Once the correctness of the test has been verified, we must use the method index() of the class ContactsBookMain in our application, replacing the code in index.php with it.

```
--- index.php ---
require_once('lib/ContactsBookMain.php');

$contacts_book_main = new ContactsBookMain();
$contacts_book_main->index();
```

To be sure that our first step in refactoring is going to succeed, we run all tests, both functional and unit.

```
PHPUnit 3.4.1 by Sebastian Bergmann.

......

Time: 44 seconds

OK (6 tests, 101 assertions)
```

Add Action

After the index action, we turn to the second action, adding a new contact record. As we have seen, first of all we create a new unit test that verifies the creation of a new record. As for the other tests, we use the same strategy and verify that the output the method add() returns is a valid DOM document.

```
--- tests/unit/ContactsBookMainTest.php ---
...
class ContactsBookMainTest extends PHPUnit_Extensions_Database_TestCase
{
  ...
  public function testAdd()
  {
    ob_start();
    $contacts_book_main = new ContactsBookMain();
    $contacts_book_main->add();
    $output = ob_get_contents();
    ob_end_clean();

    error_reporting(E_ALL | E_STRICT);

    try
    {
      $dom = new DOMDocument();
      $dom->loadHTML($output);
    }
    catch (Exception $e)
    {
      $this->fail('Not valid dom document - '.$e->getMessage());
    }

    $xpath = new DOMXPath($dom);
  }
}
```

We create the add() method in the class ContactsBookMain and we copy inside the code of a new.php script, adjusting the paths of included files and PHP tags.

```
--- lib/ContactsBookMain.php ---
...
class ContactsBookMain
{
  ...
  public static function add()
  {

    include(dirname(__FILE__).'/../config.php');

    if($_SERVER['REQUEST_METHOD'] == 'POST')
    {
      $errors = validate(array('firstname', 'lastname', 'phone'), $_POST);

      if(count($errors) == 0)
      {
        $db = @mysql_connect($database['host'], $database['username'], $database['password']) ↵
or die('Can\'t connect do database');
        @mysql_select_db($database['name']) or die('The database selected does not exists');

        $query = sprintf("INSERT INTO contacts (firstname, lastname, phone, mobile) VALUES ↵
('%s', '%s', '%s', '%s')",
                              mysql_real_escape_string($_POST['firstname']),
                              mysql_real_escape_string($_POST['lastname']),
                              mysql_real_escape_string($_POST['phone']),
                              mysql_real_escape_string($_POST['mobile'])
                            );

        $rs = mysql_query($query);

        if (!$rs)
        {
          die_with_error(mysql_error(), $query);
        }

        mysql_close($db);

        header('Location: index.php');

      }
    }
    ?>

    <?php include(dirname(__FILE__).'/../header.php') ?>
    <?php include(dirname(__FILE__).'/../_form.php') ?>
    <?php include(dirname(__FILE__).'/../footer.php'); ?>
  }
}
```

We run the test, and it fails.

```
PHPUnit 3.4.1 by Sebastian Bergmann.

.E

Time: O seconds

There was 1 error:

1) ContactsBookMainTest::testNew
Undefined index:  REQUEST_METHOD

bigrefactoring/lib/ContactsBookMain.php:72
bigrefactoring/tests/unit/ContactsBookMainTest.php:92

FAILURES!
Tests: 2, Assertions: 25, Errors: 1.
```

After the test we notice that the index REQUEST_METHOD of the super global variable $_SERVER is not set. That's right, because we are in the CLI environment and not in the web environment. PHP CLI doesn't populate the super global variable $_SERVER as does PHP on the web. Therefore we introduce the method setUp() in tests that will create the PHP environment like we're on the web.

```
--- tests/unit/ContactsBookMainTest.php ---
...
class ContactsBookMainTest extends PHPUnit_Extensions_Database_TestCase
{
  ...
  public function setUp()
  {
    parent::setUp();
    $_SERVER['REQUEST_METHOD'] = 'GET';
  }
}
...
```

We perform the test ContactsBookMainTest again and it fails again.

```
PHPUnit 3.4.1 by Sebastian Bergmann.

.

    <form method="post">

<input type="hidden" name="id" value="E

Time: O seconds

There was 1 error:

1) ContactsBookMainTest::testAdd
Undefined index:  id

/Users/cphp/Dropbox/Progetti/Libri/Apress/ProPHPRefactoring/chapters/bundled_code/↵
bigrefactoring/_form.php:11
```

```
/Users/cphp/Dropbox/Progetti/Libri/Apress/ProPHPRefactoring/chapters/bundled_code/↵
bigrefactoring/lib/ContactsBookMain.php:105
/Users/cphp/Dropbox/Progetti/Libri/Apress/ProPHPRefactoring/chapters/bundled_code/↵
bigrefactoring/tests/unit/ContactsBookMainTest.php:97

FAILURES!
Tests: 2, Assertions: 25, Errors: 1.
```

The test fails again due to a bug that was already in our application but that we find only now, as we have ability to E_STRICT errors. The test fails because the index "ID" in the super global variable $_POST is not set. This is correct when the form is empty; it was our code that didn't check the condition. Finding bugs while you do refactoring always makes you feel good. Fix the bug by checking if the index is set, then print it, otherwise print an empty string. Add the same condition in all other form fields.

```
--- form.php ---
...
<input type="hidden" name="id" value="<?php echo isset($_POST['id'])?$_POST['id']:''?>" />
...
```

We run the unit test again and everything is running correctly. Having fixed a bug, before going forward, we run all the tests and verify that all functional tests still resolve properly. Only with green text can we continue our work. At this point we increase the unit test checking the output of the form and the correct creation of a record. Like the previous test, we use the functional test AddTest as a starting point for the unit test code and fix it a little bit because we don't use a Selenium extension here.

```
--- tests/unit/ContactsBookMainTest.php ---
...
class ContactsBookMainTest extends PHPUnit_Extensions_Database_TestCase
{
  ...
  private function isElementPresent(DOMXPath $xpath, $query)
  {
    if ($xpath->query($query)->length == 0)
    {
      throw new Exception('Element with name '.$name.' not found');
    }

    return true;
  }

  private function type($name, $value)
  {
    $_POST[$name] = $value;
  }

  public function testAdd()
  {
    ...
    $xpath = new DOMXPath($dom);

    $this->assertEquals('Contacts Book', $this->getText($xpath, '//head/title'));
    $this->assertEquals('Contacts Book', $this->getText($xpath, '//div[@id="header"]/h1'));

    $this->assertEquals("First Name*", $this->getText($xpath, ↵
"//div[@id='content']/form/label[1]"));
    $this->assertEquals("Last Name*", $this->getText($xpath, ↵
"//div[@id='content']/form/label[2]"));
```

```
    $this->assertEquals("Phone*", $this->getText($xpath, "//div[@id='content']/form/label[3]"));
    $this->assertEquals("Mobile", $this->getText($xpath, "//div[@id='content']/form/label[4]"));

    $this->assertTrue($this->isElementPresent($xpath, '//input[@name="firstname"]'));
    $this->assertTrue($this->isElementPresent($xpath, '//input[@name="lastname"]'));
    $this->assertTrue($this->isElementPresent($xpath, '//input[@name="phone"]'));
    $this->assertTrue($this->isElementPresent($xpath, '//input[@name="mobile"]'));
    $this->assertEquals("Cancel", $this->getText($xpath, "//a"));

    $this->assertEquals("(* Mandatory fields)", $this->getText($xpath, ↩
"//div[@id='content']/em"));
    $this->assertRegExp("/All © Francesco Trucchia &grave; Jacopo Romei - Pro PHP Refactoring/",
$this->getText($xpath, '//div[@id="footer"]'));

    $this->type("firstname", "Girolamo");
    $this->type("lastname", "Pompei");
    $this->type("phone", "098245678");
    $this->type("mobile", "3402343879");

    $_SERVER['REQUEST_METHOD'] = 'POST';

    $contacts_book_main->add();
    }
}
```

To comply with the interfaces used in our functional tests, we have created the new methods isElementPresent(), which checks for an element within the document, and type(), which populates the super global variable $_POST. At the end of the test we simulate a POST call to verify that the record is inserted. We launch the test and the test fails.

```
PHPUnit 3.4.1 by Sebastian Bergmann.

.E

Time: 1 second

There was 1 error:

1) ContactsBookMainTest::testAdd
Cannot modify header information - headers already sent by (output started at
/Applications/MAMP/bin/php5/lib/php/PHPUnit/Util/Printer.php:173)

bigrefactoring/lib/ContactsBookMain.php:97
bigrefactoring/tests/unit/ContactsBookMainTest.php:163

FAILURES!
Tests: 2, Assertions: 38, Errors: 1.
```

The test fails because our code calls the header() function, which cannot be called here, because the headers are already sent by the test environment. We can use the error to test that the behavior is correct, because this error ensures that the function header() is called. To capture the error we use the PHP try catch construct.

```
--- tests/unit/ContactsBookMainTest.php ---
...
class ContactsBookMainTest extends PHPUnit_Extensions_Database_TestCase
{
  ...
  public function testAdd()
  {
    ...
    try
    {
      ContactsBookMain::add();
      $this->fail();
    }
    catch(Exception $e)
    {
      $this->assertRegExp('/Cannot modify header information/', $e->getMessage());
    }
  }
}
```

We run the test and now it passes.

```
PHPUnit 3.4.1 by Sebastian Bergmann.

...

Time: 0 seconds

OK (3 tests, 39 assertions)
```

Now we can replace the procedural code of the new.php script with a call to the add() method of the
ContactsBookMain class.

```
--- new.php ---
require_once('lib/ContactsBookMain.php');

$contacts_book_main = new ContactsBookMain();
$contacts_book_main->add();
```

Finally we run all tests and verify that the behavior of our application has not changed.

Edit Action

As already seen in the refactoring of the two previous actions, first of all we prepare the unit test for the
new method edit() of the ContactsBookMain class and check that the output of the methods is a valid DOM
document passing the ID of the record in GET parameters.

```
--- tests/unit/ContactsBookMainTest.php ---
...
class ContactsBookMainTest extends PHPUnit_Extensions_Database_TestCase
{
  ...
  public function testEdit()
  {
```

```
    $_GET['id'] = 1;

    ob_start();
    $contacts_book_main = new ContactsBookMain();
    $contacts_book_main->edit();
    $output = ob_get_contents();
    ob_end_clean();

    error_reporting(E_ALL | E_STRICT);

    try
    {
      $dom = new DOMDocument();
      $dom->loadHTML($output);
    }
    catch (Exception $e)
    {
      $this->fail('Not valid dom document - '.$e->getMessage());
    }

    $xpath = new DOMXPath($dom);
  }
  ...
}
```

We implement the edit() method and copy the code in the edit.php script to the new method. As we did previously, we fix the code where needed and modify the path of included files.

```
--- lib/ContactsBookMain.php ---
...
class ContactsBookMain
{
  ...
  public static function edit()
  {
    include(dirname(__FILE__).'/../config.php');

    if(!$_GET['id'])
    {
     die('Some error occured!!');
    }

    $db = @mysql_connect($database['host'], $database['username'], $database['password']) ↵
or die('Can\'t connect do database');
    @mysql_select_db($database['name']) or die('The database selected does not exists');

    if($_SERVER['REQUEST_METHOD'] == 'POST')
    {
      $errors = validate(array('id', 'firstname', 'lastname', 'phone'), $_POST);

      if(count($errors) == 0)
      {
        $query = sprintf("UPDATE contacts set firstname = '%s',
                                               lastname = '%s',
                                               phone = '%s',
                                               mobile = '%s' WHERE id = %s",
```

```php
                          mysql_real_escape_string($_POST['firstname']),
                          mysql_real_escape_string($_POST['lastname']),
                          mysql_real_escape_string($_POST['phone']),
                          mysql_real_escape_string($_POST['mobile']),
                          mysql_real_escape_string($_POST['id'])
                        );

      $rs = mysql_query($query);

      if (!$rs)
      {
        die_with_error(mysql_error(), $query);
      }

      header('Location: index.php');
    }
  }
  else
  {
    $query = sprintf('SELECT * FROM contacts WHERE id = %s', ↵
mysql_real_escape_string($_GET['id']));

    $rs = mysql_query($query);

    if (!$rs)
    {
      die_with_error(mysql_error(), $query);
    }

    $row = mysql_fetch_assoc($rs);

    $_POST['id'] = $row['id'];
    $_POST['firstname'] = $row['firstname'];
    $_POST['lastname'] = $row['lastname'];
    $_POST['phone'] = $row['phone'];
    $_POST['mobile'] = $row['mobile'];
  }

  mysql_close($db);

  ?>

  <?php include(dirname(__FILE__).'/../header.php') ?>

  <?php include(dirname(__FILE__).'/../_form.php') ?>

  <?php include(dirname(__FILE__).'/../footer.php'); ?>
  }
}
```

We run the test and make sure everything is correct.

```
PHPUnit 3.4.1 by Sebastian Bergmann.

...

Time: 0 seconds

OK (3 tests, 39 assertions)
```

Looking at our test class, we note that in the methods testIndex(), testAdd(), and testEdit() there is a piece of duplicated code that calls a different method of ContactsBookMain but always gets output and verifies the validity of the DOM document. For the rule of three times, this portion of code should be refactored. Through the "Extract Method" technique we create a new assertDomReturnXPath() method, moving the block of code and replacing all of the duplicate blocks of code or other methods with the method we just created.

```
...
class ContactsBookMainTest extends PHPUnit_Extensions_Database_TestCase
{
  ...
  private function assertDomReturnXPath($action)
  {
    ob_start();
    $contacts_book_main = new ContactsBookMain();
    $contacts_book_main->$action();
    $output = ob_get_contents();
    ob_end_clean();

    error_reporting(E_ALL | E_STRICT);

    try
    {
      $dom = new DOMDocument();
      $dom->loadHTML($output);
    }
    catch (Exception $e)
    {
      $this->fail('Not valid dom document - '.$e->getMessage());
    }

    return new DOMXPath($dom);
  }
  ...
  public function testEdit()
  {
    $_GET['id'] = 1;

    $xpath = $this->assertDomReturnXPath('edit');
  }
}
```

After performing this step of refactoring, we go on integrating our method testEdit() with more assertions. As with other actions we use the functional test EditTest as a starting point and we fix our calls where needed.

```
...
class ContactsBookMainTest extends PHPUnit_Extensions_Database_TestCase
{
  ...
  public function testEdit()
  {
    $_GET['id'] = 1;

    $xpath = $this->assertDomReturnXPath('edit');

    $this->assertEquals('Contacts Book', $this->getText($xpath, '//head/title'));
    $this->assertEquals('Contacts Book', $this->getText($xpath, '//div[@id="header"]/h1'));

    $this->assertEquals("First Name*", $this->getText($xpath, ↵
"//div[@id='content']/form/label[1]"));
    $this->assertEquals("Last Name*", $this->getText($xpath, ↵
"//div[@id='content']/form/label[2]"));
    $this->assertEquals("Phone*", $this->getText($xpath, "//div[@id='content']/form/label[3]"));
    $this->assertEquals("Mobile", $this->getText($xpath, "//div[@id='content']/form/label[4]"));

    $this->assertTrue($this->isElementPresent($xpath, '//input[@name="firstname"]'));
    $this->assertTrue($this->isElementPresent($xpath, '//input[@name="lastname"]'));
    $this->assertTrue($this->isElementPresent($xpath, '//input[@name="phone"]'));
    $this->assertTrue($this->isElementPresent($xpath, '//input[@name="mobile"]'));
    $this->assertEquals("Cancel", $this->getText($xpath, "//a"));

    $this->assertEquals("Jacopo", $this->getValue($xpath, '//input[@name="firstname"]'));
    $this->assertEquals("Romei", $this->getValue($xpath, '//input[@name="lastname"]'));
    $this->assertEquals("0543123543", $this->getValue($xpath, '//input[@name="phone"]'));
    $this->assertEquals("34012345", $this->getValue($xpath, '//input[@name="mobile"]'));

    $this->assertEquals("(* Mandatory fields)", $this->getText($xpath, ↵
"//div[@id='content']/em"));
    $this->assertRegExp("/All © Francesco Trucchia &grave; Jacopo Romei - Pro PHP ↵
Refactoring/", $this->getText($xpath, '//div[@id="footer"]'));

    $this->type("firstname", "Jack");
    $this->type("lastname", "Brown");
    $this->type("phone", "1234");
    $this->type("mobile", "4321");
    $this->type("id", "1");

    $_SERVER['REQUEST_METHOD'] = 'POST';

    try
    {
      $contacts_book_main = new ContactsBookMain();
      $contacts_book_main->edit();
      $this->fail();
    }
    catch(Exception $e)
    {
      $this->assertRegExp('/Cannot modify header information/', $e->getMessage());
    }

    $xpath = $this->assertDomReturnXPath('index');
```

```
    $this->assertEquals('Brown', $this->getText($xpath, '//table/tr[2]/td[1]'));
    $this->assertEquals('Jack', $this->getText($xpath, '//table/tr[2]/td[2]'));
    $this->assertEquals('1234', $this->getText($xpath, '//table/tr[2]/td[3]'));
    $this->assertEquals('4321', $this->getText($xpath, '//table/tr[2]/td[4]'));
  }
}
```

We run the test case and verify that all tests are OK.

```
PHPUnit 3.4.1 by Sebastian Bergmann.

...

Time: 0 seconds

OK (3 tests, 61 assertions)
```

Now we replace the code in the edit.php script with the call to the method edit() of the class ContactsBookMain and run all unit and functional tests again.

```
--- edit.php ---
require_once('lib/ContactsBookMain.php');

$contacts_book_main = new ContactsBookMain();
$contacts_book_main->edit();
```

Remove Action

Finally we prepare the unit test for the last action, that of removal. We verify that when calling the method a record is deleted. To verify the removal, we call the method index() at the beginning, and we count how many rows are in the list table. Then we call to the remove() method, and at the end we call index() again and check that the number of row has decreased.

```
--- tests/unit/ContactsBookMainTest.php ---
...
class ContactsBookMainTest extends PHPUnit_Extensions_Database_TestCase
{
  ...
  public function testRemove()
  {
    $xpath = $this->assertDomReturnXPath('index');
    $this->assertEquals(3, $this->getXPathCount($xpath, '//table/tr'));

    $_GET['id'] = 1;
    try
    {
      $contacts_book_main = new ContactsBookMain();
      $contacts_book_main->remove();
      $this->fail();
    }
    catch(Exception $e)
    {
      $this->assertRegExp('/Cannot modify header information/', $e->getMessage());
    }

    $xpath = $this->assertDomReturnXPath('index');
```

```
      $this->assertEquals(2, $this->getXPathCount($xpath, '//table/tr'));
  }
}
```

We create the remove() method in the class ContactsBookMain and copy the code of the remove.php script code inside the method, replacing include_once() with include() and adjusting the path of the included files.

```
<code>
--- lib/ContactsBookMain.php ---
<?php
class ContactsBookMain
{
  ...
  public static function remove()
  {
    include(dirname(__FILE__).'/../config.php');

    if(!$_GET['id'])
    {
     die('Some error occured!!');
    }

    $db = @mysql_connect($database['host'], $database['username'], $database['password']) ↵
or die('Can\'t connect do database');
    @mysql_select_db($database['name']) or die('The database selected does not exists');

    $query = sprintf('DELETE FROM contacts where ID = %s',
                     mysql_real_escape_string($_GET['id']));

    if(!mysql_query($query))
    {
      die_with_error(mysql_error(), $query);
    }

    mysql_close($db);

    header('Location: index.php');
  }
}
```

Run the test and verify that everything is OK.

```
PHPUnit 3.4.1 by Sebastian Bergmann.

....

Time: 0 seconds

OK (4 tests, 64 assertions)
```

Now replace the code in the script remove.php with the call to the remove() method of the class ContactsBookMain.

```
--- remove.php ---
require_once('lib/ContactsBookMain.php');

ContactsBookMain::remove();
```

We run all functional tests and unit tests for the last time and verify that all tests are still correct.

```
PHPUnit 3.4.1 by Sebastian Bergmann.

.........

Time: 45 seconds

OK (9 tests, 140 assertions)
```

With this refactoring, we transformed our procedural code into object code, and we were able to test it at the unit level. We have opened the way to further improving the design of our code, which still has a lot of bad smells. The next steps will be introducing an ORM, introducing a Template Engine, and, finally, implementing the MVC architecture.

Replace SQL with ORM

Problem: "We have an application that doesn't use data structure objects, but only scalar values extracted from SQL queries."

Solution: "Introduce an Object Relationship Mapper to convert data between incompatible types."

Motivation

Classical relational databases can handle only scalars and records, not objects. An object, compared to a record, can be easily reusable and have behaviors and properties. A record, however, is merely the expression of a set of primitive data. This approach is very limited when we work with objects and leads to a very impressive duplication of code, as well as a difficult management of SQL queries needed to query the database.

> *Object-relational mapping (ORM, O/RM, and O/R mapping) in computer software is a programming technique for converting data between incompatible type systems in relational databases and object-oriented programming languages. This creates, in effect, a "virtual object database" that can be used from within the programming language.*

—Wikipedia

Introducing an ORM can transform our model from record-relational to object-relational and benefit from all the characteristics of the object-oriented paradigm.

In most cases, a disadvantage of ORM is the difficulty in being tested, because it is very coupled with the database adapter. Another disadvantage is performance. Many ORMs can not easily scale with increasing data, and sometimes it is needed to return to a procedural management of our data.

Mechanism

1. Install a PHP ORM library.

2. Configure the database connection and the bootstrapping.

3. Replace calls to the primary database with the adapter library.

4. Generate the classes that map the database tables.

5. Replace the SQL relational method calls of the model.

Example

In the example we will see how to insert the open-source ORM library Doctrine, in our application "Contacts Book," after having succeeded, in the first step of big refactoring, in transforming our code from procedural to object through the Façade pattern.

Saying that our code respects the object-oriented paradigm, at the point where we have come earlier in our Contacts Book application, it is still too strong a statement. The methods of the Main class are still too procedural, while our goal is to have an object-oriented design. Following this goal, to improve the design we can insert an Object Relationship Mapper, which helps us to map the structure of the database into objects.

In the PHP world there are many ORM libraries competing with each other. We decided to use Doctrine[2] because we believe it is very easy to use and has a very active community behind it.

From the official site, www.doctrine-project.org, comes this brief description that highlights the strengths of the library:

> *Doctrine is an object relational mapper (ORM) for PHP 5.2.3+ that sits on top of a powerful database abstraction layer (DBAL). One of its key features is the option to write database queries in a proprietary object-oriented SQL dialect called Doctrine Query Language (DQL), inspired by Hibernates HQL. This provides developers with a powerful alternative to SQL that maintains flexibility without requiring unnecessary code duplication.*

We install the Doctrine library in the folder lib/vendor/doctrine of our application. For installation refer to the official documentation on the web site: www.doctrine-project.org/documentation/manual/1_2/en/getting-started.

To use Doctrine we must configure a bootstrapping file. We create a new file in the lib folder named bootstrap.php and we copy the following code inside:

```
--- lib/bootstrap.php ---
require_once(dirname(__FILE__) . '/vendor/doctrine/Doctrine.php');
spl_autoload_register(array('Doctrine', 'autoload'));
Doctrine_Manager::connection('mysql://root@localhost/contacts', 'ContactsBook');
```

With this code we register the Doctrine autoloader and we configure the database connection. We include this file in the ContactsBookMain.php file and run all tests. The advantage to including an ORM as Doctrine is to be able to change the database transparently, simply by changing the connection string, and all of our code will still work.

---

[2] www.doctrine-project.org

```
$ phpunit lib/tests
PHPUnit 3.4.1 by Sebastian Bergmann.

.........

Time: 45 seconds

OK (9 tests, 140 assertions)
```

Once you configure the library, the next step is to replace primitive calls used to query our MySql database with calls of the MySql adapter for Doctrine.

We begin first with the method index() in the class ContactsBookMain. To replace the primitive calls we must, first of all, create mock functions that help us to switch to Doctrine. We create an object called DatabaseMock, which will help us in this step, and we make each primitive call to MySql a static call to the DatabaseMock method. Any static method keeps the same name as its primary function.

For example, replace the call mysql_connect() with DatabaseMock::mysql_connect(), the call mysql_select_db() with DatabaseMock::mysql_select_db(), and so on. The final result of the index() method of the class ContactsBookMain will be the following:

```
--- lib/ContactsBookMain.php ---
...
class ContactsBookMain
{
  public static function index()
  {
    include(dirname(__FILE__).'/../config.php');

        $db = DatabaseMock::mysql_connect($database['host'], $database['username'], ↵
$database['password']) or die('Can\'t connect do database');
      DatabaseMock::mysql_select_db($database['name']) or die('The database selected does ↵
not exists');

      $query = 'SELECT * FROM contacts ORDER BY lastname';
      $rs = DatabaseMock::mysql_query($query);

      if (!$rs)
      {
        die_with_error(DatabaseMock::mysql_error(), $query);
      }

      $num = DatabaseMock::mysql_num_rows($rs);

      include_once(dirname(__FILE__).'/../header.php') ?>

      <div class="actions">
        <a href="new.php">New contact</a>
      </div>

      <?php if ($num) : ?>
        <table border="1" cellspacing="0" cellpadding="5">
        <tr>
          <th>Last Name</th>
          <th>First Name</th>
          <th>Phone</th>
          <th>Mobile</th>
          <th> </th>
        </tr>
```

```php
        <?php while($row = DatabaseMock::mysql_fetch_assoc($rs)) :?>
            <tr>
                <td><a href="edit.php?id=<?php echo $row['id']?>" title="Edit"><?php echo ↵
$row['lastname']?></a></td>
                <td><?php echo $row['firstname']?></td>
                <td><a href="callto://<?php echo $row['phone']?>"><?php echo $row['phone']?></a></td>
                <td><a href="callto://<?php echo $row['mobile']?>"><?php echo ↵
$row['mobile']?></a></td>
                <td>[<a href="remove.php?id=<?php echo $row['id']?>" title="Delete" onclick="if ↵
(confirm('Are you sure?')) {return true;} return false;">X</a>]</td>
            </tr>
        <?php endwhile;?>
        </table>

        <?php else: ?>
        Database is empty
        <?php endif ?>

        <?php
            include_once(dirname(__FILE__).'/../footer.php');
            DatabaseMock::mysql_free_result($rs);
            DatabaseMock::mysql_close($db);
    }
}
...
```

We run the test cases ContactsBookMainTest and let ourselves be guided by the test failures, implementing only the simplest code block so that each assertion passes. We implement the DatabaseMock class in the easy way, so that the text does not give errors. The first result is the following. Of course we need to include the class file in the ContactsBooksMain.php file.

```php
--- test/lib/mock/DatabaseMock.php ---
...
class DatabaseMock
{
    public static function mysql_connect()
    {
        return true;
    }

    public static function mysql_select_db()
    {
        return true;
    }

    public static function mysql_query()
    {
        return true;
    }

    public static function mysql_fetch_assoc(){}

    public static function mysql_error(){}

    public static function mysql_num_rows(){}

    public static function mysql_free_result(){}
```

```
  public static function mysql_close(){}
}
```

At this point, the test still does not pass, because the methods do not effectively query to the database, and they do not return any results.

```
PHPUnit 3.4.1 by Sebastian Bergmann.

E.EE

Time: 1 second

There were 3 errors:

1) ContactsBookMainTest::testIndex
Exception: Element not found with query //table/tr/th[1]

bigrefactoring/tests/unit/ContactsBookMainTest.php:33
bigrefactoring/tests/unit/ContactsBookMainTest.php:40
bigrefactoring/tests/unit/ContactsBookMainTest.php:100

2) ContactsBookMainTest::testEdit
Exception: Element not found with query //table/tr[2]/td[1]

bigrefactoring/tests/unit/ContactsBookMainTest.php:33
bigrefactoring/tests/unit/ContactsBookMainTest.php:40
bigrefactoring/tests/unit/ContactsBookMainTest.php:213

3) ContactsBookMainTest::testRemove
Exception: Element not found with query //table/tr

bigrefactoring/tests/unit/ContactsBookMainTest.php:33
bigrefactoring/tests/unit/ContactsBookMainTest.php:56
bigrefactoring/tests/unit/ContactsBookMainTest.php:222

FAILURES!
Tests: 4, Assertions: 35, Errors: 3.
```

Since our goal is to replace primitive calls with ORM calls, in the DatabaseMock class we implement only the methods needed to run the tests, keeping the others empty.

The connection to the database, the database selection, the connection closure, and the memory management are already initialized and managed by ORM in the bootstrapping, so we can leave the related mock calls empty. To run the tests we implement only the methods mysql_query(), mysql_fetch_assoc(), and mysql_num_rows(). PDO, that is, the driver behind the PHP Doctrine ORM, gives us all the interfaces to handle these calls. The DatabaseMock final class will be as follows:

```
--- test/lib/mock/DatabaseMock.php ---
class DatabaseMock
{
  public static function mysql_connect()
  {
    return true;
  }

  public static function mysql_select_db()
  {
```

```php
        return true;
    }

    public static function mysql_query($query)
    {

        $connection = Doctrine_Manager::connection()->getDbh();
        return $connection->query($query);
    }

    public static function mysql_fetch_assoc(PDOStatement $statement)
    {
        return $statement->fetch();
    }

    public static function mysql_error(){}

    public static function mysql_num_rows(PDOStatement $statement)
    {
        return $statement->rowCount();
    }

    public static function mysql_free_result(){}

    public static function mysql_close(){}

}
```

We run the test cases ContactsBookMainTest and everything still works properly. The next step is to remove the null database method from the index() method, so we remove the method calls to mysql_connect(), mysql_select_db(), mysql_error(), mysql_free_result(), and mysql_close(). We can also remove the condition over the result set and the subsequent death in case of error in the query, as we delegate responsibility to PDO, which is able to independently manage all these controls. We can also remove the inclusion of the config.php file, because of the database connection parameters we have moved to the bootstrap, moving the inclusion it made in the boostrap.php file. Less is better.

```php
--- lib/ContactsBookMain.php ---
class ContactsBookMain
{
    public static function index()
    {
        $rs = DatabaseMock::mysql_query('SELECT * FROM contacts ORDER BY lastname');
        $num = DatabaseMock::mysql_num_rows($rs);

        include_once(dirname(__FILE__).'/../header.php') ?>

        <div class="actions">
          <a href="new.php">New contact</a>
         </div>

        <?php if ($num) : ?>
          <table border="1" cellspacing="0" cellpadding="5">
          <tr>
            <th>Last Name</th>
            <th>First Name</th>
            <th>Phone</th>
            <th>Mobile</th>
            <th> </th>
```

```
          </tr>
          <?php while($row = DatabaseMock::mysql_fetch_assoc($rs)) :?>
            <tr>
              <td><a href="edit.php?id=<?php echo $row['id']?>" title="Edit"><?php echo ↵
$row['lastname']?></a></td>
              <td><?php echo $row['firstname']?></td>
              <td><a href="callto://<?php echo $row['phone']?>"><?php echo $row['phone']?></a></td>
              <td><a href="callto://<?php echo $row['mobile']?>"><?php echo $row['mobile']?></a></td>
              <td>[<a href="remove.php?id=<?php echo $row['id']?>" title="Delete" onclick="if ↵
(confirm('Are you sure?')) {return true;} return false;">X</a>]</td>
            </tr>
          <?php endwhile;?>
          </table>

        <?php else: ?>
          Database is empty
        <?php endif ?>

        <?php
          include_once(dirname(__FILE__).'/../footer.php');
      }
}
```

I would say that this is already a better result than that of our old code. Delegating responsibility for the management of the database to an ORM and removing it tfrom our code is a great way to beautify our code. The last step is to extract code from the DatabaseFake method and replace the static calls with this code. The DatabaseMock class is only a temporary support. We adjust the code, also removing the temp variable.

```
--- lib/ContactsBookMain.php ---
class ContactsBookMain
{
  public static function index()
    {
    $connection = Doctrine_Manager::connection()->getDbh();
    $rs = $connection->query('SELECT * FROM contacts ORDER BY lastname');

    include_once(dirname(__FILE__).'/../header.php') ?>

    <div class="actions">
      <a href="new.php">New contact</a>
    </div>

    <?php if ($rs->rowCount()) : ?>
      <table border="1" cellspacing="0" cellpadding="5">
      <tr>
        <th>Last Name</th>
        <th>First Name</th>
        <th>Phone</th>
        <th>Mobile</th>
        <th> </th>
      </tr>
      <?php while($row = $rs->fetch()) :?>
        <tr>
          <td><a href="edit.php?id=<?php echo $row['id']?>" title="Edit"><?php echo ↵
$row['lastname']?></a></td>
          <td><?php echo $row['firstname']?></td>
          <td><a href="callto://<?php echo $row['phone']?>"><?php echo $row['phone']?></a></td>
```

```
            <td><a href="callto://<?php echo $row['mobile']?>"><?php echo $row['mobile']?></a></td>
            <td>[<a href="remove.php?id=<?php echo $row['id']?>" title="Delete" onclick="if ↵
(confirm('Are you sure?')) {return true;} return false;">X</a>]</td>
          </tr>
        <?php endwhile;?>
        </table>

      <?php else: ?>
        Database is empty
      <?php endif ?>

      <?php
        include_once(dirname(__FILE__).'/../footer.php');
    }
    ...
}
```

After performing the same steps in all other class methods of ContactsBookMain, we can remove the class DatabaseMock. Run all tests and verify that everything is still correct.

The next step is to generate our model, mapping relational database entities to objects. In this way we could remove the SQL query and use a logical object.

Doctrine provides the tools to create model classes automatically by querying a database. To use this feature we create a PHP script that could run from the shell. Create a new folder called bin and add the file build_model.php file inside. We also need to create a folder called model inside the lib folder, where the script will put the model classes. Copy the following code inside the build_model.php file:

```
--- bin/build_model.php ---
require_once(dirname(__FILE__).'/../lib/bootstrap.php');

Doctrine::generateModelsFromDb(dirname(__FILE__).'/../lib/model', array('ContactsBook'),
array('generateTableClasses' => true));
```

Run the script, and it creates the following files inside the model folder:

```
$ php bin/build_model.php
$ ls -al lib/model
total 16
drwxr-xr-x  3 cphp   staff   170 22 Apr 22:10 .
drwxr-xr-x  5 cphp   staff   238 22 Apr 22:05 ..
-rw-r--r--  1 cphp   staff   307 22 Apr 22:10 Contacts.php
-rw-r--r--  1 cphp   staff   356 22 Apr 22:10 ContactsTable.php
drwxr-xr-x  2 cphp   staff   102 22 Apr 22:10 generated
```

The script generated all the classes of our model in the lib/model folder. To include them, add the following code in the script bootstrap.php.

```
--- lib/bootstrap.php ---
...
Doctrine::loadModels(dirname(__FILE__).'/model/generated');
Doctrine::loadModels(dirname(__FILE__).'/model/');
...
```

Now we can replace the SQL query in class methods of ContactsBookMain using the interfaces of the models just created. We begin with the index() method.

Here is the old code:

```
--- lib/ContactsBookMain.php ---
class ContactsBookMain
{
  ...
  public function index()
  {
    ...
    $connection = Doctrine_Manager::connection()->getDbh();
    $rs = $connection->query('SELECT * FROM contacts ORDER BY lastname');
    ...
    <?php while($row = $rs->fetch()) :?>
      <tr>
        <td><a href="edit.php?id=<?php echo $row['id']?>" title="Edit"><?php echo ↵
$row['lastname']?></a></td>
        <td><?php echo $row['firstname']?></td>
        <td><a href="callto://<?php echo $row['phone']?>"><?php echo $row['phone']?></a></td>
        <td><a href="callto://<?php echo $row['mobile']?>"><?php echo $row['mobile']?></a></td>
        <td>[<a href="remove.php?id=<?php echo $row['id']?>" title="Delete" onclick="if ↵
(confirm('Are you sure?')) {return true;} return false;">X</a>]</td>
      </tr>
    <?php endwhile;?>
    ...
  }
}
```

That becomes:

```
--- lib/ContactsBookMain.php ---
...
class ContactsBookMain
{
  ...
  public function index()
  {
    ...
    $contacts = Doctrine::getTable('Contacts')->
                        createQuery()->
                        orderBy('lastname ASC')->
                        execute();
    ...
    if (count($contacts))
    ...
    <?php foreach($contacts as $contact) :?>
      <tr>
        <td><a href="edit.php?id=<?php echo $contact->id?>" title="Edit"><?php echo ↵
$contact->lastname?></a></td>
        <td><?php echo $contact->firstname?></td>
        <td><a href="callto://<?php echo $contact->phone?>"><?php echo ↵
$contact->phone?></a></td>
        <td><a href="callto://<?php echo $contact->mobile?>"><?php echo ↵
contact->mobile?></a></td>
        <td>[<a href="remove.php?id=<?php echo $contact->id?>" title="Delete" onclick="if ↵
(confirm('Are you sure?')) {return true;} return false;">X</a>]</td>
      </tr>
```

```
    <?php endforeach;?>
    ...
  }
  ...
}
```

Through the model class, the procedural SQL code is automatically converted into object code. Through the model we can query our database and see the results as objects rather than as an array, so we can use the model with this behavior in other parts of our software.

Run all tests and verify that all tests are correct.

If we want to insert a new record through the ORM, we need to replace the SQL code in the edit() method of the class ContactsBookMain with the following code:

```
--- lib/ContactsBookMain.php ---
...
class ContactsBookMain
{
  ...
  public function edit()
  {
    ...
    $connection = Doctrine_Manager::connection()->getDbh();
    $statement = $connection->prepare('INSERT INTO contacts (firstname, lastname, phone, ↵
mobile) VALUES (:firstname, :lastname, :phone, :mobile)');
    $statement->bindValue(':firstname', $_POST['firstname'], PDO::PARAM_STR);
    $statement->bindValue(':lastname', $_POST['lastname'], PDO::PARAM_STR);
    $statement->bindValue(':phone', $_POST['phone'], PDO::PARAM_STR);
    $statement->bindValue(':mobile', $_POST['mobile'], PDO::PARAM_STR);
    $statement->execute();
    ...
  }
  ...
}
```

That becomes:

```
--- lib/ContactsBookMain.php ---
...
class ContactsBookMain
{
  ...
  public function edit()
  {
    ...
    $contact = new Contacts();
    $contact->firstname = $_POST['firstname'];
    $contact->lastname = $_POST['lastname'];
    $contact->phone = $_POST['phone'];
    $contact->mobile = $_POST['mobile'];
    $contact->save();
    ...
  }
}
```

Run the tests for the last time and make sure everything is still correct.

Separate Business Logic from View

Problem: "The representation of the application (GUI) is coupled with the business logic."

Solution: "Separate the business logic from its representation through the Decorator pattern and Template View pattern."

Motivation

Many PHP applications are written in a procedural manner with business logic, that is, code delegated to the retrieval of data, such as from a database, fully coupled with the logic of representation, usually HTML. The common portions of the code related to view such as the header, footer, or sidebar are included as PHP script. This type of design is very complex to maintain. For example, if we want to add a new view for some of our data to the database, such as a view for mobile devices, we should duplicate all the business logic in a new script and then write the new logic of the representation. If, for example, we want to reuse the same representation with a different header, footer, and sidebar, we can do that only duplicating the code.

To solve this problem of software design inside this kind of PHP script, once again we are helped by design patterns, especially by the Decorator Design pattern and the Template View pattern.

The Decorator Design pattern allows you to draw a certain object in different ways by attaching different responsibilities dynamically. For example, we can have a basic layout that it is needed to render the content in the simplest way. To this layout we can dynamically attach a layout with a header, then a layout with a footer, and finally a layout with a sidebar. In practice, I can make my layout quite dynamic.

The second pattern that helps us represent our data in a totally flexible way is the Template View pattern. Creating the HTML code dynamically is much more difficult than it may seem, but a static HTML page does not fit to represent the data that can change dynamically based on demand. The best way to create dynamic web pages is to compose the pages as if they were static pages, but put markers that can be translated into calls providing dynamic information.

The Template View pattern is implemented with a template engine that can parse the HTML pages and replace the markers with the correct values. In PHP there are many template engines. Smarty is probably the most famous, although, lately, for the simple nature of PHP itself, there are some template engines using PHP itself as a marker in the template. Obviously if you use PHP as markers, you must make the logic simple, as the templates may also be modified by non-expert developers, such as graphics or UX experts.

The advantage of using a template engine is the ease of amending the code of representation and reusing the same code.

Mechanism

- Extract the logic of view towards the Decorator pattern.

- Implement a simple Decorator.

- Install a template engine.

- Extract the representational logic in templates.

- Implement the rendering of views through the template engine.

Example

In the following example we will see how to implement the Decorator Design pattern and then the Template View pattern in our application "Contacts Book." After some refactoring steps, we transformed our procedural code into object code, and we included an ORM to map our database related to the object model.

Decorator Design Pattern

The first step is to implement the Decorator pattern. We must change the logic of how we include HTML code around the content in the methods of the class ContactsBookMain. Instead of including the header and footer, we need to extract the included files and make only the content return to the method, delegating the rendering of the content to the class Decorator, which decorates content with the right layout.

In all methods we include header.php and footer.php after and before the rendering of content. The first step is delegating the rendering of the header and footer to a class called Decorator. With small steps, by refactoring we will extract the class Decorator.

First of all we extract two methods that include header.php and footer.php in the ContactsBookMain class.

```
--- lib/ContactsBookMain.php ---
class ContactsBookMain
{
  ...
  public function header()
  {
    include(dirname(__FILE__).'/../header.php');
  }

  public function footer()
  {
    include_once(dirname(__FILE__).'/../footer.php');
  }
  ...
}
```

Remove all headers and footers from the ContactsBookMainTest methods except from the header() and footer() methods, just extracted, and fix the test cases class ContactsBookMainTest, calling the two methods header() and footer() before the call to action.

```
--- tests/unit/ContactsBookMainTest.php ---
class ContactsBookMainTest extends PHPUnit_Extensions_Database_TestCase
{
  ...

  public function setUp()
  {
    ...
    $this->contacts_book_main = new ContactsBookMain();
    ...
  }

  private function assertDomReturnXPath($action)
  {
    ob_start();
```

```
    $this->contacts_book_main->header();
    $this->contacts_book_main->$action();
    $this->contacts_book_main->footer();
    $output = ob_get_contents();
    ob_end_clean();
    ....
  }
}
```

Run the unit test and verify that the tests are OK. At this point we can modify the index.php script so that it directly calls the methods header() and footer().

```
--- index.php ---
require_once('lib/ContactsBookMain.php');

$contacts_book_main = new ContactsBookMain();
$contacts_book_main->header();
$contacts_book_main->index();
$contacts_book_main->footer();
```

And run functional test case tests/functional/contact/ListTest.php.

```
PHPUnit 3.4.1 by Sebastian Bergmann.

.

Time: 9 seconds

OK (1 test, 24 assertions)
```

With the "Extract Class" technique, we extract a new class called Decorator delegated to render the header and footer of the HTML page.

```
--- lib/Decorator.php ---
...
class Decorator
{
  public function header()
  {
    include(dirname(__FILE__).'/../header.php');
  }

  public function footer()
  {
    include(dirname(__FILE__).'/../footer.php');
  }
}
```

We modify the index.php script and the test cases ContactsBookMain so that they use the Decorator class instead of the methods header() and footer() of the ContactsBookMain class and remove these useless methods.

```
--- index.php ---
require_once('lib/ContactsBookMain.php');

$decorator = new Decorator();
```

```
$contacts_book_main = new ContactsBookMain();

$decorator->header();
$contacts_book_main->index();
$decorator->footer();

--- test/unit/ContactsBookMainTest.php ---
class ContactsBookMainTest extends PHPUnit_Extensions_Database_TestCase
{
  ...
  public function setUp()
  {
    ...
    $this->contacts_book_main = new ContactsBookMain();
    $this->decorator = new Decorator();
    ...
  }

  private function assertDomReturnXPath($action)
  {
    ob_start();
    $this->decorator->header();
    $this->contacts_book_main->$action();
    $this->decorator->footer();
    $output = ob_get_contents();
    ob_end_clean();
    ....
  }
}
```

We run the unit test and check that everything is still working.

```
PHPUnit 3.4.1 by Sebastian Bergmann.

....

Time: 1 second

OK (4 tests, 66 assertions)
```

A unit test should test only one class, so putting the class Decorator in ContactsBookMainTest unit test is wrong, because we're creating coupling in the test. To decouple, we need to create a new unit test called DecoratorTest and remove the code of the class Decorator from the test ContactsBookMainTest. Since we are delegating the class Decorator to rendering the header and footer, we move the tests for this output into the test case class DecoratorTest.

```
--- tests/unit/DecoratorTest.php ---
...
class DecoratorTest extends PHPUnit_Framework_TestCase
{
  protected $object;

  protected function setUp()
  {
    $this->decorator = new Decorator;
  }
```

```php
  public function testHeader()
  {
    ob_start();
    $this->decorator->header();
    $output = ob_get_contents();
    ob_end_clean();

    $this->assertRegExp('/<h1>Contacts Book<\/h1>/', $output);
    $this->assertRegExp('/<div id=\"content\">/', $output);
  }

  public function testFooter()
  {
    ob_start();
    $this->decorator->footer();
    $output = ob_get_contents();
    ob_end_clean();

    $this->assertRegExp('/<div id="footer">/', $output);
    $this->assertRegExp('/All &copy; Francesco Trucchia &amp; Jacopo Romei - Pro PHP ↵
Refactoring/', $output);
    $this->assertRegExp('/<\/div>/', $output);
  }
}
```

Run the test and verify that everything is OK. Then we modify the test ContactsBookMainTest, removing the instance of Decorator and removing the test of the header and footer output. Then, following the Decorator pattern, we can implement the render method that will decorate a content string with the right layout. We write the unit test first.

```php
--- tests/unit/DecoratorTest.php ---
....
class DecoratorTest extends PHPUnit_Framework_TestCase
{
  ...
  public function testRender()
  {
    ob_start();
    $this->decorator->render('Hello World');
    $output = ob_get_contents();
    ob_end_clean();

    $this->assertRegExp('/<h1>Contacts Book<\/h1>/', $output);
    $this->assertRegExp('/<div id=\"content\">/', $output);
    $this->assertRegExp('/Hello World/', $output);

    $this->assertRegExp('/<div id="footer">/', $output);
    $this->assertRegExp('/All &copy; Francesco Trucchia &amp; Jacopo Romei - Pro PHP ↵
Refactoring/', $output);
    $this->assertRegExp('/<\/div>/', $output);
  }
}
?>
--- lib/DecoratorTest.php ---
<?php
class Decorator
{
  ...
```

```
  public function render($content)
  {
    $this->header();
    echo $content;
    $this->footer();
  }
}
```

The test checks that the content represented by the "Hello World" string is decorated with the right header and footer.

Last but not least, move the buffering output from the test to the render() method, so we can decide whether to print the output and simplify testing.

```
--- tests/unit/DecoratorTest.php ---
....
class DecoratorTest extends PHPUnit_Framework_TestCase
{
  ...
  public function testRenderPrinting()
  {
    ob_start();
    $this->decorator->render('Hello World');
    $output = ob_get_contents();
    ob_end_clean();

    $this->assertRegExp('/<h1>Contacts Book<\/h1>/', $output);
    $this->assertRegExp('/<div id=\"content\">/', $output);
    $this->assertRegExp('/Hello World/', $output);

    $this->assertRegExp('/<div id="footer">/', $output);
    $this->assertRegExp('/All &copy; Francesco Trucchia &amp; Jacopo Romei - Pro PHP ↵
Refactoring/', $output);
    $this->assertRegExp('/<\/div>/', $output);
  }

  public function testRender()
  {
    $output = $this->decorator->render('Hello World', false);

    $this->assertRegExp('/<h1>Contacts Book<\/h1>/', $output);
    $this->assertRegExp('/<div id=\"content\">/', $output);
    $this->assertRegExp('/Hello World/', $output);

    $this->assertRegExp('/<div id="footer">/', $output);
    $this->assertRegExp('/All &copy; Francesco Trucchia &amp; Jacopo Romei - Pro PHP ↵
Refactoring/', $output);
    $this->assertRegExp('/<\/div>/', $output);
  }
}

--- lib/DecoratorTest.php ---
class Decorator
{
  ...
  public function render($content, $print = true)
  {
    ob_start();
    $this->header();
```

313

```
      echo $content;
      $this->footer();
      $output = ob_get_contents();
      ob_end_clean();

      if ($print) echo $output;
      return $output;
  }
}
```

Run the DecoratorTest test and verify that everything is OK. Now we need to replace the calls header() and footer() in the index.php script with the render() call, finding a way to pass the output of the class ContactsBookMain to the render() method.

```
--- index.php ---
require_once('lib/ContactsBookMain.php');
require_once('lib/Decorator.php');

$decorator = new Decorator();
$contacts_book_main = new ContactsBookMain();

ob_start();
$contacts_book_main->index();
$content = ob_get_contents();
ob_end_clean();

$decorator->render($content);
```

To pass the output of the index() method to the render() method, we use the output buffer functions. Having to bufferize the output in all of the other scripts of our actions, to not duplicate the code, we decide to move the code into a new method called getContent() inside the class ContactsBookMain. The method takes as input the name of the string and returns the output of the content. We prepare the new test for this method and then we implement it.

```
--- tests/unit/ContactsBookMainTest.php ---
class ContactsBookMainTest extends PHPUnit_Extensions_Database_TestCase
{
  ...

  public function actionExceptionProvider()
  {
    return array(array(), array(''), array('invalid'));
  }

  /**
   * @expectedException Exception
   * @dataProvider actionExceptionProvider
   */
  public function testGetContentException($action)
  {
    $this->contacts_book_main->getContent($action);
  }

  public function testGetContent()
  {
    $output = $this->contacts_book_main->getContent('index');
```

```
      $dom = new DOMDocument();
      $dom->loadHTML($output);

      $this->assertIndexOutput(new DOMXPath($dom));

  }
  ...
}

--- lib/ContactsBookMain.php ---
class ContactsBookMain
{
  ...
  public function getContent($action)
  {
    if (!method_exists($this, $action))
    {
      throw new Exception('Method '.$action.' does not exists');
    }

    ob_start();
    $this->$action();
    $content = ob_get_contents();
    ob_end_clean();

    return $content;
  }
  ...
}

--- index.php ---
...
$decorator = new Decorator();
$contacts_book_main = new ContactsBookMain();

$decorator->render($contacts_book_main->getContent('index'));
```

We run the listTest.php functional test and check that everything is correct. Then we can add in all the other PHP script logic of the Decorator pattern. Through this pattern, it becomes easy to decorate the output in any way, creating new classes that extend our Decorator.

Template View Pattern

The second major step is to separate business logic from the logic of representation within the class methods ContactsBookMain. The business logic is now coupled with the logic of representation. To solve this problem, we will use the Template View pattern, which will move the logic of representation in a template managed by a template engine.

We decide to use the template engine library Savant3 (http://phpsavant.com), a simple open-source template engine for PHP5 that uses PHP language as the template language. We install the library in the lib/vendor/savant folder. For installation details refer to the online document http://phpsavant.com/docs.

We need to include the class Savant3 in the bootstrap so that it is always available when needed.

```
--- lib/bootstrap.php ---
...
require_once(dirname(__FILE__) . '/vendor/savant/Savant3.php');
...
```

To simplify the job of extracting the logical representation in the template, starting from the index()
method of the class ContactsBookMain, we can extract the logic of representation in the method
viewIndex() of the same class with the "Extract Method" refactoring technique.

```
--- lib/ContactsBookMain.php ---
class ContactsBookMain
{
  ...
  public function viewIndex($contacts)
  {
    ?>
    <div class="actions">
      <a href="new.php">New contact</a>
    </div>

    <?php if (count($contacts)) : ?>
      <table border="1" cellspacing="0" cellpadding="5">
      <tr>
        <th>Last Name</th>
        <th>First Name</th>
        <th>Phone</th>
        <th>Mobile</th>
        <th> </th>
      </tr>
      <?php foreach($contacts as $contact) :?>
        <tr>
          <td><a href="edit.php?id=<?php echo $contact->id?>" title="Edit"><?php echo ↩
$contact->lastname?></a></td>
          <td><?php echo $contact->firstname?></td>
          <td><a href="callto://<?php echo $contact->phone?>"><?php echo ↩
$contact->phone?></a></td>
          <td><a href="callto://<?php echo $contact->mobile?>"><?php echo ↩
$contact->mobile?></a></td>
          <td>[<a href="remove.php?id=<?php echo $contact->id?>" title="Delete" onclick="if ↩
(confirm('Are you sure?')) {return true;} return false;">X</a>]</td>
        </tr>
      <?php endforeach;?>
      </table>

    <?php else: ?>
      Database is empty
    <?php endif;
  }

  public function index()
  {
    $contacts = Doctrine::getTable('Contacts')->
                        createQuery()->
                        orderBy('lastname ASC')->
                        execute();
```

```
    $this->viewIndex($contacts);
  }
  ...
}
```

Run the unit test ContactsBookMainTest and verify that everything is OK. Now create a new folder named templates in the root of the project and create a new file called index.tpl.php inside, where we'll move all the code inside the method viewIndex().

```
--- templates/index.tpl.php ---
<div class="actions">
  <a href="new.php">New contact</a>
</div>

<?php if (count($contacts)) : ?>
  <table border="1" cellspacing="0" cellpadding="5">
  <tr>
    <th>Last Name</th>
    <th>First Name</th>
    <th>Phone</th>
    <th>Mobile</th>
    <th> </th>
  </tr>
  <?php foreach($contacts as $contact) :?>
    <tr>
      <td><a href="edit.php?id=<?php echo $contact->id?>" title="Edit"><?php echo ↵
$contact->lastname?></a></td>
      <td><?php echo $contact->firstname?></td>
      <td><a href="callto://<?php echo $contact->phone?>"><?php echo $contact->phone?></a></td>
      <td><a href="callto://<?php echo $contact->mobile?>"><?php echo $contact->mobile?></a></td>
      <td>[<a href="remove.php?id=<?php echo $contact->id?>" title="Delete" onclick="if ↵
(confirm('Are you sure?')) {return true;} return false;">X</a>]</td>
    </tr>
  <?php endforeach;?>
  </table>

<?php else: ?>
  Database is empty
<?php endif; ?>
```

We implement in the method viewIndex() all the logic to use the template with the template engine Savant3.

```
class ContactsBookMain
{
  ...
  public function viewIndex($contacts)
  {
    $tpl = new Savant3();
    $tpl->contacts = $contacts;
    $tpl->addPath('template', dirname(__FILE__).'/../templates/');
    $tpl->display('index.tpl.php');
  }
?>
```

If we need to pass some variable to the template we just can pass it as a Savant3 attribute. In the template we have to change the variable $contacts to $this->contacts, because we can access the variable passed to the template only as attributes of the class.

```
--- templates/index.tpl.php ---
...
<?php if (count($this->contacts)) : ?>
  ...
  <?php foreach($this->contacts as $contact) :?>
  ...
```

Since the method viewIndex() is not used by anybody but the method index() and because it is a very simple method, we decide to remove its code to the end of the index() method.

Now we can perform all the same steps for all other class methods of ContactsBookMain, where business logic is coupled with representational logic.

To improve our code, we make the instance of Savant3 an attribute of the ContactsBookMain class, so we can remove code duplication in the method.

```
class ContactsBookMain
{
  protected $tpl;

  public function __construct()
  {
    $this->tpl = new Savant3();
    $this->tpl->addPath('template', dirname(__FILE__).'/../templates/');
  }
  ...
  public function index()
  {
    ...
    $this->tpl->contacts = $contacts;
    $this->tpl->display('index.tpl.php');

  }
}
```

We run all the tests again and if everything is correct, we have succeeded in this big refactoring, which has made our code more maintainable, easier to use, and more object-oriented.

```
PHPUnit 3.4.1 by Sebastian Bergmann.

...............

Time: 47 seconds

OK (15 tests, 170 assertions)
```

A useful exercise, which we leave to the reader, is to use the template engine in the Decorator class, making it more configurable. In this way we can make the layout of our application more dynamic, such as customizing the title or changing the CSS, depending on the action.

MVC Architecture

Problem: "The actions of the software are separated into many different scripts, in which the view and the model are coupled."

Solution: "Implement the Model View Controller architecture to separate the model from view and have a controller that tries to create a response by invoking the right action."

Motivation

The essential purpose of MVC is to bridge the gap between the human user's mental model and the digital model that exists in the computer.

—Trygve M. H. Reenskaug[REE78]

The coupling of models, which corresponds to the logic and data of our domain, with the view, which is how we can represent the logic of our domain (GUI), with the controller, delegated to receive input and send a response to the client, is a bad smell, because the application makes it very difficult to test and maintain.

The Model View Controller is an architectural pattern that solves problems about the right design of these components, decoupling and explaining how they communicate. MVC is often seen in web applications where the view is the HTML or XHTML generated by the application. The controller receives GET or POST input and decides what to do with it, handing it over to domain objects (i.e., the model) that contain the business rules and know how to carry out specific tasks such as processing a new subscription.

In PHP there are many MVC frameworks that can be used in our application, however, we recommend passing first through a simple implementation of an MVC architecture, as we shall see in the example, then maybe moving to a more mature open-source MVC framework, respecting the principle of small steps.

Mechanism

If we start from procedural code, first we need to implement a Façade class through the technique of "Transform Procedural Code into Object Code."

Then if I have a relational database and I query it with simple SQL, I could introduce an ORM to map my relational database into objects through the technique "Replace With SQL ORM."

Finally, if I have business logic coupled with view logic, I could introduce a template engine to the decoupling component through the technique of "Separate Business Logic from View."

Once these preliminary steps are made, implementing an MVC architecture becomes very simple, and I can do it with the following steps:

Extract the Controller class from the Façade class.

1. Delegate the execution of the Façade actions to the Controller class.

2. Replace client calls to the class Façade with calls to the Controller class.

3. Delegate the Controller class to render the whole response.

4. Extract from the Façade class the Actions class that implements only the user actions.

5. Remove the Façade class.

Example

We will use the "Contacts Book" application as an example for this refactoring, starting from the state we achieved in the previous section. We have a Façade class ContactsBookMain delegated to the execution of individual actions, an ORM delegated to manage our model, and a template engine delegated to represent the model.

The target of this last step of refactoring is to remove the Façade class, which serves only as a support to improve the procedural code initially, and delegate the execution of the right action called by the client rendered with the correct view to a Controller class.

The Façade class implements a method called getContent(), which is the controller of our application, since it takes as input an action name, executes it, and returns the output.

```
--- lib/ContactsBookMain.php ---
class ContactsBookMain
{
  ...
  public function getContent($action)
  {
    if (!method_exists($this, $action))
    {
      throw new Exception('Method '.$action.' does not exists');
    }

    ob_start();
    $this->$action();
    $content = ob_get_contents();
    ob_end_clean();

    return $content;
  }
  ...
}
```

The method getContent() should not be in the Façade class, but in the Controller class. We extract the Controller class and the method getContent()from the class ContactsBookMain. Before doing so, we write a simple unit test for the Controller class.

```
--- tests/unit/ControllerTest.php ---
...
class ControllerTest extends PHPUnit_Extensions_Database_TestCase
{
  public function setUp()
  {
    $this->controller = new Controller();
  }

  public function testGetContent()
  {
    $output = $this->controller->getContent('index');
    $this->asserTrue(is_string($output));
  }
}
```

Run the test, which will fail because the Controller class doesn't exist. Then we create it and include it in the test.

```
--- lib/Controller.php ---
class Controller
{ }
```

After running the unit test, it fails again because the method getContent() doesn't exist. We move the getContent() method from the ContactsBookMain class to the Controller class.

```
--- lib/Controller.php ---
class Controller
{
  public function getContent($action)
  {
    if (!method_exists($this, $action))
    {
      throw new Exception('Method '.$action.' does not exists');
    }

    ob_start();
    $this->$action();
    $content = ob_get_contents();
    ob_end_clean();

    return $content;
  }
  ...
}
```

Run the test again. It fails again, notifying that the method index() does not exist. The method index() doesn't exist because it is a method of the ContactsBookMain class. Creating a new instance of the class ContactsBookMain inside the method getContent() would couple the Controller class with the ContactsBookMain class, which is wrong because it makes the Controller test dependent on ContactsBookMain. So we decide to pass the class name to use as a parameter of the Controller constructor. We also check that if the class and action passed don't exist, the method will throw an exception.

```
--- tests/lib/mock/ModuleMock.php ---
class ModuleMock
{
  public function index()
  {
    echo 'Hello World';
  }
}
```

```
--- tests/unit/ControllerTest.php ---
class ControllerTest extends PHPUnit_Framework_TestCase
{
  ...
  public function testGetContent()
  {
    $output = $this->controller->getContent('ModuleMock', 'index');
    $this->assertTrue(is_string($output));
    $this->assertEquals('Hello World', $output);
  }

  /**
   * @expectedException Exception
```

```
    */
  public function testExceptionGetContentNotValidClassName()
  {
    $output = $this->controller->getContent('NotValidClassName', 'index');
  }

  /**
   * @expectedException Exception
   */
  public function testExceptionGetContentNotValidModuleName()
  {
    $output = $this->controller->getContent('ModuleMock', 'invalidMethod');
  }
  ...
}
```

Edit the getContent() method in order to create a new instance of the class passed and a call to right action.

```
--- lib/Controller.php ---
class Controller
{
  private $module;

  public function getContent($module, $action)
  {
    if (!class_exists($module))
    {
      throw new Exception('Class '.$module.' does not exists');
    }

    $this->module = new $module();

    if (!method_exists($this->module, $action))
    {
      throw new Exception('Method '.$action.' does not exists');
    }

    ob_start();
    $this->module->$action();
    $content = ob_get_contents();
    ob_end_clean();

    return $content;
  }
}
```

We run the test and everything is correct.

```
PHPUnit 3.4.1 by Sebastian Bergmann.

...

Time: 0 seconds

OK (3 tests, 4 assertions)
```

Finally, we transform the method getContent() in the ContactsBookMain class in a proxy method to the getContent() method of the Controller class.

```
--- lib/ContactsBookMain.php ---
class ContactsBookMain
{
  ...
  public function getContent($action)
  {
    $controller = new Controller();
    return $controller->getContent('ContactsBookMain', $action);
  }
  ...
}
```

Run all tests and verify that the behavior of our application has not changed.

```
PHPUnit 3.4.1 by Sebastian Bergmann.

.................

Time: 46 seconds

OK (18 tests, 174 assertions)
```

Replace the instance of the ContactsBookMain class in all our scripts with the instance of the Controller class and remove the method getContent() from the class ContactsBookMain. Run the test and verify that everything is OK.

For example, in the index.php script the result at the end of the replacement will be the following:

```
--- index.php ---
require_once('lib/ContactsBookMain.php');
require_once('lib/Decorator.php');

$decorator = new Decorator();
$controller = new Controller();
$decorator->render($controller->getContent('ContactsBookMain', 'index'));
```

In MVC architecture, the controller is delegated to prepare the whole response to be sent to the client. For this reason, the class Decorator must be passed to the Controller class. Let's change the interface of the Controller construct passing a new instance of the Decorator class and delegating the method getContent() to call the render() method of the Decorator class. In the test we use a stub to verify that the render() method is called successfully.

```
--- tests/unit/ControllerTest.php ---
...
class ControllerTest extends PHPUnit_Framework_TestCase
{
  public function setUp()
  {
    $this->decorator = $this->getMock('Decorator', array('render'));
    $this->controller = new Controller($this->decorator);
  }

  public function testGetContent()
  {
    $this->decorator->
```

```
              expects($this->once())->
              method('render')->
              with($this->equalTo('Hello World'));

    $output = $this->controller->getContent('ModuleMock', 'index');
    $this->assertTrue(is_string($output));
    $this->assertEquals('Hello World', $output);
  }
  ...
}
```

Modify the Controller class to accommodate the instance of the Decorator class and perform the call to render() method.

```
--- lib/Controller.php ---
class Controller
{
  private $module;
  private $decorator;

  public function __construct(Decorator $decorator)
  {
    $this->decorator = $decorator;
  }

  public function getContent($module, $action)
  {
    ...
    $this->decorator->render($content);
    return $content;
  }
}
```

Replace client calls to the Controller class passing an instance of the Decorator class. For example, the index.php script becomes

```
--- index.php ---
require_once('lib/ContactsBookMain.php');
require_once('lib/Decorator.php');

$controller = new Controller(new Decorator());
$controller->getContent('ContactsBookMain', 'index');
```

The method getContent() of the class Controller initially simply returns the content; now it also performs other activities. It is delegated to dispatch input and render the representation. Through the "Extract Method" technique, we want to separate the two actions, extracting a new method called dispatch() from the method getContent(). We prepare a unit test.

```
--- tests/unit/ControllerTest.php
class ControllerTest extends PHPUnit_Framework_TestCase
{
  ...
  public function testDispatch()
  {
    $this->decorator->
            expects($this->once())->
            method('render')->
```

```
          with($this->equalTo('Hello World'));

    $this->controller->dispatch('ModuleMock', 'index');
  }
  ...
}
```

Transform the getContent() method in a proxy method to dispatch().

```
--- lib/Controller.php ---
class Controller
{
  ...
  public function dispatch($module, $action)
  {
    if (!class_exists($module))
    {
      throw new Exception('Class '.$module.' does not exists');
    }

    $this->module = new $module();

    if (!method_exists($this->module, $action))
    {
      throw new Exception('Method '.$action.' does not exists');
    }

    ob_start();
    $this->module->$action();
    $content = ob_get_contents();
    ob_end_clean();

    $this->decorator->render($content);

    return $content;
  }

  public function getContent($module, $action)
  {
    return $this->dispatch($module, $action);
  }
}
```

Run all tests and verify that the code is still correct. Finally, as the last step, we transform the variable $content in the dispatch() method, in the attribute $content of the Controller class. Then, we replace all the client calls to the method getContent() with calls to the dispatch() method, and then we make sure that the method getContent() is only a getter method of the $content attribute.

The end result of the Controller class is as follows:

```
--- lib/Controller.php ---
...
class Controller
{
  private $module;
  private $decorator;
  private $content;
```

```php
  public function __construct(Decorator $decorator)
  {
    $this->decorator = $decorator;
  }

  public function dispatch($module, $action)
  {
    if (!class_exists($module))
    {
      throw new Exception('Class '.$module.' does not exists');
    }

    $this->module = new $module();

    if (!method_exists($this->module, $action))
    {
      throw new Exception('Method '.$action.' does not exists');
    }

    ob_start();
    $this->module->$action();
    $this->content = ob_get_contents();
    ob_end_clean();

    $this->decorator->render($this->content);
  }

  public function getContent()
  {
    return $this->content;
  }
}
```

Changing client calls, the index.php script, for example, is as follows:

```php
--- index.php ---
require_once('lib/ContactsBookMain.php');
require_once('lib/Decorator.php');

$controller = new Controller(new Decorator());
$controller->dispatch('ContactsBookMain', 'index');
```

Finally, we have to extract from the ContactsBookMain class the ContactsActions class, which implements all the actions that the user can perform in our software with the Contacts entity. Through the techniques of the "Pull Up Field" and "Pull Up Method" seen in Chapter 12, move all methods and attributes from the class ContactsBookMain to the class ContactsActions. Finally, with the technique "Collapse Hierarchy" shown in Chapter 12, remove the class ContactsBookMain. Remove all of the reference in the code also, changing it with the ContactsActions reference.

```php
--- lib/ContactsActions ---
class ContactsActions
{
  ...
}
```

We also have to change in all PHP scripts the first parameters passed to the dispatch() method of the Controller class from "ContactsBookMain" to "ContactsActions." For example, in index.php the code is the following:

```
--- index.php ---
...
$controller = new Controller(new Decorator());
$controller->dispatch('ContactsActions', 'index');
```

Fix all unit tests and run all functional and unit tests again.

```
PHPUnit 3.4.1 by Sebastian Bergmann.

..............

Time: 49 seconds

OK (15 tests, 152 assertions)
```

All tests builds are green, and now our software has MVC architecture.

Summary

In this chapter we transformed our procedural application in an object-oriented application on MVC architecture. After the first essential step, using the Façade pattern, we succeeded with refactoring techniques presented in previous chapters and design patterns, moving in small steps, to achieve a better design of our application.

Surely there is still work to do to make our application better, but now we know the techniques of refactoring that at any time will allow us to improve a software's design. So now, adding new features or fixing bugs, through refactoring, we will constantly improve the quality of our application without losing any value.

Index

INDEX

refactoring techniques (*continued*)
remove the middle man, 127–130
for removing speculative code, 20
rename method, 20, 187–189
replace arrays with objects, 140–143
replace constructor with factory method,
206–207
replace data value with object, 135–137
replace delegation with inheritance, 247–249
replace error code with exception, 208–210
replace exception with test, 210
replace inheritance with delegation, 243–247
replace magic number with constant, 149–150
replace method with method object, 102–104
replace parameter with explicit method,
196–199
replace parameter with method, 201
replace SQL with ORM, 298–307
replace subclass with fields, 161–166
replace temp with query, 95–98
replace type code with state/strategy, 156–160
replace type code with subclasses, 151–155
self-encapsulate field, 133–134
separate business logic from view, 308–318
separate query from modifier, 192–193
split temporary variable, 99–102
substitute algorithm, 6, 104–105
refactoring tools, 63–84
IDEs, 63–64
PHPUnit, 64–77
Selenium, 77–82
reference objects, 137
changing value objects to, 137–140
changing to value objects, 140
regression tests, 264–276
remove control flag technique, 175–179
remove parameter technique, 20, 191–192
remove setting method technique, 21, 204–205
remove the middle man technique, 127–130
remove() method, 296–298
rename, 63
rename method technique, 20, 187–189
render() method, 13, 312–314, 323–324
replace conditional with polymorphism technique,
182–185
replace constructor with factory method
technique, 139, 206–207
replace data value with object technique,
135–137
replace delegation with inheritance technique,
247–248

replace error code with exception technique,
208–209
replace exception with test technique, 210
replace inheritance with delegation technique,
243–246
replace nested conditional with guard clause
technique, 179–181
replace parameter with explicit method technique,
196–198
replace parameter with method technique, 201–202
replace SQL with ORM technqiues, 298–307
replace subclass with fields technique, 161–166
replace temp with query method technique, 95–98
REQUEST_METHOD, 288
return exit point, replacing control flag with,
177–179
return on investment (ROI), 2
rule of three, 51–52

S

Savant3 template engine library, 315
second law of thermodynamics, 26
Selenium
functional testing using, 77–82
installation, 78–79
integration with PHPUnit, 82–84
organizing tests, 81
overview, 77–78
recording and running functional tests, 79–81
Selenium Grid, 78
Selenium IDE, 78–81
Selenium Remote Control (RC), 78, 82
self-encapsulate field technique, 133–134
separate business logic from view technique,
308–318
separate query from modifer technique, 192–193
$_SERVER variable, 288
setter classes, 21
setter methods, 64, 133, 151
removing, 21, 204–205
setUp() method, 69, 83, 288
single responsibility principle, 99
small classes, 115
Smarty template engine, 308
software
adding functionality to, 52
divergent changes in, 13–15
functionality of, 54
rewriting, 5
techniques for making changes to, 60
improvement of design, with refactoring, 47

334

software development
   after initial release, 60
      automatic tests and process of, 58–60
      productivity in, 50–51
software development teams, 61
software value, 2–3, 266
speculative code, 20
split temporary variable technique, 99–102
SQL, replace with ORM, 298–307
SQL injection, 261
state object, replacing type code with, 156–161
structural design patterns, 278
structure, 26
structured data type, 17
Stub Object, 75–76
subclasses
   extracting, 10–11, 20–21, 226–231
   moving fields to, 223–226
   moving methods to, 220–222
   replacing type code with, 151–155
   replacing with fields, 161–165
substitute algorithm technique, 6, 104–105
suite tests, 275–276
super class constructors, 216–219
super classes
   extracting, 231–234, 275
   moving attributes to, 211–213
   moving methods to, 213–216
switch statements, 18–19
system under test (SUT), 74

■ T

tearDown() method, 69
template engine, 308
template pattern, 238
Template View design pattern, 278, 308, 315–318
temporary fields, 20
temporary variables, 86, 90
   inline, 94–95
   introducing, as explaining variable, 98–99
   replacing with query, 95–98
   splitting, 99–102
@test annotation, 66
test doubles, 74–77
test-driven development (TDD), 49, 61–62
test-first development, 57–62

tets/testing
   automated, 58–61, 266
   before refactoring, 53
   functional tests, 58–61, 77–84
   integration tests, 40
   with PHPUnit, 64–77
   regression tests, 264–276
   replacing exceptions with, 210
   suite tests, 275–276
   unit tests, 39, 58–59, 64–77, 267, 282
__toString() method, 120, 246
trust, 61
two-way references, 143–148
type code
   replacing with class, 17
   replacing with state/strategy pattern, 17, 156–161
   replacing with subclasses, 17, 151–155

■ U

unidirectional association
   changing bidirectional to, 146–148
   changing to bidirectional, 143–146
unit tests, 39, 58–59, 267, 282
   organizing, 71–74
   running, 70–71
   test doubles, 74–77
   with PHPUnit, 64–77
   writing, 66–70

■ V

value objects, 137
   changing reference values to, 140
   changing to reference values, 137–140
variables
   global, 12
   local, 86, 88–92
   temporary, 86, 90, 94–102
viewIndex() method, 316–318

■ W

whole object, preservation of, 199–201
working code, value of, 2–3